Praise for *YouTube for Business*, Second Edition

"Mike Miller provides an excellent guidebook for utilizing the tremendous flexibility of YouTube as a powerful business-building tool. This idea-packed book provides step-by-step instructions for growing any business, through the marketing and promotional benefits of video production and sharing."

—Wayne Hurlbert—Blog Business World and host of Blog Business Success Radio

"Social media arguably has made the possibility of brand awareness easier. However, within that simplicity lies a complexity for business…How can we make sense of and how do we make the most of this new marketing approach? That is what I loved about this book—it not only explains the why but most importantly the how…brilliantly written, a must-read book for business people who want to really understand the power of YouTube."

—Anna Farmery, Managing Director—The Engaging Brand

"*YouTube for Business* is chock-full of great ideas and examples for marketing your business with video. Whether you are brand new to using YouTube and need some help with ideas for your first video or you've already got a few videos under your belt but want to up your technical production game, *YouTube for Business* is definitely worth the read. Engaging, easy-to-understand, authoritative."

—Kate Trgovac Kate Trgovac, Co-founder—LintBucket Media

"YouTube for Business is another well written, informative book. On my show, I always refer to Michael's books as wonderful desktop reference guides, filled with practical advice. They're not filled with engineered techno talk."

—John Iasiuolo, Host/Executive Producer

"YouTube For Business: Online Video Marketing for Any Business, 2nd Edition is another example of why Michael Miller's book is considered *The* definitive book about YouTube! This latest edition is a *must read* book for any business owner wanting to implement a successful inbound video marketing campaign for their business, product or service! I highly recommend it!!"

—Rey Ybarra, Host/Producer of "*The New Media Radio Hour*"
www.newmediaradiohour.com

YouTube®

Online Video Marketing for Any Business

for Business

Second Edition

Michael Miller

800 East 96th Street
Indianapolis, Indiana 46240 USA

YouTube for Business, Second Edition

Copyright © 2011 by Que Publishing

ISBN-13: 978-0-7897-4726-6

ISBN-10: 0-7897-4726-X

First Printing: January 2011

Library of Congress Cataloging-in-Publication data is on file.

Trademarks

All terms mentioned in this book that are known to be trademarks or service marks have been appropriately capitalized. Que Publishing cannot attest to the accuracy of this information. Use of a term in this book should not be regarded as affecting the validity of any trademark or service mark.

Warning and Disclaimer

Every effort has been made to make this book as complete and as accurate as possible, but no warranty or fitness is implied. The information provided is on an "as is" basis. The author and the publisher shall have neither liability nor responsibility to any person or entity with respect to any loss or damages arising from the information contained in this book.

Bulk Sales

Que Publishing offers excellent discounts on this book when ordered in quantity for bulk purchases or special sales. For more information, please contact

U.S. Corporate and Government Sales
1-800-382-3419corpsales@pearsontechgroup.com

For sales outside of the U.S., please contact

International Salesinternational@pearsoned.com

Associate Publisher
Greg Wiegand

Acquisitions Editor
Michelle Newcomb

Development Editor
The Wordsmithery LLC

Managing Editor
Sandra Schroeder

Project Editor
Seth Kerney

Indexer
Erika Millen

Proofreader
Sheri Cain

Technical Editor
Steve Baldwin

Publishing Coordinator
Cindy Teeters

Book Designer
Anne Jones

Page Layout
Bronkella Publishing, LLC

CONTENTS AT A GLANCE

Introduction 1

I Marketing Your Business Online with YouTube

1 How YouTube Can Help You Market Your Business 5
2 Developing Your YouTube Marketing Strategy 21
3 Creating Informative Videos 37
4 Creating Educational Videos 49
5 Creating Entertaining Videos 57
6 Incorporating YouTube Videos in Your Overall Web
     Marketing Mix 63

II Producing Your Own YouTube Videos

7 Understanding Audio/Video Technology 69
8 Shooting Webcam Videos 79
9 Shooting Semi-Pro Videos 89
10 Shooting Professional Videos 115
11 Editing and Enhancing Your Video 123
12 Tips for Producing More Effective YouTube Videos 141

III Managing Your YouTube Videos

13 Uploading Your Videos to YouTube 153
14 Annotating and Linking Your Videos 161
15 Managing Comments 169
16 Establishing Your YouTube Channel 179
17 Leveraging the YouTube Community 191
18 Incorporating YouTube Videos on Your Own Website 199

IV Promotion and Monetization

19 Tracking Performance 207
20 Marketing Your YouTube Videos 223
21 Optimizing Your Videos for Search 237
22 Advertising Your YouTube Videos 243
23 Using Call-to-Action Overlays on Your Videos 255
24 Generating Revenues from Your YouTube Videos 261
25 Using YouTube for B2B Marketing 267
     Index 275

TABLE OF CONTENTS

I   MARKETING YOUR BUSINESS ONLINE WITH YOUTUBE

Introduction **1**

How This Book Is Organized 2

Conventions Used in This Book 3

Web Pages 3

Special Elements 3

There's More Online 4

Get Ready to YouTube 4

1   How YouTube Can Help You Market Your Business **5**

A Short History of YouTube 6

YouTube: The Early Days 6

YouTube Launches—and Gets Acquired 7

YouTube Today 7

Who Watches YouTube—and What Do They Watch? 8

Is Video Right for Your Business? 9

Low-Cost Online Marketing 9

Attracting Eyeballs 10

Everybody's Doing It 11

How Can You Use YouTube to Market Your Business? 11

YouTube for Brand Awareness 11

YouTube for Product Advertising 12

YouTube for Retail Promotion 13

YouTube for Direct Sales 14

YouTube for Product Support 14

YouTube for Internal Training 15

YouTube for Employee Communications 16

YouTube for Recruiting 17

What Kinds of Promotional Videos Should You Produce? . . . 17

Informative Videos 17

Educational Videos 18

Entertaining Videos 19

The Big Picture 19

2 Developing Your YouTube Marketing Strategy **21**

What Is the Purpose of Your YouTube Videos? 22

Who Is Your Customer? 22

What Does Your Customer Want or Need? 24

What Are You Promoting? 24

What Is Your Message? 25

How Will You Measure the Results of Your YouTube
Videos? 26

What Type of Video Content Is Best for Your Goals? 27

Repurposed Commercials 27

Infomercials 29

Instructional Videos 31

Product Presentations and Demonstrations 31

Real Estate Walk-Throughs 32

Customer Testimonials 33

Company Introductions 33

Expert Presentations 33

Business Video Blogs 33

Executive Speeches 33

Company Seminars and Presentations 34

User or Employee Submissions 34

Humorous Spots 34

The Big Picture 35

3 Creating Informative Videos **37**

Why Informative Videos Work 38

Different Types of Informative Videos 39

Information = News 39

Information = Facts 40

Producing an Informative Video 41

Producing a Video Newscast 42

Producing a Video Product Tour 44

The Big Picture 48

4   Creating Educational Videos **49**

Why Educational Videos Work 50

What Kinds of How-To Videos Should You Produce? 50

Product Instruction Videos 50

Project Videos 51

Producing a How-To Video 53

The Big Picture 55

5   Creating Entertaining Videos **57**

What's Entertaining? 58

Understanding Viral Videos 60

Producing an Entertaining Video 61

The Big Picture 61

6   Incorporating YouTube Videos in Your Overall Web Marketing Mix **63**

Defining YouTube's Role in Your Marketing Strategy 64

Formulating Your New Marketing Mix 64

Coordinating Your Online Marketing Activities 65

Making YouTube Co-Exist with Television Marketing 66

Repurposing 67

Extending and Expanding 67

Starting Fresh 68

The Big Picture 68

II   PRODUCING YOUR YOUTUBE VIDEOS

7   Understanding Audio/Video Technology **69**

Understanding Video Resolution 70

Standard Versus High Definition 70

YouTube Resolution 70

Choosing the Right Resolution 72

Understanding Video File Formats 73

Understanding Compression and Codecs 73

Comparing File Formats 73

Choosing the Right Format for Your YouTube Videos 75

Converting Existing Videos to YouTube Format 77

The Big Picture 77

8 Shooting Webcam Videos **79**

Understanding Webcam Video 80

When a Webcam Makes Sense 81

Creating a Video Blog 82

Reporting from the Road or Special Events 82

Responding to Immediate Issues 82

Capturing Customer Testimonials 83

Tips for Shooting an Effective Webcam Video 83

Make It Immediate 83

Keep It Simple 83

Watch the Lighting 84

Minimize the Background Noise 84

Uploading Webcam Video to YouTube 85

Uploading Webcam Video Files 85

Uploading Live Webcam Video 85

The Big Picture 88

9 Shooting Semi-Pro Videos **89**

Understanding Consumer Video Equipment 90

How Camcorders Work 90

Examining Camcorder Storage 91

Standard or High Definition? 92

Choosing a Camcorder 92

Selecting Essential Accessories 96

Building a Computer for Video Editing 100

When a Semi-Pro Video Makes Sense 101

   Video Blogs 101

   Informational Videos 102

   Product Demonstrations and Overviews 102

   On-the-Scene Reports 103

Shooting a Semi-Pro Video 103

   Shooting in the Office 103

   Shooting Outside the Office 104

Transferring Videos to Your PC for Editing 105

Tips for Shooting an Effective Semi-Pro Video 106

   Shoot Digitally 106

   Keep the Proper Resolution in Mind 106

   Use a Tripod 106

   Lighting Matters 107

   Use an External Microphone 107

   Watch the Background 108

   A Little Movement Is Good... 108

   ...But Too Much Movement Is Bad 108

   Shoot from Different Angles 109

   Close-Ups Are Good 109

   Don't Center the Subject 109

   Shoot to Edit 111

   Use a Teleprompter 111

   Dress Appropriately 112

The Big Picture 114

10 Shooting Professional Videos **115**

Why Create a Professional Video for YouTube? 116

   Advantages of Professional Videos 116

   Disadvantages of Professional Videos 117

What Makes a Professional Video Professional 118

   Shooting in the Studio 118

   Shooting in the Field 119

   Preparing for a Professional Video Shoot 120

   Learn Your Shooting Angles 121

Wait for the Lighting 121

Prepare for Multiple Takes 122

The Big Picture 122

11 Editing and Enhancing Your Videos 123

Choosing a Video-Editing Program 124

Tier One: Free Programs 124

Tier Two: Mid-Level Programs 126

Tier Three: High-End Programs 130

Using a Video-Editing Program 133

Editing Together Different Shots 134

Inserting Transitions Between Scenes 135

Inserting Titles and Credits 136

Creating Other Onscreen Graphics 137

Adding Background Music 137

Getting Creative with Other Special Effects 138

Converting and Saving Video Files 138

The Big Picture 139

12 Tips for Producing More Effective YouTube Videos 141

Tips for Creating Better-Looking Videos 142

Shoot for the Smaller Screen 142

Accentuate the Contrast 143

Slow and Steady Wins the Race 143

Invest in Quality Equipment 143

Shoot Like a Pro 144

Use Two Cameras 144

Look Professional—Or Not 145

Don't Just Recycle Old Videos—Re-Edit Them, Too 145

Consider Creating a Slideshow 145

Hire a Pro 145

Break the Rules 146

Tips for Improving Your Video Content 146

Be Entertaining 146

Be Informative 146

Go for the Funny 147

Keep It Short 147

Keep It Simple 148

Stay Focused 148

Communicate a Clear Message 148

Avoid the Hard Sell 148

Keep It Fresh 149

Design for Remixing 149

Tips for Generating Sales 149

Include Your Website's Address in the Video 149

Include Your URL in the Accompanying Text 151

Link from Your Channel Page 151

The Big Picture 152

III   MANAGING YOUR YOUTUBE VIDEOS

13   Uploading Your Videos to YouTube 153

Uploading Videos from Your Computer 154

Selecting a File to Upload 154

Entering Information About Your Video 155

Sharing Options 158

Editing Video Information 158

Removing a Video from YouTube 160

The Big Picture 160

14   Annotating and Linking Your Videos 161

Understanding Annotations 162

Uses for Video Annotations 163

Annotating a Video 164

Watching an Annotated Video 166

The Big Picture 167

15   Managing Comments 169

Enabling Comments—and Other User Response Features .. 170

Comments 171

Comment Voting 172

Video Responses 172

Ratings 172

Embedding 172

Syndication 173

Approving Comments and Video Responses 173

Dealing with Negative Comments 174

Removing Viewer Comments and Responses 175

Blocking Specific Viewers from Leaving Comments 175

Responding to Negative Comments 175

The Big Picture 177

16   Establishing Your YouTube Channel **179**

Understanding YouTube Channels 180

Viewing a Channel Page 180

Personalizing Your Channel Page 181

Editing Channel Settings 182

Editing Channel Themes and Colors 182

Editing Channel Modules 184

Choosing Videos and Playlists 185

Establishing a Brand Channel 186

Understanding Brand Channels 186

Benefits of a Brand Channel 188

Applying for a Brand Channel 189

The Big Picture 190

17   Leveraging the YouTube Community **191**

Working the YouTube Community 192

Posting Bulletins to Your Channel's Subscribers 193

Working with Friends and Contacts 194

Adding a Friend to Your List 195

Sending Messages to Your Friends 195

Reading Messages from Other Users 196

The Big Picture 197

18   Incorporating YouTube Videos on Your Own Website **199**

Why You Should Let YouTube Host Your Videos 200

Adding YouTube Video Links to a Web Page 200

Linking to an Individual Video 201

Linking to Your YouTube Channel 202

Embedding YouTube Videos in a Web Page 202

The Big Picture 204

IV   PROMOTION AND MONETIZATION

19   Tracking Performance **207**

Why Tracking Is Important 208

Fine-Tuning Your Efforts 208

Measuring Effectiveness 208

Planning Future Activities 208

Tracking Views, Ratings, and Comments 209

Measuring Views 209

Judging Likes and Dislikes 210

Reviewing Comments 210

Tracking Basic Metrics 210

Tracking More Advanced Metrics 212

Views 212

Discovery 214

Demographics 215

Community 216

Hot Spots 216

Call-to-Action 217

Tracking Effectiveness 218

Tracking Interactivity 218

Tracking Traffic 218

Tracking Conversions 219

Tracking Direct Sales 220

The Big Picture 220

20   Marketing Your YouTube Videos **223**

Start with Great Content... 224

Entertain, Inform, or Educate 224

Target Your Content 225

Write a Compelling Title 225

Pick the Best Thumbnail Image 225

Take Advantage of YouTube's Community Features 227

Sharing with Subscribers and Friends 227

Guerilla Comments 228

Use Email Marketing 229

Reach Out to the Blogosphere 229

Post to Other Web Forums 230

Work the Social Media 230

Run a Contest 233

Promote Traditionally 233

Upload to Other Video-Sharing Sites 234

Advertise Your Video 235

The Big Picture 235

21   Optimizing Your Videos for Search **237**

How YouTube Searches for Videos 238

Choosing the Right Keywords 238

Optimizing Your Tags 239

Optimizing Your Title 240

Optimizing Your Description 241

Optimizing Embeds and Links 241

Optimizing Views 241

Optimizing Comments and Ratings 242

The Big Picture 242

22   Advertising Your YouTube Videos **243**

Understanding YouTube Promoted Videos 244

How PPC Advertising Works 244

How YouTube Promoted Videos Work 245

Creating a Promoted Videos Campaign 246
  Getting Started 246
  Creating an Account and Setting a Budget 247
  Writing Your Ad 248
  Choosing Keywords 249
  Setting CPC 250
  Confirming the Promotion 251
Using the Promoted Videos Dashboard 251
  Examining Key Metrics 252
  Analyzing Individual Video Performance 252
  Editing Your Promotion 254
  Editing Your Bids 254
  Revising Your Budget 254
  Pausing, Resuming, and Deleting Ads 254
The Bottom Line 254

23 Using Call-to-Action Overlays on Your Videos   **255**
Understanding Call-to-Action Overlays 256
Creating a Call-to-Action Overlay 257
Tracking the Performance of Your Call-to-Action
  Overlays 258
The Big Picture 259

24 Generating Revenues from Your YouTube Videos   **261**
Create a Video with Value 262
Direct Viewers to Your Website 262
Close the Sale on Your Website 264
The Big Picture 265

25 Using YouTube for B2B Marketing   **267**
Why Use YouTube for B2B Marketing 268
Different Ways B2B Companies Can Use YouTube ... 268
  Using YouTube for Additional Information 269
  Using YouTube to Reinforce Existing Relationships ... 269
  Using YouTube for After-the-Sale Support 269

Different Types of B2B Videos 270

    Product Demonstrations and Walk-Throughs 270

    How-To Videos 270

    Case Studies and Testimonials 270

    Conferences and Events 270

    Management Messages and Video Blogs 271

Best Practices for B2B Marketing on YouTube 271

    Upload All Existing Video Assets 271

    Publicize Your Videos 271

    Optimize Your Videos for Search 272

    Embed Your YouTube Videos on Your Own Website 272

    Optimize Your Channel Page 272

    Keep Your Content Fresh 273

    Include a Call to Action 273

The Bottom Line 273

Index **275**

About the Author

Michael Miller is a successful and prolific author. He is known for his casual, easy-to-read writing style and his ability to explain a wide variety of complex topics to an everyday audience.

Mr. Miller has written more than 100 nonfiction books over the past two decades, with more than a million copies in print worldwide. His most popular books include *The Ultimate Web Marketing Guide, Facebook for Grown-Ups, Windows 7 Your Way, Selling Online 2.0, Using Google AdWords and AdSense, Sams Teach Yourself Google Analytics in 10 Minutes*, and *Sams Teach Yourself YouTube in 10 Minutes*.

You can email Mr. Miller directly at youtube4business@molehillgroup.com. His website is at www.molehillgroup.com, and his YouTube channel is www.youtube.com/user/trapperjohn2000/.

Dedication

To Sherry. It's even better now.

Acknowledgments

Thanks to the usual suspects at Que, including but not limited to Greg Wiegand, Michelle Newcomb, Charlotte Kughen, and technical editor Steve Baldwin.

We Want to Hear from You!

As the reader of this book, *you* are our most important critic and commentator. We value your opinion and want to know what we're doing right, what we could do better, what areas you'd like to see us publish in, and any other words of wisdom you're willing to pass our way.

As an associate publisher for Que, I welcome your comments. You can email or write me directly to let me know what you did or didn't like about this book—as well as what we can do to make our books better.

Please note that I cannot help you with technical problems related to the topic of this book. We do have a User Services group, however, where I will forward specific technical questions related to the book.

When you write, please be sure to include this book's title and author, as well as your name, email address, and phone number. I will carefully review your comments and share them with the author and editors who worked on the book.

Email: feedback@quepublishing.com

Mail: Greg Wiegand
Que Publishing
800 East 96th Street
Indianapolis, IN 46240 USA

Reader Services

Visit our website and register this book at www.quepublishing.com/register for convenient access to any updates, downloads, or errata that might be available for this book.

Introduction

Unless you've been living in a cave for the past few years, you've no doubt heard of YouTube, the video-sharing site owned by Google. YouTube lets anyone post videos online so that anyone else can watch. It's a fun site and a popular one, constantly ranking in the top five of all sites on the Web with more than 130 million visitors per month. With hundreds of millions of videos on the YouTube site, it would take a viewer half a millennium to watch them all!

When I wrote the first edition of this book, back in 2008, YouTube was a lot smaller than it is today—still big, and still a major site, but less half the size. It's more than doubled in visitors and videos in the two years since then, which is somewhat astounding. YouTube just keeps getting bigger.

It's this size that makes YouTube attractive to businesses—as well as the relatively low cost of entry. The cost of making a YouTube video is next to nothing; you don't need much more than a camcorder and a computer. If you can reach even a fraction of YouTube's 130 million users, you can get a very big bang for your marketing buck.

That's why I wrote this book, to help you learn how to add YouTube to your company's online marketing mix. Judging from the number of interviews I give and questions I get asked, it's obviously a topic of interest for a lot of organizations, large and small.

I try to answer as many of these questions as possible in this book. You'll learn how you can use YouTube to market your company, brand, products, and services online; what types of videos you should create; how to create those videos; and how to promote and make money from your YouTube videos. It's easy enough that any business can do it.

The new edition of *YouTube for Business* adds to what I first presented two years ago, to cover YouTube's new features for marketers. You'll learn how to promote your videos on the YouTube site, insert pop-up notes and annotations, add clickable overlays to your videos, and create a customized brand channel. I even address how to use YouTube for B2B marketing, which is always a hot topic.

Know that the information included in this book is both strategic and technical. That means you'll find general marketing advice alongside specific technical instructions; you'll learn how to use YouTube as a marketing tool as well as how to create, post, and manage YouTube-friendly videos. If you do it right, YouTube can become an important part of your marketing mix and drive a lot of traffic (and sales) to your existing website.

How This Book Is Organized

YouTube for Business, Second Edition is part marketing text, part computer book; that's because you need both marketing and technical skills to take best advantage of YouTube as a marketing channel. To that end, I organized this book into four main parts, as follows:

- **Part I, "Marketing Your Business Online with YouTube,"** helps you incorporate YouTube as part of your online marketing strategy. You'll learn how YouTube can help you market your business, as well as discover the three types of videos that can lead to YouTube success.

- **Part II, "Producing Your YouTube Videos,"** is all about the technical aspect of creating videos for online videos. You'll learn the necessary audio and video technology, as well as how to create webcam, semi-pro, and professional videos. You'll even learn how to edit your videos by using any desktop personal computer, and discover tips for producing more effective videos.

- **Part III, "Managing Your YouTube Videos,"** shows you how to upload your videos to the YouTube site, create a presence in the YouTube community, customize your YouTube channel page, manage viewer comments, and even incorporate your YouTube videos into your own website.

- **Part IV, "Promotion and Monetization,"** is all about the money. You'll learn how to track your videos' performance, get your videos noticed on the YouTube site, advertise your videos, create clickable overlays, generate revenues from your videos, and use YouTube for B2B marketing.

Conventions Used in This Book

I hope that this book is easy enough to figure out on its own, without requiring its own instruction manual. As you read through the pages, however, it helps to know precisely how I've presented specific types of information.

Web Pages

Obviously, there are a lot of web page addresses in the book, like this one: www.youtube.com. When you see a web page address (also known as a *URL* or *uniform resource locator*), you can go to that web page by entering the URL into the address box in your web browser. I've made every effort to ensure the accuracy of the web addresses presented here, but given the ever-changing nature of the Web, don't be surprised if you run across an address or two that's changed. I apologize in advance.

Special Elements

As you read this book, you'll note several special elements, presented in what we in the publishing business call *margin notes*. There are different types of margin notes for different types of information, as you see here.

 Note

This is a note that presents some interesting information, even if it isn't wholly relevant to the discussion in the main text.

Tip

This is a tip that might prove useful for whatever it is you're in the process of doing.

 Caution

This is a warning that something you might accidentally do might have undesirable results—so take care!

There's More Online

While you're online checking out the videos on the YouTube site, you might want to browse over to my personal website, located at www.molehillgroup.com. Here you'll find more information on this book and other books I've written—including an errata page for this book, in the inevitable event that an error or two creeps into this text. (Hey, nobody's perfect!)

In addition, know that I love to hear from readers of my books. If you want to contact me, feel free to email me at youtube4business@molehillgroup.com. I can't promise that I'll answer every message, but I do promise that I'll read each one!

Get Ready to YouTube

Now that you know how to use this book, it's time to get to the heart of the matter. To learn more about YouTube, and how to make it an essential part of your online marketing mix, get ready and turn the page!

1

How YouTube Can Help You Market Your Business

YouTube is a site where you can watch just about any type of video imaginable. There are videos of cute kittens, indie rock bands, stand-up comedy routines, stupid human tricks, vintage television commercials, high school musicals, film school projects, home movies, breaking news clips, personal video blogs—you name it. Users have uploaded literally millions of video clips, and any-one can watch them in his or her web browser at no cost.

Most of the videos on YouTube are amateurish, produced by nonprofessionals with simple webcams or consumer camcorders—and that's okay; it's personal, but stuff that people like to watch. But there is an increasing number of more professional clips, many designed to service or pro-mote a particular product or business.

That's right: Businesses small and large have discovered YouTube. In fact, YouTube is the hottest new medium for online marketing; if your business has an online component, you could, and should, be promoting it via YouTube videos.

A Short History of YouTube

If you've never visited the YouTube website (shown in Figure 1.1), you've missed out on the hottest thing on the Internet today. It's hard to believe that YouTube is barely five years old; what did we do online before there were YouTube videos to watch?

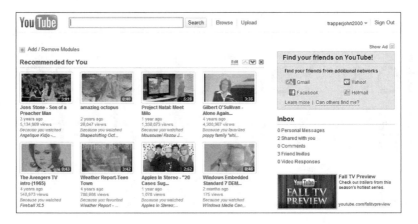

Figure 1.1   *The YouTube site—home base for all your online video marketing.*

YouTube: The Early Days

YouTube was the brainchild of three former PayPal employees: Chad Hurley, Steven Chen, and Jawed Karim. The three founders had left their former company and were looking for a new business opportunity. After exploring a few less interesting ideas, they eventually realized there was a real need for a service that facilitated the process of uploading, watching, and sharing videos. Hence the development of YouTube.

The trio registered the domain name YouTube.com on February 15, 2005 and then started developing the technology for the site—in Hurley's garage. Chen, the programmer of the bunch, worked with Adobe's Flash development language to stream video clips inside a web browser. Hurley, a user interface expert, adopted the concept of *tags* to let users identify and share the videos they liked. Together they came up with a way to let users paste video clips onto their own web pages, which expanded the reach of the site.

The development work done, a public beta test version of the site went live in May 2005. After a few months of working the kinks out of the site, the three men officially launched YouTube in December 2005.

YouTube Launches—and Gets Acquired

YouTube proved immensely popular from virtually the first day in business. Site traffic that first month was three million visitors, which is pretty good for a startup. The number of visitors tripled by the third month (February), tripled again by July (to 30 million visitors), and reached 38 million visitors by the end of the site's first year in business. That made YouTube one of the top 10 sites on the Web, period—and one of the fastest growing websites in history.

That kind of growth didn't go unnoticed, especially by competing websites. The biggest of the competing sites, Google, set out to buy the company, and did so in October 2006. Google paid $1.65 billion for YouTube—an incredible sum for such a young company, and one that had yet to generate significant revenues.

This put YouTube smack in the middle of the mighty Google empire. That said, YouTube continues to operate independently of the mother ship; the site looks and acts pretty much the same today as it did in the pre-Google days. The only big difference is volume.

YouTube Today

The number of videos and users on the site continues to grow, which is great for businesses looking to take advantage of the opportunity. In fact, the growth has been nothing short of stratospheric; traffic to the site has doubled in just the past two years. (Figure 1.2 shows this growth, graphically.)

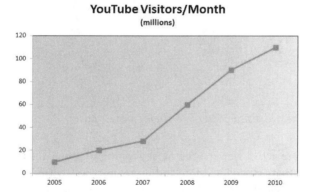

Figure 1.2   *YouTube visitors per month—tremendous growth through the years.*

How big is YouTube today? According to the market research firm comScore, YouTube is the number-three site on all the Web, with more than 146 million visitors per month (as of August 2010). And those visitors are watching a lot of videos—more than two billion videos a day, representing more than 40% of all videos watched online.

Who Watches YouTube—and What Do They Watch?

Not surprisingly, it appears that YouTube is replacing traditional television viewing for many users. According to Google, an average YouTube viewer spends 164 minutes online every day; in contrast, viewers spend just 130 minutes per day watching traditional television. Where would you rather put your marketing message?

YouTube's viewers come from all ages and demographic groups. Figure 1.3 details the age distribution of YouTube's user base; the attractive 18–44 demographic represents 56% of YouTube's viewers. In terms of gender distribution, it's a fairly even 55% male/45% female split.

YouTube Age Distribution

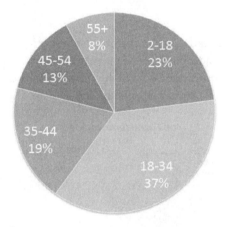

Figure 1.3   *The age distribution of YouTube's viewer base.*

These viewers are active viewers. Yes, most people still watch YouTube on their computers, but that's changing. More and more users watch YouTube on their mobile phones while they're on the go; the YouTube app is one of the most popular applications for the iPhone. And an increasing number of people are watching YouTube in their living rooms, as an increasing number of flat screen TVs and Blu-ray players come with Internet connectivity—and a YouTube widget—built in.

What are these people watching? Lots and lots of different videos, that's what. Sysomos recently analyzed YouTube usage by category, and came up with the numbers shown in Figure 1.4. Music is the big category, at 31% of all videos viewed, but after that it breaks down a lot more evenly.

YouTube Video Viewership by Category

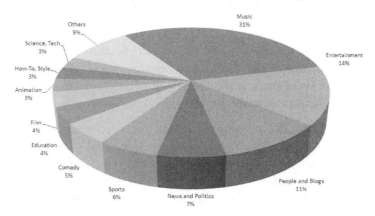

Figure 1.4   *What people watch on YouTube, by category.*

Is Video Right for Your Business?

I'll give you the bottom line up front: If done right, YouTube can provide a huge bang for your marketing buck. That's because YouTube delivers a huge audience for very little investment. It's a marketer's dream channel.

That said, YouTube isn't right for all businesses. And there's a lot of competition for eyeballs on the YouTube site. You have to do a lot of things right to get the payback you desire.

Low-Cost Online Marketing

Let's look at the cost thing first. Large businesses have long embraced video marketing, in the form of traditional television advertising. But television ads are expensive, and typically outside the purview of smaller businesses—except, perhaps, for little-seen late night spots on local channels.

Thanks to YouTube, however, businesses both large and small can afford to market themselves via online videos. The cost of posting a video to the YouTube site is zero; YouTube doesn't charge anything to upload, host, or stream videos. The only cost you have is the expense of shooting and editing the video, which can be as low as you want it to be; not a lot of YouTube videos are high-priced professional affairs. This makes YouTube marketing affordable for virtually any business.

Attracting Eyeballs

But is video the right way to promote your business? If you've never produced a video or television ad, you might not be sure. But in many cases, a short video can have tremendous positive effect on your website's traffic or in orders generated via 800-number.

Let's face it: Consumers love to watch videos. We're becoming less a society of readers and more one of watchers; the average consumer would rather watch a video than read a text-based advertisement. Like it or not, you need to be aware of and adapt your marketing mix to this trend.

And here's the thing: The more interesting the video, the bigger the audience it will attract. You can include a lot of information in a short three-minute video, and you can present that information in an entertaining and engaging fashion. People like to be entertained, educated, and informed, and online video can do all three things—and, in the process, provide a clear picture of the product or service you're offering.

DoubleClick conducted a survey in 2006 that codified the benefits of online video advertising. Here's what it found:

- A high percentage of audiences interact with video ads, via mouseovers, use of the video control buttons, and so forth.

- Viewers click the Play button in video ads twice as often as they click traditional image ads. In addition, click-through rates are four to five times higher than with traditional text or image ads.

- Viewers actually watch video ads. On average, video ads play two thirds of the way through.

Here's how Rick Bruner, research director at DoubleClick, assessed the results:

Online video ads are quickly becoming the medium of choice to drive both brand awareness and sales. The results show that there are clear ROI advantages to placing video ads. We expect to see strong growth in the number of companies reaping the benefits of online video advertising in the coming months and years.

Done effectively, a YouTube video can add a viral component to your company's web marketing strategy. You see, when you post a video to YouTube, that video takes on a life of its own. It will be viewed by thousands of YouTube users, posted to numerous websites and blogs, emailed around the Internet—you name it. Just make sure you tailor your message to the YouTube crowd and you can start generating traffic from the millions of people who frequent YouTube each day. Any user watching your video is now a potential customer—assuming that you include your website's address or other contact information in the video itself.

Everybody's Doing It

It doesn't matter what type of business you run or how large that business is. You can create effective videos that will attract YouTube viewers and drive more business to your website or 800-number. All types of businesses are getting into the YouTube scene: local businesses, major national marketers, ad agencies, real estate agencies, consultants and motivational speakers, Internet-only retailers, B2C, B2B—you name it.

On the big side of things, consider the major brands that are incorporating YouTube into their overall marketing mix. YouTube's big-name adherents look like a who's who of brand marketing today: American Express, Coca Cola, Ford, Home Depot, Old Spice, Progressive Insurance, Sears, Starbucks… the list goes on and on. (And I haven't even mentioned all the big media companies, from CBS to Disney, that distribute their content on the YouTube site.)

As far as smaller companies go, there are too many to even start mentioning them here. I've seen videos from companies that make or sell aquarium accessories, computer cables, motorcycle parts, you name it. Realtors use YouTube to show video walk-throughs of their properties; travel agencies use YouTube to show off their prize destinations. Pottery companies use the site to sell their wares; credit card companies use the site to show merchants how to use their terminals.

In short, YouTube is used by companies of all sizes to do many things. If what you're selling is in any way visual, which almost everything is, YouTube is a perfect medium for your company's promotional message.

How Can You Use YouTube to Market Your Business?

Given the huge number of companies that embrace YouTube videos, it should come as no surprise that there are a lot of different ways to use the site. Every company has its own unique goals for their YouTube marketing.

Some companies use YouTube to generate brand awareness. Some use YouTube to promote a particular product or drive sales to their retail store or website. Others incorporate YouTube as part of their product or customer support mix, use videos for product training, or even use YouTube for recruiting and employee communications. Anything you can say in person or to a group of people, you can say in a video and distribute via YouTube.

YouTube for Brand Awareness

Large national companies and major advertisers often use YouTube to enhance the awareness of their brands. Instead of focusing on individual products or services, these videos push the company's brand, often in the same fashion used in traditional television advertising.

In fact, online videos are better at imparting brand awareness than are traditional TV ads. A Millward Brown study found that online viewing led to 82% brand awareness and 77% product recall, compared to just 54% brand awareness and 18% product recall for similar television ads. Experts believe this is because online viewers are more engaged than television viewers; the Web is a more interactive medium than the passive viewing inherent with television.

Brand awareness videos are typically entertaining, using a soft-sell approach to ingrain the brand's name and image in the minds of viewers. A good example is the series of videos produced by Old Spice (www.youtube.com/user/OldSpice), like the one shown in Figure 1.5, capitalizing on the popularity of its 2010 "The Man Your Man Could Smell Like" commercials. I love these videos; they're clever, intelligent, and entertaining as hell. They're also extremely popular, garnering millions of views apiece on the YouTube site. Very successful brand building, indeed.

Figure 1.5   *A brand-building video from Old Spice.*

YouTube for Product Advertising

If you can use YouTube to push an overall brand, you can use it to push individual products, too. This requires a more direct approach, although it's still important to make the video informative, educational, or entertaining.

To promote a product, you want to show the product in your advertising, as Nike (www.youtube.com/user/nikefootball) does with its Bootcamp Drill videos, shown in Figure 1.6. You can show the product in action or used as part of a demonstration or tutorial. Just make sure you include lots of close-up product shots and link back to your own website—where more product information is available.

Figure 1.6   *Promoting Nike soccer (football) shoes in a Bootcamp Drill video.*

YouTube for Retail Promotion

You can also use YouTube to promote a company's retail stores. These videos can be general in nature (which gives the videos a long shelf life), or more specifically targeted to shorter-term promotions ("check out this weekend's specials!").

But a video that is nothing more than a store advertisement probably won't attract a lot of viewers. A better approach is to find a way to showcase the store without resorting to claims of 20% off and "this weekend only" specials. For example, you might want to record a short store tour or highlight individual departments or services within the store. You can even produce educational videos that demonstrate the products or services your store offers, like the one for Home Depot (www.youtube.com/user/homedepot) shown in Figure 1.7. Make the video informative, and you stand a better chance of grabbing eyeballs.

Figure 1.7   *Showing off the latest grills in a Home Depot video.*

YouTube for Direct Sales

YouTube is a terrific channel for generating direct sales for products and services. All you have to do is show the product in action or provide a clip of the service in question, and then ask for the sale by directing the viewer to your own website.

One of the best ways to showcase a product is in an instructional video—the online equivalent of an old-school infomercial. Do you remember Ron Popeil's late-night TV ads for slicers and dicers? Create a shorter version of said Ronco ads, but focusing on the useful attributes of your product, and you'll gain YouTube viewership.

The key to converting eyeballs to dollars is to generously highlight your company's website address or 800-number within the body of the video. Put the contact information at the front of the video, at the end of the video, and overlaid at the bottom of the screen during the body of the clip, as Sign Warehouse (www.youtube.com/ user/signwarehouse) does in the video shown in Figure 1.8. Make it easy for interested viewers to find more information or place an order. (And, to that end, there's nothing wrong with mentioning the product's price somewhere in the video.)

Figure 1.8   *A direct sales video from Sign Warehouse.*

YouTube for Product Support

Not all companies use YouTube to generate new business; some companies do so to support existing customers. Consider some of the most common customer problems and questions, and produce one or more videos addressing those issues. If you can help your customers help themselves, you provide them with a useful service and reduce your company's support costs—all with a free YouTube video.

For example, AutoDesk Inventor is a high-end computer program for 3D mechanical design from AutoDesk (www.youtube.com/user/autodesk). Knowing that their customers need a lot of post-sales support, the company put together a series of YouTube videos (such as the one in Figure 1.9) showing how to install, configure, and use the program. It's extremely useful—and helps to cut down on traditional tech support costs, as well.

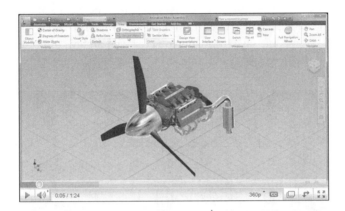

Figure 1.9 *Post-sales customer support for AutoDesk Inventor.*

 Note

> You can also embed your YouTube support video into your own website. It doesn't matter where customers view the video, YouTube or your site; what matters is that they get their problems solved at little or no expense to you. Learn more about embedding YouTube videos on your company's site in Chapter 18, "Incorporating YouTube Videos on Your Own Website."

The same goes if you have specific product support or technical support issues. If you're a computer manufacturer, you might create a video showing users how to install more memory or connect an external hard drive. If you're a car manufacturer, you might create a video showing drivers how to change a brake light or check their car's oil level. You get the idea—use YouTube to turn a problem area into a public relations victory.

YouTube for Internal Training

Your company can also use YouTube for internal purposes. Take, for example, the issue of sales or product training. You have a new product to introduce and a sales force to train. How best to reach them? In the old days, you'd fly salespeople from around the country to a central office and put on a day's worth of hands-on training. Doing so, however, is both time-consuming and expensive.

Instead, consider using YouTube for your product training. Create a series of short training videos, like the one in Figure 1.10 for Cree LED Lighting (www.youtube.com/user/CreeLEDLighting). All you have to do is upload the videos to YouTube and provide access to all your company's salespeople. (They don't have to be public videos.) Sales force personnel can watch the videos at their leisure, without losing valuable sales time trekking back to the office for training. You save money, your salespeople save time, and you create an archive of product information that anyone can access at any time.

Figure 1.10 *A product training video for Cree LED Lighting.*

 Note

If you create a video for internal use, make it a private video so that it won't be viewable by the public. Learn how to do this in Chapter 13, "Uploading Your Videos to YouTube."

YouTube for Employee Communications

You can use YouTube for all manner of company communications. Instead of holding a big company meeting just so that the big boss can give his yearly state of the company address, have him record the address and post it on a private channel on YouTube. Employees can watch the prez say his thing from the comfort of their own desks, while they're on the road, or even at home.

In fact, many companies find that YouTube is a fast and effective way to disseminate all kinds of employee information. Done right, it gets information out there in near–real-time, with all the benefit of face-to-face communication, which is a lot better than sending impersonal memos via email.

YouTube for Recruiting

Finally, don't underestimate YouTube as a recruitment tool for new employees. If you have a company welcome video, post it on YouTube and make it public. Think of this as a PR exercise to attract new talent to your company, which means doing it up right—it's as much a marketing project as it is something from the HR department.

You can link to the video from all your recruiting materials, even from any traditional ads you place. Don't limit yourself to a single long puff video: Produce separate videos for individual departments, as well as to illustrate company values, employee benefits, facilities, and the like.

 Tip

Your current employees are your best recruitment tools. Include plenty of employee interviews in your recruitment videos to help personalize your company and to put a friendly face on the corporation.

What Kinds of Promotional Videos Should You Produce?

Let's narrow our focus specifically to promotional videos—those videos produced to market a company, its brands, or its products and services. What types of videos work best to get your message across?

While there's a lot of variety, depending on the type of business or product being marketed, the key is to offer a video that YouTube users actually want to watch. That means a video that has some sort of entertainment, educational, or informational value. In other words, your video needs to entertain, educate, or inform—or no one will watch it.

Informative Videos

One way to do this is to create the YouTube equivalent of an infomercial; that is, a video that provides useful information to the viewer. This information can be anything from a guided tour of a new product to a company spokesperson talking about larger industry trends. It's a newsy kind of approach, one that leaves the viewer more informed than he was before he started watching.

For example, if you're a travel agent, you can produce an informative video that provides a guided tour of one of your featured destinations. You could also take a more talking-head approach, and have one of your agents talk about travel trends in the coming season. Or maybe you put together some PowerPoint slides comparing travel costs to different destinations.

The key is to provide information that your current or potential customers find truly useful. This helps establish your company as the authority on this topic; when the customer wants to pull the trigger, he'll think of you because of the useful information you provided.

Of course, you do have to remind the customer of who you are and how he can contact you. That means placing a title card at the beginning and end of the video with your website address or toll-free phone number. You can also overlay this information onscreen during the course of the video. And don't forget to include this contact information in the descriptive text that accompanies your video.

The key is to provide enough useful information to be of practical value to viewers, and then make it easy for those viewers to click through to your site for more information or to purchase what you have for sale. It can't be a straight advertisement; it has to be real information, presented in as straight a fashion as possible.

 Note

Learn more about informative videos in Chapter 3, "Creating Informative Videos."

Educational Videos

Another approach is to educate the viewer, show him how to do something useful with the products or services you sell. This means producing a "how to" video, a step-by-step guide to doing something the viewer wants or needs to do.

For example, if you sell appliance parts, you could create a video showing how to change the water filter in a refrigerator or the light bulb in a dryer. If you offer custom woodworking services, create a video showing how to build a bookcase or install wood trim. If you're a tire store, create a video showing how to check tire pressure or change a flat. You get the picture.

The key here is to offer truly useful content. Nothing theoretical or ethereal; down-to-earth practicality is what attracts YouTube viewers. Make the task common enough to draw a large audience, produce an easy-to-follow step-by-step tutorial, and then use the video to sell other goods and services.

Note

Learn more about educational videos in Chapter 4, "Creating Educational Videos."

Entertaining Videos

Informing and educating are important, and you can draw in a fair number of YouTube viewers if you do these things right. But everybody likes to be entertained, which is why pure entertainment videos typically show up at the top of YouTube's lists of most-viewed videos.

What's entertaining? It's impossible to say. Maybe you find some funny way to use your product or service. Maybe you put your president or CEO in a funny situation. Maybe you put together a product or industry overview that focuses on the lighter side of things. Or maybe you turn the creative work over to the pros and engage a creative agency to produce your videos.

Whatever you do, it has to be something that viewers find interesting and at least a little humorous. It needs to bear up to repeat viewings, and it should be something that people might like to share with their friends. Viral videos are a result of people sharing links with each other—and people definitely like to share those videos they find most entertaining.

 Note

Learn more about entertaining videos in Chapter 5, "Creating Entertaining Videos."

The Big Picture

As you can see, there are lots of ways your company can make use of YouTube videos—from traditional brand and product marketing to customer support and employee communications. In almost all instances, you don't have to spend a fortune doing making videos for YouTube; as you'll learn, you can produce them in a quick and inexpensive fashion. And, of course, you don't have to give a penny to YouTube; everything you post on the YouTube site is completely free of charge.

The key is to not overthink or overanalyze the opportunity. Don't be afraid to get started, even if your first videos are modest with little budget behind them. YouTube makes it easy to dip your toes in the water; you can't reap the benefit until you get online!

2

Developing Your YouTube Marketing Strategy

Before you shoot your first minute of video footage, you need to determine how YouTube fits into your marketing plans. What is your YouTube marketing strategy—what do you want to achieve, and how?

Developing a YouTube marketing strategy is similar to developing any marketing strategy. You need to focus on your customer (audience), your message, your products/services/brand, and the other elements of your marketing mix. Everything has to work together to bring your chosen message to your chosen customer, and generate the desired results.

You can't just shoot a video and throw it on the YouTube site; you need to develop a plan. This chapter walks you through the elements of a successful YouTube marketing strategy—what you need to do, why, and how.

What Is the Purpose of Your YouTube Videos?

Let's start with the most basic strategic issues for any marketing professional: What is the purpose of your YouTube videos? What is your goal? Why do you want to market via YouTube?

The wrong answer to the last question is "because everyone's doing it." Equally wrong are "because it's the latest thing," "because my competitors are doing it," and "because it's neat." As a marketing professional, you can't base your marketing strategy on the latest trends and technologies or on the behaviors of other marketers. You have to pick and choose the media you use based on their strategic importance to your company and brand; you have to pick media that serves your purpose and achieves your stated results.

It's possible that there is no strategic reason for you to market on YouTube. Perhaps you run a local contracting business and you have a very loyal and satisfied customer base, enough to fill your schedule for years to come. In this instance, you might have nothing to gain by putting up a video on YouTube.

On the other hand, maybe you *do* have something to gain from producing a series of YouTube videos. Even if you don't want or need to attract new customers, you might be able to serve your existing customers better by incorporating YouTube into your media mix. Perhaps you can create a video demonstrating some of the options you have available for your customers, using YouTube as a kind of extended video catalog. Or maybe you can reinforce your new customers' choices by uploading testimonials from customers who have been pleased with your company. Possibly you can use YouTube as after-sale support by showing customers how to maintain the work you create for them.

The point is that you need to determine up front what you want to achieve and how YouTube can help you achieve that. Don't automatically assume that YouTube is just for attracting new customers or selling individual products—there are a number of ways that you can use YouTube for both pre-sale promotion and after-sale support. Figure out your goals ahead of time, and then build your plan around those goals. And, as I said, if YouTube doesn't help you achieve those goals, that's okay; you should never shoehorn a particular medium into your plans just because everybody else thinks you ought to.

Who Is Your Customer?

Another factor in determining how YouTube fits into your plans is the customers you're trying to reach. Just who do you sell to—and why?

This is Marketing 101 stuff, so forgive me if I'm stating the obvious. But many marketers, especially those working online, either don't know the basics or somehow forget them over time. Sometimes stating the obvious is the most important thing you can do.

All your marketing should revolve around the customer, so it's imperative that you know who that customer is and what he wants. Work through the following checklist to determine just who you should be focusing on:

- How old is your target customer?

- Is your customer male or female?

- Is your customer single or married?

- What is your customer's average yearly income?

- Where does your customer live?

- Where does your customer shop?

- What does your customer like to do in his or her spare time?

- How does your customer describe himself or herself?

- How does your customer prefer to receive information: via newspaper, television, radio, or the Internet?

- What websites does your customer frequent?

- How does your customer access the Internet—via a computer or mobile device, and over what speed of connection?

- What products does your customer currently use?

- Is your target customer a current client or someone who is not yet using your product?

- Does your customer know about your company or product?

- If so, what does your customer think about your company and product—what image does he have of you?

These are just a few of the things you need to know about your target customer. The more you know, of course, the better you can serve the customer's wants and needs. The less you know, the more you're guessing in the dark—and guessing in the dark is a very ineffective and inefficient way to create a marketing plan.

Of course, another set of important questions to ask, in terms of incorporating YouTube into your marketing mix, concerns YouTube itself. Does your customer visit the YouTube site? If so, how often? Why does he visit the site? What does he think of YouTube? What types of videos does he like to watch? How does he feel about "commercial" videos on YouTube?

If your customer is a heavy YouTube viewer, and if he's open to commercial messages among his entertainment, YouTube holds promise as a marketing vehicle for your company. On the other hand, if your customer never visits YouTube, or is diametrically opposed to commercial messages intruding on his entertainment, you really shouldn't include YouTube in your marketing mix. After all, you don't want to advertise in places where your customer isn't.

What Does Your Customer Want or Need?

Knowing who your customer is makes up just part of the process. Equally important is knowing what your customer wants or needs—that is, why the customer is in the market for a particular product or service.

Perhaps the customer has a problem; most do. Your customer is looking for a solution to that problem—and that solution is what you want to provide.

 Tip

Often times, the customer's problem has something to do with using your product—and the solution might be a post-sale video showing just how to set things up or access key features.

Or perhaps your customer has a basic unfulfilled need, such as food, shelter, or security. Your goal is to fulfill that basic need; the product or service you offer is how to fill the need.

What's key is to identity with your customer so that you share his wants and needs. Only then can you determine how to best meet those requirements, and communicate that fact in a compelling fashion.

What Are You Promoting?

What exactly is it that you want to promote on YouTube? Is it your overall company, a brand, or an individual product or service? You need to identify this upfront because you'll use different methods to promote different aspects of your business.

And, remember, you're not always promoting a product. That is, your product might be only the means to an end. For example, you might be selling bookcases, but what you're really promoting is a superior system for displaying your customers' libraries of books. Or maybe you're selling door locks; what you're promoting are the security and peace of mind that come from a superior lock solution.

In other words, you're promoting a solution, not a product or service. Your product or service is merely a means to accomplish that solution.

Or maybe you're not promoting anything at all. That is, you might be using YouTube to provide customer support or technical support; that's much different from using YouTube to sell products or services. It's also possible that you're using YouTube for strictly internal purposes, to support your employee base or for employee training. Again, how you intend to use YouTube will determine the types of videos you create.

What Is Your Message?

Assuming that you're using YouTube to promote your company, brand, or product/service, what message is it that you want to impart? Marketing is about more than just offering a product for sale; it's also about creating and conveying a company/brand/product image—and that image is conveyed as part of a cohesive marketing message.

Take, for example, the classic example of low-end versus high-end image. If you're selling a commodity product on price, the image you convey must resonate with a price-sensitive audience. On the other hand, if you're offering a high-end product to a brand-savvy audience, you need to convey a classier image; it's not about price, it's about appearance.

Beyond simple image, your YouTube videos need to carry the same or similar message that you use in your other advertising media. This message is critical to everything you do in your marketing efforts; it should grab your customers' attention, tell them how you can solve their problem/meet their needs, and convince them that you offer the best of all available solutions.

That last point bears reinforcement. Not only should you tell potential customers what it is you're offering, you must tell them what it is about your company/brand/product that differentiates you from your competitors. Answer the unspoken question, "why us?"—or you risk losing the sale to a better-defined competitor. Emphasize what makes you different, and what makes you better. You are selling yourself, after all.

In doing this, however, you should never forget that your message is about the customer, not about you. The biggest mistake that companies make is to communicate "what we do" instead of "what we do for you." Customers want to hear what's in it for them, not what's in it for you.

In addition, you must present your message in terms of benefits rather than features. Never describe the 22 function buttons on your new electronic gizmo; instead, describe how each button solves a particular customer want/need. Instead of saying that your gizmo has memory recall, say that "memory recall lets you remember key contacts at the touch of a single button." Again, phrase your message in terms of what you do for the customer—not in terms of what you or your product does.

How Will You Measure the Results of Your YouTube Videos?

Creating a video and posting it on YouTube is just part of the process. How do you measure the success of that video?

The first key to measuring success is to determine what kind of response you wanted. Did you design the video to generate direct sales, either via your website or 800-number? Did you design the video to drive traffic to your website? Did you design the video to enhance or reinforce your company or brand image? Or did you design the video to reduce customer or technical support costs?

This is key: To measure the success of your YouTube video, you have to first determine what it is you hope to achieve. Then, and only then, can you measure the results:

- If your goal is to generate sales, measure sales. Include your website's URL (ideally to a unique landing page) and toll-free number in the video, along with a promotion or order code, and then track sales that include that code.

- If your goal is to drive traffic to your website, measure your traffic (pageviews and unique visitors) pre- and post-YouTube video. Use site analytics to determine where site traffic originates from; specifically track the traffic that came directly from the YouTube site.

- If your goal is to build your brand image, measurement is more difficult. You'll need to conduct some sort of market research after your YouTube campaign has had a chance to do its thing, and ask customers what they think of your brand—and where they heard about it.

- If your goal is to reduce customer or technical support costs, measure the number of support requests before and after uploading the YouTube video(s). The more effective the video, the fewer the subsequent calls for support.

Of course, another way to measure your video's success is to count the number of views it achieves on YouTube. This, however, is a false measurement. Just because many people view your video doesn't mean that it has accomplished the goals you set out to achieve. A video with 100,000 views is nice, but it means nothing if you wanted to boost your sales and it didn't do that. Entertaining YouTube viewers is one thing, but generating sales (or establishing brand image or whatever) is quite another.

What Type of Video Content Is Best for Your Goals?

What type of video should you produce for YouTube? More immediately, what types of video *can* you produce?

You have a number of choices to make when determining what type of videos to produce for YouTube. It's not a one-size-fits-all situation; what works for one company might bomb completely for another. In fact, what works today might not be what you need to do tomorrow. And, of course, you're not limited to a single approach; many companies employ two or more different types of videos, each designed to achieve its own specific goal.

With that in mind, let's look at the most common types of videos that companies incorporate into their online marketing mixes.

Repurposed Commercials

Many companies think that the best way to use YouTube is as an alternative distribution channel for their existing television commercials. Their YouTube content consists of repurposed commercials—the same 30-second spots they run on television.

This might be an appropriate strategy—if your TV spots are uniquely entertaining. To be honest, however, this is a losing strategy for most firms; YouTube viewers tend to expect something new and different than the same commercials they see on TV.

In fact, some companies have experienced the ire of the YouTube community for unimaginatively commercializing the site in this manner. You win the support of the community by doing something new and innovative; you lose their support when you seemingly don't put in the effort, or treat YouTube as just another type of television station—which it most decidedly is not.

 Tip

> In my opinion, YouTube is not the place to recycle your company's commercials. Users will not go out of their way to view something online that they try to avoid otherwise in the real world. Unless you have a clever, Super Bowl–caliber commercial that people want to view again and again, keep your ads to yourself and don't upload them to YouTube.

That said, if you have no budget for new production and you do have a unique commercial message, you might want to try uploading your existing commercials to the YouTube site. Know, however, that what works on the big TV screen often works less well in the small YouTube video window.

For example, it's important to note that most YouTubers view videos in a small window in a web browser on a computer screen. That's pretty small, especially compared to what viewers are used to experiencing on a 42" or larger high definition TV. All the niggling details you can see on a bigger TV turn miniscule when viewed in a web browser. This fact alone might cause you to reshoot a busy television commercial for the smaller YouTube screen; you need to customize the look and feel of your presentation for the YouTube audience.

 Note

Learn more about optimizing your videos for the YouTube audience in Chapter 7, "Understanding Audio/Video Technology."

And then there's the envious situation where you *do* have a Super Bowl–caliber commercial. If so, congratulations! By all means, upload that commercial—and all variations—to YouTube. You can milk this one for all its worth, by creating a "making of" video, doing YouTube-only spinoffs, you name it. This is the best of both worlds, where you build on your success in traditional media by gaining even broader distribution online.

Figure 2.1 shows one such Super Bowl ad on the YouTube site, Snickers' "Game" commercial, starring Betty White. Snickers (www.youtube.com/user/SnickersBrand) has uploaded this particular commercial, of course, as well as similar follow-up ads. As of this writing, they've received more than 2.2 million views on YouTube—not bad for a free upload!

Figure 2.1   *Snickers' popular Super Bowl commercial, viewable on YouTube.*

Infomercials

Let's move beyond repurposed material into new content created expressly for the YouTube site. (Although you can, of course, also display your YouTube videos on your own website or blog.) When you're creating videos just for YouTube, you can choose from among several different approaches you can employ.

One very popular approach is to create the YouTube equivalent of an infomercial. That is, you create a video that purports to convey some type of information, but in reality exists to subtly plug your product or brand.

Let's say that you offer gift baskets for sale. You create a short video for YouTube about how to make gift baskets—something that would be of interest to anyone in the market for them. You prominently display your web page address and phone number within the video and in the descriptive text that accompanies the video on the YouTube site. Because the video has some informational content (the how-to information), it attracts viewers, and a certain percentage of them will follow through to purchase the gift baskets you have for sale.

Or maybe you're a business consultant and you want to promote your consulting services. To demonstrate what you have to offer potential clients, you create and upload some sort of short video—a motivational lecture, perhaps, or a slideshow about specific business practices, or something similar. You use the video to establish your expert status and then display your email address or web page address to solicit business for your consulting services.

Or maybe you have a full-length DVD for sale. You excerpt a portion of the DVD and upload it to YouTube, with graphics before and after (and maybe even during) the video detailing how a viewer can order the full-length DVD can.

Likewise, if you're a musician with music to sell, an author with books to sell, an artist with paintings or other artwork to sell, or a craftsman with various crafts and such to sell. The musician might create a music video to promote his music; the author might read an excerpt from her book; the artist might produce a photo slideshow of her work; and the craftsman might upload a short video walk-through of pieces he has for sale. Make sure you include details for how the additional product can be ordered, and let your placement on YouTube do the promotion for you.

Here's an example of an effective infomercial approach. Viator Travel (www.youtube.com/user/ViatorTravel) offers tours of more than 400 destinations worldwide. The company created a series of informative and entertaining videos about their top destinations, like the one in Figure 2.2, and uploaded those videos to YouTube. Interested people can view the videos and then contact the firm to schedule a vacation. It's quite synergistic.

Figure 2.2 *An online preview of a Barcelona tapas walking tour, from Viator Travel.*

Then there's futurist Dr. Patrick Dixon (www.youtube.com/user/pjvdixon), who's a popular speaker on topics about global change. He's uploaded videos of several of his speeches, like the one in Figure 2.3, and they're both entertaining and informational in regard to the services that he has to offer. Any viewers who like what they see can then go to his website to learn more or arrange a speaking engagement.

Figure 2.3 *An informative speech by Dr. Patrick Dixon.*

The key is to create a video that people actually want to watch. That means something informative, useful, or entertaining. It can't be a straight commercial because people don't like to watch commercials. It has to provide value to the viewer.

After you hook the viewers, you lead them back to your website where your goods or services are for sale. It's a two-step process: Watch the video, and then go to the website to learn more or buy something. If your video is interesting enough, viewers will make the trip to your website to close the deal.

Instructional Videos

Similar to the infomercial is the instructional or how-to video. In this type of video, you create something truly useful for your target customer, and then drive business by direct link from the instructional video.

As an example, take Drs. Foster & Smith Pet Supplies (www.youtube.com/user/drsfostersmith), a retailer of aquarium supplies. They've created a series of videos, like the one in Figure 2.4, which show users how to set up various types of aquariums and aquarium equipment. Each video exists unto itself, with the sole goal of providing practical information to the viewer; it's really useful stuff for the hobbyist.

Figure 2.4   *A how-to video from Drs. Foster & Smith Pet Supplies.*

While this type of video is not a hard sell, and shouldn't be, the company benefits when viewers need to buy related equipment.

Product Presentations and Demonstrations

You can also use YouTube for more obvious selling efforts, the most common of which is the product presentation or demonstration. Here is where you use the video medium to show customers a particular product, in the kind of detail you just can't do in print or on a web page.

Many products are good candidates for video demonstrations, from kitchen appliances and power tools to computers and other electronic gadgets. Automobiles also benefit from video presentation because there's a lot to see there; Figure 2.5 shows just such a video presentation from Audi (www.youtube.com/user/Audi). In fact, any item that's not quickly or easily understood, or that has a bevy of sophisticated features, is a good candidate for a YouTube video demonstration.

Figure 2.5   *A video preview of the Audio A7.*

Real Estate Walk-Throughs

A specific subset of the product demonstration is the real estate walk-through video. Today, most realtors take digital photographs of the houses they list, and potential buyers view those photos on the realtor's website. But there's nothing stopping you from using a camcorder to produce a video tour of the house, editing the tour into a short video, and posting the video on YouTube. As an example, Figure 2.6 shows just such a video walk-through of a luxury property offered by Coldwell Banker (www.youtube.com/user/coldwellbanker).

Figure 2.6   *A video walk-through from realtor Coldwell Banker.*

You can then direct potential buyers to the walk-through video on the YouTube website, or embed the YouTube video on your website so that visitors can view the video there. It's a great enhancement to a realtor's selling services, and it doesn't cost you a dime (beyond the cost of shooting the video, of course).

Customer Testimonials

You can also use YouTube to promote your company or reinforce a buyer's decision. To that end, the time-honored approach of using testimonials from existing customers is a viable one. Send a video crew out to the customer's location, or invite him or her to your office, and let the camera roll. Film the customer talking about her experience with your company in her own words, and you have an effective plug for who you are and what you do.

Company Introductions

For that matter, you can use YouTube to introduce your company to your customers. This could be in the form of a short brand-building video or a video welcome from the company president—even a video tour of your offices or factory. This is especially beneficial for companies that employ innovative production techniques or create especially interesting products.

Expert Presentations

If your business is a leader in its category, or if you are an industry expert, you can establish and exploit that expertise via a series of YouTube videos. All it takes is a video camera or webcam pointed at you behind a desk; you then spend three or four minutes talking about a particular topic or issue of interest. If you truly know what you're talking about, your video will help to establish your professional credentials and burnish your company's image.

Business Video Blogs

This leads us to the topic of video blogs, or *vlogs*. A vlog is like a normal text-based blog, except that it's spoken and put on video. You or someone from your company sits in front of a webcam or video camera and expounds on the issues of the day. Perhaps multiple vloggers participate so that you present a variety of faces to the viewing public. In any case, you use the video blog as you would a normal blog: to comment on contemporary issues and put a human face on your company.

Executive Speeches

If your company likes to communicate regularly to its employees, YouTube presents a better way to do so. Instead of sending a soulless memo to the worker bees or trying to gather all your employees at a single location, simply record your company executives on video and post those videos on YouTube. Create a private channel just for your company's employees, and they can receive the executive's message at any time, on their own computers. It's more efficient than a company meeting and more personal than a memo.

Company Seminars and Presentations

Along the same line, you can use YouTube to bring all your company's employees into seminars and presentations that might otherwise be limited to a select few. You might accomplish this by recording a meeting or seminar with one or more video cameras, or by uploading PowerPoint presentations in a video format with audio annotations. Again, this works best via a private company channel that authorized employees can view at their discretion.

 Tip

To convert PowerPoint presentations to video with audio accompaniment, use a software program called Camtasia (www.techsmith.com).

User or Employee Submissions

Of course, you don't have to personally create all the videos you post to YouTube. There's a wealth of talent outside your company's marketing department, in the form of other employees, customers, and other interested individuals.

You might, for example, solicit videos from your company's employee base. Run a contest, pay for participation, or just present the endeavor as a fun exercise, but let your co-workers express their creativity in ways that are hopefully suitable for YouTube broadcast.

The same goes with your customers, who have their own ways of showing brand or company loyalty. Ask for testimonials, as discussed previously, or open it up to more fully produced submissions. As with employee videos, you can roll the whole thing up into a contest, which itself serves as another form of promotion for your company.

Humorous Spots

Finally, don't fall into the trap of taking yourself too seriously. Some of the most popular videos on YouTube are humorous ones; the funnier the video, the more likely it is to gain a large audience and go viral. It's okay to make fun of your company, your product, or yourself, or just to treat the topic in an entertaining fashion.

YouTubers like to be entertained, and they'll tolerate a promotional message if it's a funny one.

The Big Picture

As you can see, a lot of thought goes into creating a successful YouTube video. It's not just a matter of recycling an existing spot, or even of setting up a camera and pressing the Record button. You need to determine what you want the YouTube video to achieve, who your audience is, how your video fits within your overall marketing mix, and how you intend to measure the results. Then, and only then, can you decide what type of video to produce—and then start working on it.

When marketing on YouTube, as with marketing in any medium, planning is everything.

3

Creating Informative Videos

Previously, we discussed the three most common types of YouTube videos used to promote brands and products. It boils down to why people watch videos on YouTube—to be informed, to be educated, and to be entertained. If your video falls into one of these three buckets, it stands a good chance of being successful in attracting new customers for your business.

In the next three chapters, we look at each of these types of business videos—starting, in this chapter, with informative videos. An informative video is one that imparts information of some sort to the viewer. As to how exactly you do that... well, that's what we talk about next.

Why Informative Videos Work

Informative videos are the YouTube equivalents of old school infomercials. The best of the bunch provide useful information for viewers, something they want or need to know, while subtly selling your product or brand beneath the surface.

With informative videos, it's the information you provide that's key. It has to be something that viewers are looking for, something that will help them perform some sort of task or make some sort of decision. It has to be both relevant and useful to what they're doing—and relevant to what you're offering, as well.

It goes without saying that random information placed on the YouTube site won't attract many viewers. The information you present has to be something that your current or potential customers are looking for, or else they'll never seek out, let alone view, your video.

Equally important, the information you impart has to be complete, accurate, and unique. Complete, in that you can't expect to attract customers by only giving them half the story; you have to provide all the answers, all the data, all the facts, in order to be fully useful. Accurate, because if you're not, viewers will abandon you without question and savage you without mercy. And unique, in that viewers can't find it elsewhere; you can't hand out the same old same old and except anyone to care. (It's a truism that if consumers can find the same information elsewhere, they will; why should they get it from you?)

Whatever it is you present, then, you have to present it in the best way possible. You have the opportunity to position yourself or your company as the authority on a given topic, but that status is not conferred lightly. To be perceived as an authority, your videos have to actually be authoritative. You have to present information that no one else has presented—at all, as well, or in the same fashion.

When you present information that helps viewers do something useful, they'll want to watch it—and they'll remember you afterward. After all, people do remember those that help them when they need help. When you provide answers to people's questions, they'll seek you out and recommend you to their friends. That's how you gain viewers—and future customers.

The key, then, is to determine what types of information your current and potential customers are seeking, and then provide them with that information, in video format. This gets down to being able to *think like the customer*, either innately or via customer research. What is it that your customers want or need to know—and why?

There's no universal answer to this question, of course; different customers need to know different things about different products and companies. For most businesses, there's a wide range of information you could provide.

For example, if you're selling a complex or expensive product or service, your customers might need information about what that product or service offers before they can commit to a purchasing decision. If you're in a complex, controversial, or fast-paced industry, your customers might need information about what's happening globally before they can get comfortable with you as a player within that industry. If your company itself is fast changing, or if you're a relatively new player, your customers might need information about *you* before they can get comfortable with the thought of doing business with you.

What's important, then, is to determine what you can do to help your customers get comfortable and enthusiastic about purchasing whatever it is you're selling. Provide information that people are looking for, that is unique and uniquely presented, and that is truly useful, and the customers you're targeting will seek you out. Present uninteresting, useless drek in a predictable fashion, and no one will care.

It's all about becoming an authority, by presenting authoritative information. When people want or need particular information, they want to be able to trust that information. They want to trust that the information is accurate, and trust that it will answer the questions or solve their problems. After they trust the information you present, that trust is transferred onto your product, brand, or company. And that sort of trust creates some very loyal customers.

Different Types of Informative Videos

What exactly, then, is an informative video? In a self-defining sort of way, it's a video that contains relevant and useful information—news or facts about an important topic.

Most often, an informative video is the YouTube equivalent of a newscast, with you (or your spokesperson) acting as reporter or anchorman, presenting the latest news about your company or industry or underlying technology or overall economy or whatever. In this instance, information equals news—news of interest to your customers, that is.

Alternately, an informative video might function as a video brochure, presenting in-depth information about you or your products. With this type of informative video, what's key is the information you present. In this instance, information equals facts—about your company, your products, or your industry.

Let's look at each type of informative video separately.

Information = News

This type of informative video most closely resembles a news report. That is, you or someone on your team (it can even be your president or CEO) sits in front of a camera and talks about the latest news of interest to your customers. This can be news about your products, your company, your industry, or even the outside world (as it affects you and your customers). It's the YouTube equivalent of a newscast.

The best of these videos address more universal issues, rather than being blatantly self-promotional about your own products and brands. This helps to establish you or your company as the authority on a given topic, someone customers will come back to when they want the straight poop about what's going on.

For example, if you're a dentist, you could go on camera and talk about the services you offer or what a great dentist you are, but that's pretty self-serving; in the end, who cares? It would be better and more interesting to talk about the latest teeth whitening techniques, or how to fight plaque, or what kind of toothbrush works best.

Likewise, if you represent a clothing retailer, you can produce informational "stories" about the latest seasonal fashions and such. If you sell computer equipment, you can talk about trends in the tech industry, the types of new machines coming out, new ways that people are using computers, and the like. Or if you're in the restaurant business, you can talk about food trends, new dining experiences, nutritional issues, and the like. You get the idea.

You don't even have to present straight news. You can offer opinions on the latest developments, or give advice to viewers. (There's an idea—a series of Q&A videos where you answer customer questions and address their issues.) Opinions are often more interesting than facts, and advice often more useful than straight data.

The key is to use the format to establish yourself or your company as the authority to turn to, so that when customers need to buy what you're selling, they'll think of you. To do this, your videos not only have to be newsworthy and authoritative, they have to be somewhat frequent. News isn't really new if you're reporting on it two weeks after the fact. If you go the news-based approach, be prepared to produce a new video at least once a week; viewers need to know that your information is timely, and will come to expect updates on a regular schedule. That might mean producing a weekly YouTube newscast, or maybe something even more frequent. Whatever the case, you must create and stick to a regular schedule; sporadic uploads won't attract a regular viewer base.

Information = Facts

Another approach is to produce videos that inform viewers about your product. This could take the form of a series of spec sheets, presented in slideshow format with accompanying background music. Or maybe you create a video based on an existing sales presentation or conference. Even better is a video that serves as an extended product guide or demonstration, where you use the medium to provide a closer look at what your product is, what it does, or how it's made.

The key is to give potential customers everything they need to make a purchasing decision, without the benefit of an actual hands-on demonstration. If you're selling aquarium pumps, show the pump in action in a typical aquarium. If you're selling drum sets, show a pro drummer putting your newest kit through its paces. If you're selling clothing, show people modeling your outfits. It's the YouTube equivalent of a direct mail catalog, with all the benefits that sound and moving pictures present.

I like how the big automakers use videos in this regard. They use the video medium to deliver virtual test drives, interior tours, product overviews, and the like; it's the next best thing to going to the dealership to take a look and a drive, with the added benefit of being able to watch it all over and over again on your computer screen. As an example of how this works, check out the video test drive in Figure 3.1, from the folks at BMW (www.youtube.com/user/bmw/).

Figure 3.1   *An informational video test drive for a BMW M3 GTS.*

Know, however, that you still need to take a soft sell approach. Any overview video you produce has to take a subtle approach; you can't whack viewers over the head with your sales message. Just present the facts, show them what you're selling, and then let them take the next step.

In this respect, an informative video is more like an infomercial than it is a commercial. It's a soft sell, not a hard one; it's the information you present that makes the video useful and attracts viewers.

Producing an Informative Video

Information videos can be simple to produce or quite complex. It depends on the type of video you're creating.

Note

Learn more about shooting a video in Chapter 9, "Shooting Semi-Pro Videos."

Producing a Video Newscast

When it comes to producing a newscast-like informative video, think "talking head." It's the same approach taken by local television news broadcasts: one, sometimes two people sitting in front of the camera and reading a script, like the video from Harris Dental (www.youtube.com/user/HarrisDentalPhoenix/), shown in Figure 3.2.

Figure 3.2 *A simple talking head video from Dr. Joseph Harris of Harris Dental.*

Let's take this kind of video at its most basic—a newscaster reading a script. That means you need to *write* a script. You can't depend on your on-air talent to improvise the entire video; this is not the time or place to be "winging it."

A script is important for a number of reasons. First, when you stick to a script, you're assured of covering all the points you want to cover; without a script, it's easy to forget something you meant to talk about. Second, sticking to a script ensures that you don't mention things you don't want to mention; again, without a script, it's easy to veer off the desired path or simply say the wrong thing. A script keeps you on track.

A script is also important if you decide to get a little fancy with your video. A basic newscast videos is a one-camera, newscaster-looking-directly-at-the-lens sort of thing. But that gets boring to viewers. You want to follow in the footsteps of professional newscasts and have the newscaster talking to multiple cameras. Maybe she talks for 30 seconds or so into the main camera and then turns to her left and starts talking into camera two. Then back to a direct shot into camera one and then maybe turning to the right for camera three. You get the idea.

Now, you probably don't have three cameras, and you wouldn't necessarily know how to sync together their video footage, anyway. That's okay, you can accomplish the same thing with a single camera. Have the newsreader read the entire script while looking straight at the camera and then reposition the camera 45 degrees or so to the left and have the newsreader turn and read the script again. (You can repeat this by positioning the camera to the right for a "camera three" effect, as well.) All you have to do is edit together a selection of shots from each camera, and you get a nice visual variety for your video newscast.

For this "multiple camera" trick to work, however, your newsreader has to read the exact same words for every take, and read them in the exact same fashion. This is another reason to write a script; it provides the exact same content when you're editing together multiple takes. It's how the big boys do it.

Back to the script, and the writing thereof. It's important that your script be easy to read, which means excising the longer and more difficult-to-pronounce words. You should also make sure that your script is no more than two to three minutes long; if you have more than that to say, consider breaking things up into multiple videos.

Of course, you also need to pay attention to the composition of the shot; it's really all you have for the viewer to look at, after all. Probably one of the biggest newbie mistakes is to have the newscaster too small in the frame. Don't be afraid to zoom in; you want to see the subject at about chest height in the frame. And, while it's okay to position a single subject dead center in the frame, it's more visually interesting to position him or her slightly off-center.

Consider, also, what's behind the newscaster. You need some sort of simple, unobtrusive background; you don't want the background to compete with the subject. A plain wall or sheet of seamless background paper or cloth is always good; try to get a good contrast between the background and the subject, to better make the subject "pop" in the frame.

You can also add visual interest by adding some graphics to the shot, as Food for Life TV (www.youtube.com/user/FoodForLifeTV/) did in the video shown in Figure 3.3. You insert these graphics in post-production, of course, using your video-editing software. You can create a graphic using your company's logo, a product photo, or just about anything that ties into what you're talking about in the script. Here again it makes sense to position your subject to the side of the frame, to allow more room for these added graphics.

Figure 3.3 *A more sophisticated YouTube newscast, complete with onscreen graphics, from Food for Life TV.*

Finally, you don't have to limit yourself to a single newscaster format. Many successful newscasts use two newsreaders, alternating the stories they read. You can even go with an interviewer/interviewee approach, as Sweetwater Sound (www.youtube.com/user/SweetwaterSound/) did in the video shown in Figure 3.4. Using questions and answers is a great way to get across information that might otherwise be a little dry.

Figure 3.4 *An interview-based news video from music retailer Sweetwater Sound, with Sweetwater's Mitch Gallagher interviewing famous recording engineer Ken Scott.*

Producing a Video Product Tour

If you decide to go the video product tour route, that's a whole different process. This type of video is much more involved, with multiple shots and scenes, lots of different camera angles, inspirational background music, you name it. In fact, this is the one type of video where it might pay to engage professional production services; you have to put your best foot forward.

A video product tour can be relatively low tech or quite sophisticated. A simple approach, as demonstrated in Figure 3.5 in a video from Seattle Coffee Gear (www.youtube.com/user/SeattleCoffeeGear/), simply has an employee talk about the product while the camera shoots the product from a variety of angles. Nothing too complex here, pretty easy to do.

Figure 3.5 *A hands-on "crew review" of the Rancilio Rocky Grinder, from Seattle Coffee Gear.*

A more sophisticated approach uses multiple shots—close-ups, long shots, even internal cutaways. Figure 3.6 shows just such a video, produced by HP (www.youtube.com/user/hpcomputers/) for one of its new computer models. This video employs fancy graphics, lots of onscreen overlays—you name it, this video has it—it in the process of showing all the features of the product in question. Lots of work went into this one.

Another approach is to demonstrate the product in action. This works well for certain types of products, such as musical instruments, sporting goods, kitchen appliances, and the like. Thus the video in Figure 3.7, where pro drummer Bryan "Brain" Mantia demonstrates a new snare drum from the Drum Workshop company (www.youtube.com/user/DrumWorkshopInc/). Done right, this is a very effective approach.

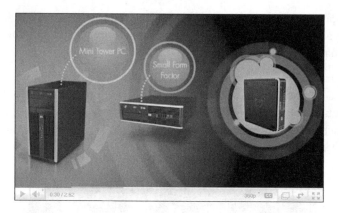

Figure 3.6   *A fancy video tour of a new HP computer.*

Figure 3.7   *A demo of a PDP snare drum from Drum Workshop.*

What all these videos have in common is a degree of complexity. You're talking multiple shots from multiple camera angles. The camera zooms in to focus on product details, zooms back to show the overall product, is repositioned to the side to show the product from a different angle, cuts to a shot of the presenter/ demonstrator, and so forth. This requires a lot of pre-production planning and post-production editing.

The pre-production stage is where this type of complicated video comes together— or not. In addition to writing the script that flows through the video, you have to plan out each shot you need to make. Although the different shots and camera angles can be spelled out in the script, as shown in Figure 3.8, I find it better to put together a *storyboard* for the entire video. This is a visual guide to each shot you need, literally sketched out in sequence, kind of like a basic animation of how the video should progress.

VIDEO	NARRATOR
1. Camera shows MILLER with a digital camera and a montage of digital photos in the background.	Hi, I'm Michael Miller, and if you're like me, you've been snapping all sorts of photographs with your digital camera. But now that you have all those photos in your camera, what do you do with them?
2. Shot of memory card.	The photos in your digital camera are stored on a removable memory card. To do anything with your photos, you first have to copy them from your camera's memory card to your personal computer. There are a couple of ways to do this.
3. Shot of PC with memory card slot.	The first way to copy photos from your digital camera to your computer is to use a memory card reader, like the one built into many PCs.

Figure 3.8 *A script with camera instructions in the left column and narration in the right column.*

Figure 3.9 shows what a blank storyboard sheet looks like. You sketch what the camera sees into each big box and then describe the shot and write the first line of dialog for that shot into the lines beneath each box. You can even add any special effects or overlays you want to add to the shot during post production.

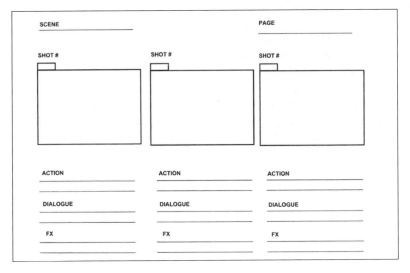

Figure 3.9 *A blank storyboard sheet.*

Tip

Your storyboard sketches don't have to be elaborate, or even good. Simple stick figures work just fine, just as long as you get across what you want the camera to shoot in each shot.

When it comes time to shoot the video, you simply follow the instructions you devised ahead of time in the storyboard. Shoot each shot you sketched out, either in sequence or in an order that is easiest to set up, and when you're done you have all the shots you need to put together the video.

Which brings us to post-production. This is where you take each of the shots you made and edit them together into the final video. You may use the audio that accompanied each shot you made, or record a new voice-over that carries across shots. You also add transitions (wipes, fades, and so on) between shots, as well as any onscreen graphics, titles, credits, and the like. The result of all this work should be an easy-to-follow overview of your product.

 Note

Learn more about video editing and post-production in Chapter 11, "Editing and Enhancing Your Videos."

The Big Picture

The first type of video you can produce for your business is an informative video. This is a video that gives your customers some sort of useful information. Some informative videos are like newscasts, where a spokesperson is positioned in front of the camera and reads from a script. Other informative videos are more sophisticated product tours or demonstrations, requiring multiple shots and camera angles. Both types of informative videos need to employ the soft sell; they shouldn't be overtly promotional, presenting just the facts that current and potential customers are looking for.

4

Creating Educational Videos

Of the three types of videos that attract potential cus-tomers on YouTube, perhaps the most widely employed is the educational video. This is a video that shows viewers how to do something—ideally, while using your com-pany's products. It's a truly useful type of video, which is why it's so popular; done right, you provide real value to your customers, which they remember when it's time to buy something you sell.

Why Educational Videos Work

Why do people log onto YouTube? A fair number are bored and want to be entertained, of course. Others want to get more information about something. But a large number of viewers turn to YouTube to learn how to do something—that is, to be educated about the topic at hand.

What does an educational video look like? Put simply, it's a how-to video—a video that shows the viewer "how to" do something. This typically takes the form of step-by-step instructions: Step 1, do this, Step 2, do that, Step 3, do something else. It's a very hands-on experience.

Why does someone watch a how-to video on YouTube? To learn how to do that something, of course. Maybe a person is looking to put together some sort of craft or project and needs instruction. Maybe a person has an item that needs repair or maintenance, and wants to learn how to do that. Maybe a person has just purchased a new product and has no idea how to put it together or get it to work. You see how it is—educational videos help people do the things they want or need to do.

So your customers get real value out of learning how to get something done. What you get out of it is the authority that comes with presenting that information. When a person learns how to do something from watching your video, he now thinks of you as the authority on that topic. When it comes to purchasing the tools or supplies necessary to complete that project (or a related project), he thinks of you and buys what you're selling. Or, if he's watching your video to learn how to use your product, he feels that he made a good purchasing decision; it reinforces the decision he made, and helps him get more value or enjoyment out of your product.

What Kinds of How-To Videos Should You Produce?

Although most how-to videos follow the same basic format (do this first, do this second, do this third), there are a few different types of instructional videos you can choose to produce. The first type is more product-focused, and the second is more generic.

Product Instruction Videos

The first type of how-to video shows customers how to install, configure, or use your products. This can be a good approach, especially if you have an item that's somehow difficult to use.

For example, if you sell aquarium supplies, you might produce a video showing people how to install one of your products. This is what you see in Figure 4.1, where the folks from Fluval (www.youtube.com/user/fluvalblog/) show how to install their newest canister filter. If you're at all familiar with the aquarium hobby, you know that a canister filter has a lot of different parts that have to be connected in just the right order, and a certain way of operation that has a bit of a learning curve. Creating a video that shows customers how to put it all together and get it working on their fish tanks is quite useful—necessary, even.

Figure 4.1   *A how-to video for installing an aquarium canister filter, from Fluval.*

This approach works for lots of different types of products. For example, if you're a pharmaceutical company selling asthma drugs, you might produce a video showing people how to use your latest inhaler. If you sell networking equipment, you might produce a video showing people how to set up a wireless router. If you sell wooden playground equipment, you might produce a video showing customers how to construct one of your more complex products.

This type of how-to video works as both a pre-purchase and post-purchase aid. For customers considering purchasing your product, it gives them a taste of what's involved, and perhaps eases some of their fears; at the very least, it demonstrates that you provide the support they might need. For customers who've already purchased your product, it's immediate assistance for getting them up and running. This type of video can actually reduce the number of customer support calls you get, minimize the need for detailed instruction manuals, and make for more satisfied customers. It's a real boon.

Project Videos

The second type of how-to video is a bit more generic in that you show viewers how to do something useful; you don't show them how to use your product, except in the course of completing the project at hand.

Let me give you an example. Lowe's (www.youtube.com/user/Lowes/) is a home improvement chain that sells all sorts of parts and supplies. What better way to show off what the company sells, as well as appeal to its do-it-yourself (DIY) customer base, than produce a series of videos showing how to complete a variety of different projects. Figure 4.2 shows just such a video, demonstrating how to install lighting under a kitchen cabinet; it walks viewers through the parts they need, the tools they use, and how to get the job done, step-by-step. It's just one of more than 300 how-to videos they offer that really establish their authority in the DIY space.

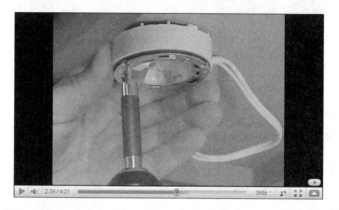

Figure 4.2   *A how-to video for installing under-cabinet lighting, from Lowe's.*

This approach can work for all sorts of companies. For example, if you sell cookware or kitchen appliances, you might produce a series of cooking videos, showing how to cook various types of dishes, such as the one from Williams-Sonoma (www.youtube.com/user/WilliamsSonoma/) in Figure 4.3.

Figure 4.3   *Learning how to cook chicken with saffron rice (yummy!) from Williams-Sonoma.*

Other examples? If you sell auto parts, you might create a series of videos showing how to change oil, replace a brake light, and so forth. If you sell guitars, you could create a series of videos showing musicians how to restring or tune their guitars, or even how to play chords and scales and such. If you provide accounting services, you could produce a series of videos showing small businesses how to set up and manage their books. If you're a dentist, you might produce videos showing kids how to brush their teeth and floss.

We can go on and on with examples of how-to videos, but you get the idea. You don't show people directly how to use your products, but instead show your products in use during the course of doing a common project. It's more infomercial-like, less of a hard sell—which is what works on YouTube.

The key with this type of video is to offer truly useful content. You have to show people how to do something they want to do (sew a quilt) or need to do (repair a leaky faucet). Attack a task common enough to draw a large audience, make the steps easy to follow, and then use the video to sell other goods and services.

That means, of course, that you can't be too shy about showing your product in action. There's nothing wrong with showing a close up of your product performing its assigned task, nor with adding an overlay stating the product's name or model number, along with a link to your website. You have to be subtle, but not so subtle that people don't notice and remember what you're selling.

Producing a How-To Video

Producing an educational video is more complex than producing a simple talking-head video. You need to plan it all out in advance, scripting and storyboarding every shot you need to make. The shooting process is likewise complex, as you have to produce each of those shots. You then feed all those shots into a video-editing program, stitch them together with the appropriate transitions and onscreen graphics, and produce yourself an easy-to-follow step-by-step video lesson.

Let's start at the top. This type of video has to be well planned in advance; you can't wing it on camera. You have to work through the steps you need to present, and the shots necessary to accomplish each step.

This means creating a pretty tight script, as well as an accompanying storyboard. Work through each step in the process, shot-by-shot, camera angle by camera angle. Know what you're showing and how, so that when it comes time to shoot, it's a simple matter of setting things up according to the storyboard.

Note

Learn more about scripts and storyboards in Chapter 3, "Creating
Informative Videos."

When you're planning your video, don't take the lazy route and overly rely on spoken instructions. Yes, your demonstrator has to tell people what he's doing, but there shouldn't be a lot of talking heads in a how-to video. You need to show people how to do it, not just tell them. Let the pictures tell the story.

That said, you should consider adding helpful text overlays for each step of the process. A (moving) picture may be worth a thousand words, but adding a few descriptive words never hurts. Add text along the lines of "Step 1: Insert the drill bit," or "Step 2: Drill a 3/4" hole." That sort of thing.

Remember to show viewers everything they need to complete the project, and do so up front, before you start the steps. Lay out all the parts they need, as well as all the tools they use. Again, this is an opportunity to reinforce your narration and visuals with onscreen text overlays.

When all the steps are done, show viewers what the completed project looks like. It's always good to have an "after" beauty shot; it lets viewers see how things are supposed to look when everything goes right. It's also a nice visual reinforcement at the end of the video.

Next comes the actual shooting of the video. This should be relatively easy if you follow your storyboard. Just be patient; most how-to videos incorporate a lot of different shots, each of which requires some degree of setup. Don't take any shortcuts; get the lighting and the angle right for each shot you need.

 Note

Learn more about shooting a video in Chapter 9, "Shooting Semi-Pro
Videos."

After you shoot all the video you need, you then have to edit it together. Use your video-editing program to place the shots in order, edit out dead space, and place transitions between scenes.

 Note

Learn more about video editing and post-production in Chapter 11,
"Editing and Enhancing Your Videos."

Of course, you want to include your website URL or toll-free phone number during the course of the video. Consider using a title card up front and a credits screen at the end, along with overlays along the way. It also might be a good idea to outline the key steps in the descriptive text that accompanies the video.

When you're putting together your how-to video, you might find that it doesn't fit comfortably within a 2- to 3-minute slot. That's okay; this is one type of video that can break the attention-span rule. If you need 6 or 7 minutes to complete the project, take it. However, if you get up to 10 minutes or longer, consider breaking the project into two or even three separate videos—Building a Deck Part 1, Building a Deck Part 2, Building a Deck Part 3, and so forth. You do have YouTube's 15-minute time limit to consider, of course, as well as a normal viewer's attention span.

The Big Picture

For many companies, the most effective way to garner new customers on YouTube is by offering some sort of step-by-step how-to video. You can show viewers how to install or use your product, or how to use your product while completing some sort of common project or task. The key is for the video to be truly useful, easy to follow, and mention your product in a subtle fashion. If you help people do something they want or need to do, they'll remember you when it comes time to make their next related purchase.

5

Creating Entertaining Videos

To create a successful promotional video, it has to be either informative, educational, or entertaining. We've already covered the first two types of videos, which leaves us with that last category—entertaining videos. This is, without a doubt, the most difficult type of video to pull off.

What exactly makes a video entertaining? And how do you go about creating an entertaining video? I'm not sure I have the answers to these questions (heck, I'm not sure there are definitive answers), but it's certainly worth discussing—which we do next.

What's Entertaining?

Informing and educating are important, and will draw a fair number of YouTube viewers if you do it right. But everybody likes to be entertained—which is why pure entertainment videos typically show up at the top of YouTube's most viewed lists.

What's entertaining? I wish I knew. I can tell you what I find entertaining, but I can't tell you what might entertain someone else. Entertainment, like all art, is in the eye of the beholder; what I laugh at might leave you cold, and vice versa.

That said, here's what I do know about entertaining videos: When they work, they work really well. It's the entertaining videos that are more likely to go viral.

When a viewer finds something really entertaining on YouTube, he watches it over and over—and then shares it with his friends. That's how viral videos are created, by one user sharing with another, who shares it with another, who shares it with another… and on and on, until that video is viewed by tens or hundreds of thousands of people. And the kind of video that most often gets passed around like that is one that entertains.

What, then, do YouTube viewers find entertaining? It's a relatively short list, including humorous videos, those that feature amazing stunts, those that include fancy special effects, and those that have some sort of shock value. And of all these, it's the funny videos that work the best. Let's face it, people like a good laugh.

One of my favorite examples of entertaining videos continues to be Blendtec (www.youtube.com/user/Blendtec/), a small company that sells high-end blenders. In a creative spurt, the company came up with a concept it calls "Will It Blend?" which it turned into a series of videos that spread across the Internet like wildfire. The videos, all extremely entertaining, show company president Tom Dickson, who gives off a bit of a mad scientist vibe, placing various objects into one of the company's blenders to see if they blend. I'm not talking bananas and cumquats here; Tom has blended (or tried to blend) things like G.I. Joe dolls, flashlights, and iPhones. It's all very entertaining, as you can see in Figure 5.1.

The result is an Internet phenomenon; Blendtec's videos, each produced on a budget of less than $100, quickly turned viral and spread across the Internet. Blendtec's example shows how a company can benefit from a creative idea, executed in an entertaining fashion. There is nothing particularly informative or educational about the "Will It Blend?" spots, but they are fun to watch. And as YouTube continues to prove, videos that are fun to watch get watched—a lot.

Figure 5.2 shows another example, for Norton Internet Security (www.youtube.com/user/norton/). It's a short one, just 12 seconds long, that pits 80's metal band Dokken against a chicken. (It's funnier to watch than it is to describe.) The point is, it's an interesting concept, a quick joke, and it gets the point across about Norton's security software.

Figure 5.1   *An entertaining "Will It Blend?" video from Blendtec. (And yes, that's an iPad that Tom is blending.)*

Figure 5.2   *A funny spot for Norton Internet Security.*

Some entertaining videos start out as entertaining commercials, and exhibit the high production values expected there. Take, for example, Evian's Roller Babies ads (www.youtube.com/user/EvianBabies/), like the one in Figure 5.3. These are not cheap videos shot with a consumer camcorder; these are professional productions, with cutting edge CGI special effects, repurposed and expanded for YouTube consumption. But they are entertaining!

If done right, then, an entertaining video is great for establishing and maintaining your brand image. But there's no guarantee that they'll work at all; you'll either succeed wildly or fail miserably.

Figure 5.3   *Roller Babies on YouTube, from Evian.*

That's because what one person finds hilarious leaves another person cold. Humor is highly subjective, and there's no guarantee you have what it takes to make someone else laugh. If you try to be funny and no one laughs, you end up with one really bad video. And, let's face it, if you had the right stuff to be funny, you'd be making your living as a stand-up comic, not as a marketing guy. Don't assume that what you find entertaining will be successful on the big stage that is YouTube.

Bottom line, entertaining videos are the riskiest types of videos you can undertake. If you decide to go this route, proceed with caution—and be prepared for failure.

Understanding Viral Videos

Several places in this book talked about *viral videos*. But just what is a viral video— and how does a video go viral?

Put simply, a viral video is one that becomes hugely popular, with hundreds of thousands or even millions of views, via Internet-based sharing. That is, a viewer finds a video that he likes and then shares it with his friends, either on the YouTube site or via email or social media, such as Facebook and Twitter. (YouTube makes it easy to share a video, literally with a few clicks of the mouse.)

Let's be honest here. As much as I like and recommend instructional and educational videos for most businesses, these types of videos seldom go viral. Instead, it's the entertaining or humorous videos that go big time. And by big time, I mean really big; the most viral of viral videos quickly move off YouTube and get picked up by traditional media. That's exposure with a capital E, and you can't buy it; it has to come organically.

Because of this potential for huge exposure, many companies think that they'll achieve success by creating a viral video, and set that as a target. While having a video that garners millions of viewers might be good for the ego (and perhaps necessary to build a huge brand like Budweiser), that might not be the most appropriate goal for the average web marketer. For most companies, attracting a thousand targeted customers is both more profitable and more realistic than getting viewed by a million strangers with no intention of ever purchasing anything from you.

So while striving for viral status might be appealing, it's probably not the best strategy for most marketers. (It's also very difficult to do; the most embarrassing videos are those that strive to be virally entertaining and instead fall flat on their faces.) Instead of shooting for the moon with a video that might be entertaining to a broad demographic, a more appropriate focus is creating a video that appeals to your target audience. For most businesses, that's the way you achieve YouTube success, in a low-key fashion.

Producing an Entertaining Video

How do you go about producing an entertaining video? I really can't tell you; no two entertaining videos are remotely similar.

That said, you definitely need to be creative. Really creative. Really, really creative. More creative than you can imagine.

Know, however, that you either have the creative spark or you don't. If you do, you create a video that people remember and want to share. If you don't, you create a video that falls flat on its face. As I've said, this is a high-risk category.

To that end, this is the one type of video where you might not want to go it alone. If you want to go the entertaining route, it may be wise to engage the services of a video production firm or advertising agency that specializes in this sort of thing. Let your agency come up with the creative ideas; they have people on staff who do this for a living. They know what works and what doesn't.

You should not, however, buy into the spiel of any firm that "guarantees" they can create a viral video for you. No one can guarantee a video going viral. Viral videos happen only rarely, when everything clicks and you hit a sweet spot in the public consciousness. Any firm promising you a viral video might as well be peddling snake oil; the best a company can promise is the production of a professional video. What happens after that is up to the YouTube universe.

The Big Picture

Of the three types of videos you can produce, entertaining videos have the biggest upside; most viral videos are entertaining videos. Entertaining videos are also the most difficult to produce, and require a degree of creativity (and luck) that not all businesses possess. That's because there's no formula for creating an entertaining video, none at all. For that reason, many businesses turn to outside firms to come up with these creative videos—and then hope that YouTube viewers find them share-worthy.

6

Incorporating YouTube Videos in Your Overall Web Marketing Mix

YouTube is just one component of a well-rounded marketing plan. You need to integrate your YouTube videos with the other marketing you do, so that all your marketing activities work toward the same common goal.

That said, how exactly should you treat YouTube videos within your larger marketing mix? Web videos aren't exactly like print ads or email newsletters, after all; it's a unique medium that somehow needs to reflect and reinforce the other marketing you do.

Defining YouTube's Role in Your Marketing Strategy

Some marketing activities are pretty direct such as direct mail, of course, but also email marketing, online and offline advertising, and the like. These methods are all fairly hard sell in their approach.

YouTube marketing, on the other hand, is all about subtlety. That is, people don't watch YouTube videos that are overtly promotional in nature. For that reason, you can't upload an existing television commercial and expect to garner an online audience; people have too many other options to watch a commercial online, on their own time.

To that end, you need to produce videos that offer true value to your intended audience. This softer sell defines YouTube's role in your marketing strategy.

This soft sell comes in the form of the information or instruction you provide. Perhaps that's a video newscast where you talk about industry news or technical developments; perhaps it's a how-to video that shows people how to use your product to do something useful. In any case, viewers watch the video because it provides valuable information; what they retain is a sense of your brand or company as a source of authority on the topic at hand.

Now, you might consider this sort of subtle sell an insidious form of corporate propaganda, and you'd be right. You're edging your way into the customer's life, hoping he'll associate your brand with the useful information he's received via your videos. WidgetCo provided value to me; WidgetCo is good; I want to make my next purchase from WidgetCo. That's much different from a paid advertisement, and ultimately more effective; you get deep into your audience's subconscious and plant your brand message in a very subtle yet long-lasting fashion.

The key is to use YouTube videos to supplement the promotional message you impart in other online and offline media. You don't use videos to broadcast blatant advertisements; instead, you build on your promotional message with the practical information you broadcast to the YouTube audience.

And here's another thing. By giving a face to your company or brand, YouTube videos can help personalize your company and develop a direct connection to your customer base. It's not an anonymous promotional message from an ad or press release, it's John Smith talking to you in person about something that interests you. This type of personal communication is particularly effective, and needs to be a part of your web marketing mix.

Formulating Your New Marketing Mix

Given the more subtle role that YouTube plays in your marketing strategy, where exactly does YouTube fit within your overall marketing mix?

Let's start by recognizing the obvious—the Internet has dramatically changed the way marketing works. A company's marketing mix today looks much different from the marketing mix of a generation ago. Go back a decade or two and you had a limited number of media to use: newspapers, magazines, radio, television, and direct mail. Now, all of these media are still around today, but the Internet has added a variety of new options one must consider.

What new media has the Internet added to the mix? Here's a short list:

- Email

- Websites

- Search engines

- Blogs

- Social networks (such as Facebook and MySpace)

- Photo-sharing sites (Flickr and so on)

- Video-sharing sites

YouTube, of course, defines that last category.

You need to consider all aspects of online marketing when fitting YouTube into your marketing plans. Does your YouTube marketing stand alone, or is it part of a larger campaign that includes seeded blog postings, banner website ads, pay-per-click search engine ads, targeted email, and viral campaigns on the key social networks? You should determine all this before you script and storyboard your first video.

In addition, you should also determine YouTube's place alongside the traditional marketing media. Do you use YouTube merely as another channel for your television commercials, or does it expand on your television advertising with additional spots, alternative takes, expanded scenarios, and the like? Does YouTube merely provide more exposure for your existing campaign, or does it change things up to fine-tune your message to the slightly younger, more interactive YouTube audience?

Answering these questions will help you determine exactly how you fit YouTube into your marketing mix.

Coordinating Your Online Marketing Activities

Whatever components you include in your marketing mix, it's important that all these components mesh with one other. They should all carry the same message; you don't want to present one image to YouTube viewers, another to Google and other search engines, another to customers viewing display ads, and yet another to blogs and social networks. Your message should be consistent, no matter where customers encounter that message.

What does that mean, in reality?

First, it means that the way you define your business has to be consistent. The keywords you choose as part of your search engine optimization should also be the keywords you purchase for your PPC advertising, should also be key words in the copy for your display ads, should also be highlighted in the promotional emails you send to customers, should also be talking points when you communicate with influential bloggers, should also be present in the electronic press releases you send to online news organizations, and should also be incorporated into the scripts of your YouTube videos. You can't describe your business one way in press releases, another way in advertisements, and yet another way in videos; you must have a consistent message.

That extends to using themes and images from your YouTube videos on your website—especially in the landing pages you create for your YouTube campaigns. When someone clicks to your website after watching a YouTube video, they should land on a page that not only repeats the message from the video, but also mirrors the look and feel of the video. Again, consistency is the key.

That doesn't mean, however, that you can't adapt the message for the medium. You need to exploit the unique nature of the YouTube community when producing your online videos; you can't just port a print ad to YouTube and expect it to work. You have to give YouTube viewers the experience they expect, not one more suited to another marketing vehicle.

That said, your videos shouldn't veer off into a totally different direction from the other marketing you do. You have to consider all your marketing activities in a holistic fashion; someone approaching your product or brand via YouTube should receive the same message as someone learning about you via email or blogs or social networking or radio or print. You need to send a similar message via all your marketing activities, traditional or Internet-based.

The point is, all of your marketing vehicles need to work together. They have to convey a consistent message and image, and should not send conflicting messages to your customer base. Your marketing mix should be a consistent whole that is greater than the sum of its parts.

Making YouTube Co-Exist with Television Marketing

If you're a larger company, chances are you're already doing some degree of television-based marketing. What's the best way to make your online and broadcast videos work together?

Tip

Whatever approach you take should be based on your particular circumstances; there's no one right way to proceed. In fact, you might choose different approaches for different campaigns over time.

Repurposing

When it comes to joint television/online marketing, there are several approaches you can take, the easiest of which is simple repurposing. If you have an established TV advertising campaign, you repurpose your television ads to YouTube, posting your 30-second TV commercials to the YouTube site.

This is a simple approach, and it might be a good one—if your commercials are compelling enough to attract YouTube viewers. But, let's face it, when given the choice of watching a million other entertaining and informative videos, why would YouTube viewers choose to spend 30 seconds of their valuable time to watch the same commercial they've seen a dozen times on TV?

If the original commercial is compelling enough, this might work. (It certainly works for Old Spice, Snickers, Evian, and other big advertisers.) But for most advertisers repurposing, although inexpensive and easy to execute, won't be very successful.

Extending and Expanding

A better approach might be to take your existing television commercial and expand it for the YouTube audience. Maybe offer an "uncut" or "uncensored" version or shoot a new commercial that starts up where the first one left off. If a commercial is really successful, you can create a series of videos playing off that first one. Or maybe you can use YouTube as a channel for similar executions that you didn't use on television. Something to extend or expand your existing campaign, not just replicate it online.

You can also use your existing campaign as the jumping off point for something new and creative. For example, some companies have created an initial video, and then encouraged viewers to produce their own variations. You can even do it in the form of a contest: Make your own YouTube video promoting our product, and the winner gets a valuable prize. Use your imagination and take advantage of the user interaction that YouTube encourages.

Starting Fresh

Finally, you can move beyond your existing campaign and create something totally new for YouTube. Play to the differences inherent in the YouTube medium; create a video campaign that exploits what's new and unique about YouTube. Just make sure your YouTube-specific activity hews to the same overall message you use in the rest of your marketing.

The Big Picture

For many businesses, YouTube can be an important component of their overall marketing mix. YouTube's role is a more subtle one, different from the hard sell approach of advertising or direct marketing. That said, your YouTube videos should reflect the same look and feel as the rest of your marketing activities, and forward the same overall message and goals. And when it comes to coordinating your online and traditional broadcast video marketing, know that repurposing is seldom the best approach—although you can use YouTube to extend and expand successful television advertising. In most instances, however, it's better to create something new and unique for YouTube, while working holistically with the other elements of your marketing strategy.

7

Understanding Audio/Video Technology

Producing professional videos for YouTube requires an understanding of the audio and video technology that YouTube uses. The more you know about the technology, the more appropriate and better-looking videos you can create.

It's important to understand not just the technology used by YouTube, but also other audio/video production technologies. For example, what video file format do you want to use when shooting your videos? What file format is best for editing? Which file formats does YouTube support for uploading? Read on to get smarter about all this.

Understanding Video Resolution

The physical size of a video picture is measured in terms of pixels. A *pixel* is, quite simply, the smallest discrete picture element. The physical size of a pixel is different on different video capture and display devices, so a picture that's 800 pixels wide might be bigger on one computer display than on another. The point, however, is that you measure resolution in pixels; the more pixels in a picture, the higher resolution—and the better the quality.

Standard Versus High Definition

A standard definition television (SDTV) picture has a resolution of 640 pixels wide by 480 pixels tall—or what we call 640×480 resolution. It doesn't matter what physical size the TV screen is; a 15" screen has the same 640×480 resolution as a 35" screen.

Notice that I used the term *standard definition*. This is different from the new high definition television (HDTV) standard—or, to be more precise, *standards*, plural. There are actually several different resolutions used in HDTV broadcasts and displays, all of which are much higher quality than the older standard resolution picture.

The two most common HD resolutions are 720×1280 (known as *720p resolution*) and 1080×1920 (used in both 1080i and 1080p displays). As you can tell from the numbers, HD packs a lot more pixels in the same screen area, resulting in much sharper pictures.

 Note

> HDTV also features a wider screen. A standard definition screen has an aspect ratio of 4:3—that is, the width is 4/3 the height. An HDTV screen has an aspect ratio of 16:9—the width is 16/9 the height. When you view a 16:9 picture on a 4:3 display, you see black bars above and below the picture, a feature known as *letterboxing*.

YouTube Resolution

Are you confused yet? There's no need to be. The bottom line is that YouTube lets you use just about any video resolution available, from standard definition to high definition—and then some.

It hasn't always been that way. When YouTube first launched, it played back every single video, no matter the original resolution, at 320×240 pixels. Now, that resolution looked okay in a small window on a small computer monitor, but really didn't hold up well at larger sizes. (It's effectively one-quarter the resolution of pre-HD standard definition television.)

It took a couple of years, but YouTube eventually upped the resolution ante, moving to what it dubbed High Quality (HQ) videos, displayed at 480×360 pixels. That's about three times the resolution of the original standard (retroactively dubbed Standard Quality, or SQ), but still below that of standard definition television. An improvement, but not much of one.

Things evolved, and YouTube embraced standard definition (640×480) video, in both standard and widescreen aspect ratios. It didn't stop there, however, as YouTube eventually let users upload and view full high definition videos, at both 720p and 1080p resolutions.

 Note

In addition to embracing today's HD videos, YouTube also lets you upload what is known as *4K video*. This is an unofficial post-HD standard that has more than six times the resolution of today's high definition videos—not widely used by the general public, but common in IMAX presentations.

In short, when it comes to video resolution, YouTube lets you have it pretty much any way you want it. (Table 7.1 compares the different video resolutions that you can use with YouTube.)

Table 7.1   YouTube Video Resolutions

Name	240p	240p Widescreen	360p	360p Widescreen	480p	480p widescreen	720p	1080p	4K
Resolution (Width×Height)	320×240	400×240	480×360	640×360	640×480	854×480	1280×720	1920×1080	4096×3072
Description	Original YouTube Standard Quality (SQ); the default for most web browsers	SQ with widescreen aspect ratio	YouTube High Quality (HQ)	HQ with widescreen aspect ratio	Standard Definition Television (SDTV)	SDTV widescreen	720p High Definition Television (HDTV)	1080p HDTV; AKA "Full HD"	Highest quality video currently available, not a current consumer standard; used in IMAX presentations
Aspect ratio	4:3	16:9	4:3	16:9	4:3	16:9	16:9	16:9	16:9
Total number of pixels	76,800	96,000	172,800	230,400	307,200	409,920	921,600	2,073,600	12,582,912

In addition, YouTube translates videos into a special, even lower resolution format for playback on smartphones and other mobile devices. The aptly named Mobile format has a 176×144 resolution (and an odd 11:9 aspect ratio), perfect for a phone's small screen.

Choosing the Right Resolution

With all these possible resolutions available to you, which should you use to shoot and edit your videos?

When I wrote the first edition of this book, I recommended shooting at the highest available resolution available at the time, which was 480×360, or what YouTube then called HQ. I didn't see much point in going with a higher resolution if YouTube wouldn't display it; in fact, YouTube would downgrade higher-resolution videos to its HQ quality.

It's a different story today, however. Now, I recommend producing high definition videos, in either the 720p or 1080p HD resolutions. An HD picture will look great on both computer monitors and big screen TVs; it's perfect for showing the detail in those close-ups you might need in a how-to video.

 Note

Both 720p and 1080p look pretty darn close on a standard computer monitor. I'd go with whichever resolution your camcorder supports.

 Note

There's no need to go the full 4K video route because that produces files that take way too long to download. The 4K format is more for professional filmmakers shooting for the super-large screen.

Note that whatever resolution you upload, YouTube will process the video so that it's available at a variety of lower resolutions, as well. That's because most viewers still watch YouTube in the default 480×360 or 640×360 (widescreen) window. In most instances, viewers have to click a button to display a video at higher resolution. (It's to ensure maximum playback capability.) As I said, YouTube does this conversion automatically; you provide a single file at the highest resolution and let YouTube do the rest.

Understanding Video File Formats

When you're producing a YouTube video, you have to take into account more than just resolution and aspect ratio. You also have to choose a video file format, and the accompanying compression used in that file format.

Understanding Compression and Codecs

Key to all video file formats is the concept of file compression. That's because raw, uncompressed video files are extremely large; video information is quite complex and requires much storage space. Rather than force users to work with unmanageably large files, the video industry adopted the concept of file compression, which works to reduce the size of the video files.

Each different method of compression is a *codec*, short for compressor/decompressor. A codec is a system for compressing a large amount of video data into a smaller, more manageable file. The more efficient the codec, the smaller the resulting files.

It isn't all about size, however. Some codecs do a better job of maintaining video quality than do others. That is, some compression schemes create videos that are noticeably inferior to the original; other compression schemes create videos that look almost identical to the source material. *Lossy* codecs result in a loss of data and degradation in audio and video quality, whereas *lossless* codecs reproduce the source material with no loss in quality.

Not only are different codecs better or worse at reproducing the source material, often you have the option of selecting different degrees of compression within a codec. That is, you can encode the video data at different rates (measured in kilobytes per second, or *kbps*). The higher the encoding rate, the better the resulting quality—and the larger the resulting file. For example, a file encoded at 256kbps would theoretically have twice the resolution or quality as a file encoded at 128kbps. Which file format and codec you choose represents a compromise between file size and audio/video quality—with the issue of compatibility thrown in for good measure.

Comparing File Formats

Codecs are important because different file formats use different forms of compression—and you have lots of file formats to choose from.

A file format is a particular way of encoding digital information. There are many different file formats for different uses; for example, Adobe's PDF file format is used to create printable documents, Microsoft's DOC file format is used to create Word documents, and the JPEG file format is used to store digital photographs. Each file format has its own unique attributes, and is generally incompatible with other, albeit similar, file formats.

There are several file formats used to store video information. Each has its own advantages and limitations, so it's important to know the ins and outs of each format before choosing the format you want to record in—in particular, the compression used and the audio/video quality that results.

With that said, you might have little choice in file format. That's because many video cameras record in just one or two formats; not all formats are always available. Fortunately, YouTube accepts uploads in most popular video file formats; you can likely upload whatever format your camcorder shoots.

Table 7.2 compares and contrasts the major video file formats you can use with YouTube.

Table 7.2   Popular Video File Formats

File Format	Extension	Characteristics
3GP	.3gpp, .3gpp2	A multimedia container file format common in 3G mobile phones
Audio Video Interleave	.avi	Container format that can store data encoded in a variety of codecs
DivX	.divx	High quality codec with equally high compression, a subset of the MPEG-4 format that supports resolutions up to 1080p; popular for Internet use
Digital Video (DV)	.dv	Lossy format used in many consumer video cameras; DV video is typically enclosed in some type of container file format, such as AVI or QuickTime
Flash Video	.flv	Adobe's popular multimedia file format; the format used by YouTube to serve videos on its site
H.264	.mpg, .mp4	A type of encoding used in many MPEG-4 , 3GP, and QuickTime files; more efficient than the normal MPEG-4 codec, records high quality video with relatively small file sizes; well suited for HD video
MPEG-1	.mpg, .mpeg	The original MPEG format, with low quality VHS-like video; not widely used today
MPEG-2	.mpg, .mpeg	Produces higher-quality audio/video than the MPEG-1 format; used in broadcast-quality television and some digital satellite services

File Format	Extension	Characteristics
MPEG-4	.mpg, .mp4	Most recent version of the MPEG format, optimized for both high definition and Internet video; used in most newer digital camcorders; the H.264 and DivX codecs build on and extend basic MPEG-4 compression
MPEG-PS	.mpg, .mpeg	PS stands for "program stream;" this is a streaming video format used with some MPEG-1 and MPEG-2 files
QuickTime	.mov, .qt	Apple's proprietary audio/video format; works with both Mac OS and Windows
RealVideo	.rm, .rv	Media file format used by RealPlayer; the RealMedia format (RM) can contain either audio or video files; a heavily compressed format that results in lower-quality video than with other competing formats
WebM	.webm	One of the newest video file formats, designed for royalty-free open-source storage; designed for use with HTML5 video; supported by Google/YouTube, Mozilla, and Opera
Windows Media Video (WMV)	.wmv	Microsoft's proprietary digital video file format, playable with Windows Media Player; offers twice the bit rate of comparable MPEG-4 files
Xvid	.xvid	Another variation of the MPEG-4 format, similar to the competing DivX codec

 Note

A *container format* is a file format that holds different types of data within the file. These formats, such as the Audio Video Interleave (AVI) and RealVideo formats, contain not only the underlying audio and video, but also metadata about the source material—chapter information, subtitles, and such.

Choosing the Right Format for Your YouTube Videos

All the technicalities out of the way, it's time to decide what formats to use when creating your YouTube videos. Now, you might think this is somewhat academic, as YouTube stores and serves its videos in a single format—Adobe's Flash Video (FLV) format, using H.264 compression. Whatever format you upload, YouTube will convert your videos to this format after you upload them.

Note

Learn more about uploading videos in Chapter 13, "Uploading Your Videos to YouTube."

 Note

While YouTube currently uses the FLV format for standard playback, it uses the 3GP format for playback on most mobile devices, and the H.264 format for playback on Apple's iPhone and iPad. YouTube is also testing the WebM format for future playback in the HTML5 world.

That said, some original file formats convert better to the FLV format. If you have a choice, here are the formats and resolutions to use:

- **File format**: MPEG-4, MPEG-2, or H.264

- **Resolution**: 720p or 1080p

- **Aspect ratio**: 16:9 widescreen

- **Length**: Up to 15 minutes

- **File size**: Up to 2GB

- **Audio format**: MP3

- **Frame rate**: 30 frames per second (FPS)

Although these are the recommended specs, know that YouTube can accept just about anything you throw at it, so you're best to work with the original file format, resolution, frame rate, and such from start to finish through the process, rather than converting midstream to MPEG-4 or whatever. That's because you lose a little something each time you go through the conversion process; you'll get worse results if you reconvert a file in another format to one of these formats.

You should also keep the same resolution and aspect ratio throughout the entire video production process. That means you shouldn't change formats when you move the video from your camcorder to your video-editing program, or anywhere else in the process. Keep the original file format, the original codec, the original frame rate, and the original resolution. Every time a conversion is made, some quality is lost; knowing that YouTube will make the final conversion, don't add to the degradation.

You should also work with the highest available quality that your equipment and software allow. Remember, YouTube will downgrade a higher resolution picture, but can't upgrade a lower resolution one. That is, you can't turn a standard resolution picture into high definition; you can't add resolution that isn't there to begin with.

Converting Existing Videos to YouTube Format

When creating a new video from scratch, it's easy enough to configure your recording device to use the recommended settings. But what do you do if you want to upload an existing video that's in a different format?

The task of converting videos from one format to another is the province of a video converter program. This type of software automatically performs video file format conversion and in the process can convert files from one resolution or size to another. If you have a lot of existing videos you want to upload to YouTube, you need one of these programs. Some of the most popular video conversion programs include

- AVS Video Tools (www.avsmedia.com/VideoTools/)
- M^{2}Convert Professional (www.m2solutionsinc.com/products/pro.html)
- Movavi VideoSuite (www.movavi.com/suite/)
- Power Video Converter (www.apussoft.com)
- RER Video Converter (www.rersoft.com/video/video-converter.html)
- VIDEOzilla (www.videozilla.net)
- Xilisoft Video Converter (www.xilisoft.com/video-converter.html)

Using one of these converter programs is typically as easy as selecting the file to convert, choosing an output format, and then clicking the Convert button. Other settings (such as resolution or frame rate) are sometimes available, but the basic conversion process is most often a one-click operation.

The Big Picture

There's a lot you could learn about video technologies, but you don't have to knock yourself out—unless you really want to. Just remember to shoot in the highest possible resolution (720p or 1080p HD are great), using any popular video file format. You can then upload said file to the YouTube site, which will automatically convert it to the FLV file format and make it available at lower resolutions for those viewers with slower Internet connections or smaller displays.

8

Shooting Webcam Videos

There are three ways to record a video for YouTube. If you have a big budget, you can go with a professional recording, complete with lights, sound, professional-grade video cameras, and the like. If that's outside your budget, and it probably is, you can record with a consumer-grade camcorder. And if even that sounds pricey to you, you can record your videos with a standard computer webcam.

In fact, recording YouTube videos with a webcam has some benefits, chief among them the immediacy and flexibility that come from the format. And it's a very low cost solution: You can purchase a webcam for as little as $30.

Should you record your business videos with a webcam? And if so, how do you do it? That's what we cover in this chapter.

Understanding Webcam Video

A *webcam* is a small camera, typically with an accompanying miniature microphone, which attaches to any computer via USB port. As you can see in Figure 8.1, most webcams fit on top of your monitor screen; some notebook PCs come with a webcam built in.

Figure 8.1   *Logitech's QuickCam Pro 9000 webcam, mounted on top of a computer screen.*

Given the webcam's small footprint, it is a relatively unobtrusive way to shoot YouTube videos. Also, when attached to a notebook PC operating on battery power (or when you use a notebook with a built-in webcam), it lets you shoot videos just about anywhere—a truly portable solution.

Webcams do not always produce the highest quality video and audio. Typical lower-priced webcams shoot video at a resolution of 640×480, but with a lower-quality lens that neither works well in darkened conditions nor reproduces especially sharp images. Today's higher-end webcams, however, can shoot in high definition, and some include a higher-quality lens. Still, if you want broadcast-quality video, a webcam is the least satisfactory of the three different shooting options.

The audio you get with a webcam is not the best either. In most instances, you speak into a small microphone embedded within the webcam itself; the farther away you are from the webcam, the less clear your voice recording will come out. (Some webcams include a separate clip-on microphone, for just this reason.) And, let's be honest, this isn't studio quality audio here; webcam audio is barely satisfactory for voice, and not for much of anything else.

With that said, the lower-quality picture and sound inherent in webcam capture lends your webcam videos a sense of immediacy; the effect is one of raw, "you are there," citizen journalism. The effect is also one of directness, a one-on-one communication between the speaker and the viewer, with little in the way of fancy production in between.

Figure 8.2 shows a screenshot from a webcam video I shot in my local coffeehouse. As you can see, the raw nature of the webcam makes for a very personal effect. As you can also see, shooting with a webcam puts you at the mercy of your environment; in this instance, a bright side light coming from a nearby window. You might not have this problem when you're shooting in your office, but it is something to watch out for when shooting on the go.

Figure 8.2   *A webcam video shot "in the field" at a local coffeehouse.*

Webcams can capture video and audio to your hard drive, typically in AVI (Audio Video Interleave) file format, using the software that comes with most webcam packages. Webcams can also stream live video over the Internet, which is common when using the webcam to chat via instant messaging or in chat rooms—but is also useful when you want to upload videos directly from your webcam to YouTube, a process we discuss later in this chapter.

When a Webcam Makes Sense

So, when might you want to shoot your business videos with a webcam? Let's look at some of the different types of videos that benefit from webcam capture.

Creating a Video Blog

The most common use of webcam video is in the creation of a *video blog* or *vlog*. Think of a video blog as a video version of a traditional text blog—an opportunity for you or someone from your company to offer regular personal insights into business trends and events.

With a video blog, the low-quality immediacy of a webcam works to your advantage. If you shoot a vlog in a professional recording studio, the result might be too slick for the viewer to take seriously. You almost need the nonprofessional nature of a webcam to give your vlog legitimacy.

In addition, if you're vlogging on a frequent basis, it's a lot easier to plug in a webcam than it is to set up a camcorder, lights, and an external microphone. When you have something to say, just plug in, turn on, and start talking. The ease-of-use alone should encourage more frequent vlogging—which is a good thing.

Reporting from the Road or Special Events

A webcam is essential when you're traveling and still need to contribute to your company's vlog or YouTube videos. It doesn't matter where you are. It's a simple setup, no need to carry any additional equipment (such as a camcorder); all you need is a webcam and a notebook computer, which you probably take with you anyway, and you're good to go.

This makes sense, of course, if you're a traveling salesperson or an executive with a busy travel schedule. It's also great when you're attending special events: trade shows, conferences, seminars, and the like. With your webcam and notebook PC in tow, you can contribute up-to-the-minute reporting from just about anywhere, including the convention floor or conference room. Your equipment does not limit you at all.

Responding to Immediate Issues

In the unfortunate event of a serious event hitting your company, you can immediately address the issue with the use of a quick-and-dirty webcam video. When disaster strikes, you want to get in front of the issue and minimize the bad PR. What better way than a personal response from the company president, recorded live to webcam?

This is another instance where a professionally produced video would be counterproductive. It would appear too impersonal and take too long to create. You can create a webcam video a lot faster, and the results speak more directly to interested viewers.

Capturing Customer Testimonials

Finally, if you're utilizing customer testimonials as part of your online marketing mix, there's no better way to capture those testimonials than via webcam—that is, by encouraging your customers to send in their own webcam videos.

First, you get the immediacy effect; your customers will appear more "real" on webcam than they might in a studio. Second, it's an inexpensive approach; customers create their own videos, with their own computers and webcams. Instead of laying out tens of thousands of dollars in travel expenses and professional video production, you're out about a hundred bucks for a webcam. What's not to like?

Tips for Shooting an Effective Webcam Video

If you decide to use webcam video as part of your YouTube video mix, how do you best take advantage of the medium? In other words, how do you make the best looking and most effective webcam video possible?

Make It Immediate

Webcam video works best when it conveys immediacy. That means you don't want it to look *too* professional. It's okay to make a few verbal mistakes and leave them in the video. Make it look as if you're speaking off the cuff, even if you are working from a script. You want your video to have the feel of a deskside chat, just you talking directly to the audience. Nothing fancy, nothing too polished. Just you and the webcam, one-to-one.

Keep It Simple

Webcam video is typically of lower quality than other types of video you might shoot. You need to keep the picture simple; fiddly details are lost in the lower-resolution picture.

What works best? Just you, close to the webcam, and talking directly to the camera. Don't try to fit two people into the frame; doing that on a webcam just looks silly. And don't even think about moving around: Sit still, directly in front of the camera, and keep your movements to a minimum. Action captured via webcam often looks jerky.

Simplicity counts in terms of visual composition. Sit in front of a plain background of either white or light gray; a busy background is distracting on YouTube. You should also avoid overly bright background colors, which can also be distracting.

In terms of composition, move close to the camera. Although you might be tempted to show yourself from the waist up, that shot makes your face too small for the YouTube viewing window. Go for a head-and-shoulders shot or move even closer for a pure headshot. Remember, it's you talking directly to the viewer—so make sure the viewer can see you!

Watch the Lighting

Most webcams don't handle extremes in lighting very well. For example, you get a lousy picture if the room light is too dark. So, you want lots of light—as long as it's shining on your face.

What you don't want is backlight shining from behind you, which tricks the webcam into darkening the picture and throwing your face into shadow. That rules out shooting with an open window behind you; close the drapes or blinds to cut out all the rear light.

You need good lighting on your face, and no lights behind you, so you might need to rearrange some room lights. This doesn't have to be a big deal; you can dramatically improve the look of the video by positioning a simple desk lamp behind or to the side of the webcam, pointing directly at your face.

 Tip

If you're not sure whether you have the right light, shoot a test video and see how it looks—before you upload your real video to the YouTube site.

Minimize the Background Noise

Most webcams don't include a high quality microphone, which means that the sound you get on a webcam video is often of lower quality than you might want. You can compensate by sitting as close to the webcam as possible and speaking loudly and clearly. Don't mumble and don't whisper; enunciate as if you're speaking to an auditorium full of people.

You should also know that the webcam will pick up any background noise in the room, which can be distracting to YouTube viewers. Turn off any noisy mechanical or electronic devices, including fans, coffee machines, printers—you name it. (Air conditioners are particularly noisy, with their low humming.) And make sure that anyone else in the room with you stays quiet!

Uploading Webcam Video to YouTube

Another nice thing about shooting with a webcam is that YouTube makes it easy to upload webcam videos. You can save your webcam video to a standard video file and then upload it, or you can use YouTube's Quick Capture feature to upload a video as you record it, in real time. The latter method is quite easy to use, even if it doesn't allow you the luxury of editing the videos you record.

Uploading Webcam Video Files

The standard approach to uploading webcam video is to take your time while recording, using multiple takes if necessary, and then to save your results in an AVI or similar format file. Most webcams come with software for capturing video in this fashion; follow the instructions to save your video files.

From there, you can edit the webcam video files using a video-editing program, and then upload the resulting file to the YouTube site. We cover this method of uploading in more detail in Chapter 13, "Uploading Your Videos to YouTube;" turn there for more information.

 Note

Learn more about editing your webcam videos in Chapter 11, "Editing and Enhancing Your Videos."

Uploading Live Webcam Video

An alternative to uploading video files is to upload your webcam video as you shoot it, live from your webcam. Here's how it works.

 Note

When you upload live webcam videos to YouTube, you don't have the opportunity to edit those videos. Whatever you record is what YouTube shows, warts and all.

With your webcam connected and running, click the Upload link on any YouTube page. When the Video File Upload page appears, click the Record from Webcam link.

You now see the Record Video from Webcam page, shown in Figure 8.3. Pull down the list boxes at the top of the video window to select your webcam video and audio options; you should now see the picture from your webcam in the video window.

Figure 8.3 *Recording a live webcam video for YouTube.*

 Note

If, when you first access the Record Video from Webcam page, you see an Adobe Flash Player Settings dialog box, click the Allow button.

 Tip

The audio level is displayed in a vertical meter to the right of the picture on the Record Video from Webcam page. As you talk, watch the audio level meter rise and fall. Try to keep the audio level in the green range; if the meter goes higher into the red, you're talking too loud and the sound on your recording could be distorted.

To start recording, click the big onscreen Record button, or the little Record button below the video window. While you're recording, the Record button changes to a red Stop button.

When you finish recording your video, click the Stop button. YouTube now prepares a preview of your video, as shown in Figure 8.4; click the Preview button to watch what you just recorded, click Re-record to do it over, or click Publish to accept and publish the video.

Figure 8.4   *Previewing and publishing a webcam video.*

When you click Publish, YouTube automatically uploads the video to the site and displays the video page shown in Figure 8.5. You now have to enter information about the video—title, description, tags, category, and the like. Do so and then click the Save Changes button. Your video will soon be available for public viewing.

Figure 8.5   *Entering information about your webcam video.*

Note

Learn more about entering information about a video in Chapter 13, "Uploading Your Videos to YouTube."

The Big Picture

The easiest way to create videos for YouTube is to use an inexpensive computer webcam. A webcam lets you capture videos from just about anywhere, with an immediacy often lacking in other types of video capture.

YouTube lets you upload webcam videos in one of two ways. You can save your webcam video to a video file and upload that file, or you use the Quick Capture feature to upload live video as you record it—no editing necessary (or possible)!

9

Shooting Semi-Pro Videos

As you learned in the previous chapter, the easiest and most affordable way to create a YouTube video is to use a computer webcam. But webcam video is low quality and limiting, not ideal for most business uses. How, then, can you shoot a more professional-looking YouTube video without spending the bucks for truly professional production?

For many businesses, the best bang for the buck comes from using consumer-grade video equipment, but in a professional manner. We're talking the kinds of video camcorder you can find at your local Best Buy or Circuit City, augmented by sophisticated video-editing software and the appropriate accessories. The resulting videos can look almost identical to professionally made videos, but without expensive professional involvement.

Understanding Consumer Video Equipment

When I was a kid, my dad shot home movies using a Super 8 film camera. The movies themselves were about what you would expect—lots of cute little kids mugging about in a dark, shaky, poorly focused little film.

Well, all that's changed. Thanks to today's digital video technology, you can now shoot videos in high resolution and edit them on your home computer. The results are often indistinguishable from what you'd get from a professional video production house, complete with sophisticated editing and special effects. And the costs are no more, in today's terms, than what my dad spent back when I was a youth.

It's amazing: Digital video recording lets you use your PC as a movie-editing studio to create sophisticated videos for YouTube distribution.

How Camcorders Work

The key to successful semi-pro video production is to start with a digital camcorder. Fortunately, now that older analog VHS camcorders have been relegated to the garbage bin or to Craigslist classified ads, virtually every camcorder sold today records in a digital format.

The nice thing about today's digital camcorders is that they're easy enough for even an executive to use, and they produce high quality results. Just point the camcorder, press the Record button, and zoom into the shot. Some higher-end camcorders feature image stabilization technology, so shaky pictures are a thing of the past. And, with today's digital recording formats, the movies you shoot are at professional quality levels.

Let's start with the basics. As you can tell from its name, a camcorder is actually two devices in one, combining a video *camera* and video *recorder* into a single unit. The camera part of the unit senses the image, and the recorder section records it.

In the camera part of the camcorder, the process starts when the image is seen through the camera's lens. The higher quality the lens, the more light passes through it without distortion of the image.

The image as seen by the lens is beamed onto a charge-coupled device (CCD), which is an electronic chip that captures the light falling on it and converts the light to electrical signals. Most consumer-level camcorders use a single CCD to capture the video image. Some high-end camcorders, however, use three CCDs, one for each of the primary colors (red, green, and blue), which provides better detail and color. Most professional video cameras use a three-CCD design.

The CCD generates the digital signal transmitted to the camcorder's recording section. Today, most camcorders record to a built-in hard disk drive, recordable flash memory, or mini DVD disk; older camcorders recorded to videotape.

Because the audio and video signals are recorded digitally, you can transfer them (typically via a USB connection) to any personal computer and then edit them using digital movie-editing software. When you record digitally, edit digitally, and then transfer the digital files to YouTube, you keep a fully digital signal path, which results in extremely high quality picture and sound.

Examining Camcorder Storage

If you used a camcorder a decade or so ago, chances are it used either the VHS or VHS-C tape format. Both of these formats were analog formats with limited image resolution. Today, however, virtually every camcorder records in a digital format, capable of much better picture quality than was delivered in the past.

The earliest digital camcorders recorded to MiniDV cassette tape. The MiniDV format is pretty much abandoned today, but you still might have an old unit sitting in the closet. This format recorded broadcast-quality standard definition video (500+ lines of resolution), at the standard 4:3 aspect ratio.

The MiniDV format was superseded by the HDV format, which recorded high definition video on the same MiniDV cassettes. Depending on the camcorder, this format recorded at either 720p or 1080i resolution, along with Dolby Digital surround sound.

Cassette tape, even in the MiniDV or HDV formats, has inherent disadvantages; it's hard to queue to a specific point, and it takes longer to transfer files from the tape to a computer for editing. For these reasons, most camcorders today record to some sort of tapeless medium for easier queuing and file transfer.

DVD-based camcorders record directly to small (8cm diameter) discs, using the DVD-R, DVD-RW, or DVD+RW disk formats. Depending on the picture quality level you select, each disc can hold between 20 to 60 minutes of video. DVD camcorders record video in MPEG-2 format. Transferring files from a mini DVD to your computer is a little convoluted, in that you have to rip the files from the disk to your computer's hard drive.

A better solution is to use a camcorder that contains and records to a built-in hard disk drive (HDD), just like the kind you have on your personal computer. It's relatively easy to connect a cable between an HDD camcorder and your computer to transfer the video files you shoot. Current models incorporate hard drives from 30GB to 120GB in size. HDD camcorders record video in MPEG-2 format.

Some camcorders today use flash memory storage instead of a hard disk drive. The advantages are pretty much the same, in that file transfer is a snap. These camcorders record directly to a CompactFlash, SD/MMC, or Memory Stick flash memory device in MPEG-2 format. Because of the small size of the storage card, these are typically compact camcorders.

Which is the best type of storage to use? If you intend to transfer your videos to a PC for editing, I recommend an HDD or flash-based camcorder. It's very easy to transfer digital video files from a camcorder's hard drive to a PC's hard drive via either a FireWire or USB connection.

Standard or High Definition?

Just a year or two ago, you had to spend a considerable amount of money to get a camcorder that shot in high definition (HD). That's not the case today. You can find HD camcorders for as little as $150, and even when you're looking at higher-end models, there isn't much of a premium for the HD feature.

In addition to the higher 720p or 1080p resolution, all HD camcorders shoot in the 16:9 widescreen aspect ratio. Shooting in widescreen is a must these days; YouTube viewers pretty much expect a widescreen picture for new videos.

In short, there isn't much of an excuse not to move up to an HD camcorder. YouTube viewers expect high definition, and you don't pay much (if any) more to get an HD model. So when you're shopping for a new camcorder, put high definition recording at the top of your feature list.

Choosing a Camcorder

You don't have to spend a lot of money to buy a camcorder. As it always does, developing technology helps to bring you better performance at a significantly lower price than you would have paid just a few years ago. The challenge is picking the right camcorder for your needs.

As you might expect, the more money you spend on a camcorder, the more bells and whistles you get. In particular, a bigger budget typically buys you better picture quality, a bigger zoom lens, and various special features (such as transition effects, night-vision shooting, and so on). That's not to say that you have to spend a fortune to get a decent performing unit; budget somewhere in the $300 to $600 range for the best performance for dollars spent.

What should you look for in a new camcorder? Beyond HD recording, you should consider a model that includes a good quality zoom lens, image stabilization (to keep your pictures steady, even if your hands aren't), various automatic exposure modes, and some sort of built-in video editing. This last feature lets you perform in-camera edits between scenes, including audio dubbing, fade in and out, and other special effects.

You should also pay particular attention to the camcorder's image-sensing system. Most lower-priced camcorders use a single CCD to capture the video image. Higher-priced models use a three-CCD system that optically splits the image and feeds color-filtered versions of the scene to three CCD sensors, one for each color: red, green, and blue. Naturally, a three-CCD camera delivers better color than a single-CCD model.

 Tip

> For a better quality picture, look for a camcorder with a bigger CCD. For example, 1/3" CCDs are better than 1/6" ones.

With these features in mind, there are three levels of camcorders available today. So-called pocket or "flip" camcorders are the smallest, lowest priced, and easiest to use. Mid-level camcorders comprise the bulk of the market, with a nice mix of features and usability. And semi-pro models are priced several orders of magnitude higher than mid-level models, but offer a range of features that aspiring professionals often drool over.

Pocket Camcorders

Let's look at the pocket camcorders first. These are often called "flip" camcorders, after the company (Flip Video—now owned by Cisco) that first came up with the concept. But many companies, including Sony, Kodak, and Samsung, offer these compact marvels, small enough to fit in a shirt pocket. (Figure 9.1 shows the Flip MinoHD, a high definition pocket camcorder.)

The advantages of a pocket camcorder are many. First, they're inexpensive, priced in the $100–$200 range. Second, they're easy to use, pretty much a point-and-shoot affair. Third, they're optimized for YouTube shooting, automatically recording in the right file formats, so you don't even have to use video-editing software if you don't want to.

There are also some definite disadvantages to shooting with a pocket camcorder, all pretty much quality related. Most pocket camcorders have unimpressive lenses, which results in no better than average picture quality. Most don't have much in the way of zoom, either, so you can't zoom into your subject, at least not much. And don't expect any fancy features, either, or the ability to add an external microphone. These are bare bones point-and-shoot camcorders, nothing more, nothing less.

As such, I don't recommend pocket camcorders for most businesses. They're okay if you're shooting a static talking head video, but not for much else.

Figure 9.1   *Cisco's Flip MinoHD camcorder.*

Mid-Level Camcorders

For most businesses, the better choice is a mid-level camcorder, such as the Canon VIXIA HF R10 shown in Figure 9.2. These camcorders run from $300 to $800 or so, and offer the best combination of price and features for shooting YouTube videos.

Figure 9.2   *Canon's VIXIA HF R10 midlevel HD camcorder.*

You can find mid-level camcorders from all major manufacturers, including Canon, JVC, Panasonic, Samsung, and Sony. Most of these camcorders record to either hard disk drive or flash memory, and offer high definition widescreen recording in either 720p or 1080p formats.

Camcorders at this level typically include a large (20X or so) zoom lens, decent-sized CMOS image sensor, image stabilization, and a big LCD display for viewing what you're recording. Look for a model that includes an input for an external microphone; some have this, some don't.

Semi-Pro Camcorders

Most consumer-level camcorders are small enough to hold in the palm of your hand. But if you want the best possible picture quality, or have an itch to be an independent filmmaker, you have to move to a larger model. These camcorders, called *semi-pro* or *prosumer* models, are often big enough to require a shoulder rest. As you can see in Figure 9.3, these units look, feel, and perform just like the type of camcorder you see TV news crews or independent filmmakers lugging around.

Figure 9.3 *Sony's HDR-AX2000 Handycam semi-pro camcorder.*

Many prosumer camcorders let you use interchangeable lenses for more shooting versatility and shoot in the 16:9 widescreen HD format. More important, they come with a bevy of automatic recording modes and manual adjustments that enable you to custom-tailor your movies to a variety of shooting styles and situations. Their picture quality is second to none, especially under difficult lighting conditions.

As you might suspect, these are not inexpensive camcorders. Expect to spend any-where from $2,000 to $3,500 for one of these pricey puppies. This is probably overkill for shooting YouTube videos; you're better off sticking to a lower-priced mid-level model.

Selecting Essential Accessories

One of the keys to shooting more professional videos is to take advantage of avail-able accessories such as tripods, lighting kits, and the like. Let's take a quick look at what you need to make sure your videos don't look like the majority of amateurish YouTube videos out there today.

Tripod

Let's talk stability first. Many amateur videos (and professional movies trying for an artsy "shaky cam" effect) bounce around like a monkey on caffeine. That's because it's hard to hold a camcorder steady in your hand; you end up shaking the cam-corder and producing a shaky video.

What you need is a way to steady your camera when you shoot. The answer is to mount your camcorder on a tripod (such as the one shown in Figure 9.4) or mono-pod. Spend $40 or less and get a rock-solid picture; it's an essential accessory.

Figure 9.4 *The sturdy 515QF tripod from Slik.*

Lighting

One of the easiest ways to make your videos look more professional is to improve the lighting. Videos shot with existing indoor lighting typically look dark and grainy, and have trouble reproducing correct colors. You'd be surprised how much of improvement you get by shining more light on the subject.

To this end, you want to supplement your existing internal lighting with some sort of auxiliary lighting. You can go with a camera-mounted light, like the one in Figure 9.5, or a more versatile multi-unit lighting kit, like the one in Figure 9.6. I like going the lighting kit route, with either two or three external photofloods; this provides the most versatility and best results for lighting just about any kind of scene. And you don't have to spend an arm and a leg for this, either; you get a camera mounted light for under $5, and a decent lighting kit for $150–$200.

Figure 9.5   *Sima's Universal Pro LED camcorder light.*

Seamless Background

When you're planning your videos, think about where the subject will be sitting or standing, and what's behind him or her. You don't want to position the subject in front of an open window or cluttered bookcase, which can be distracting to the viewer.

Figure 9.6   *The Alzo 250 2-light "Cool Lite" kit.*

Instead, consider investing in a roll or two of seamless photographic background paper and accompanying stands, such as the one shown in Figure 9.7. Also good are patterned muslin or cloth backdrops, all of which you can find at better photo retailers. You might spend $100 or so on a full setup, but like all these accessories, it's a one-time investment; you can reuse it over and over again for future video shoots.

Figure 9.7   *A seamless background roll, mounted between two stands.*

Tip

You can find most of these accessories at your local camera store. These are the same tripods, lighting kits, and seamless backgrounds used by still photographers, and most camera stores carry a large selection.

External Microphone

So far, we've talked about ways to improve the quality of your video's picture, but you should also pay attention to the sound. Unfortunately, using a camcorder's built-in microphone often produces sub-par audio, as the subject's voice has to travel clear across the room to be picked up by the mic; you also pick up a lot of extraneous noise along the way.

To enhance the audio in your videos, look for a camcorder that lets you connect an external microphone. You can choose from all sorts of high-quality microphones, including boom mics, stereo mics, and surround sound mics. For most YouTube videos, the best choice is a lavalier or lapel mic, such as the one shown in Figure 9.8, that clips onto the front of the subject's shirt or blouse. Just make sure that the mic you choose has the same connector as found on your camera—they're not all the same.

Figure 9.8 *Shure's SM11-CN lavalier microphone.*

Tip

You can choose from wired or wireless mics. A wired lavalier mic typically costs $50 to $150 or so, while a wireless system costs $300 or more. For most businesses, a wired model works just fine.

Building a Computer for Video Editing

The other essential component in creating a semi-pro video is the personal computer you use to edit your videos. It's important, then, to build a computer system that has the horsepower necessary for this demanding task.

Video editing is the second-most demanding operation you can do on your PC. (The most demanding activity is playing games, believe it or not.) It takes a lot of processing power, memory, and hard disk storage to edit and process full-motion video, and most older and lower-priced PCs simply aren't up to the task. It might mean, depending on your unit, that you have some upgrading to do.

So, what kind of PC do you need for video editing? If you're an Apple user, there's no better computer for video editing than a Mac Pro. This machine has all the horsepower and all the features you need to do all sorts of fancy video editing without even breaking a sweat. If you're a Windows user, you have a lot more choices. To start with, you want to go with the fastest, most powerful processor you can afford, with as much memory as possible. In most instances, a desktop model will provide more horsepower than a similarly priced notebook.

You also need lots of hard disk space, with a fast hard disk. Perhaps the best way to go is to add a dedicated external hard disk just for your video editing. Make sure the hard drive connects via FireWire because FireWire is faster for this type of data transfer than USB is.

How much hard disk space is enough? Well, I'm not sure you can ever have enough storage, especially when storing digital video files. Here's why: Video files are really, really big.

For example, 1080p HD video takes up about 7MB for every second you shoot. That's almost 26GB for a full hour of video. After you have a few videos (or even a few differently edited versions of the same video) on your hard disk, the space used starts getting big. For this reason, consider a 1TB (terabyte) or larger drive for your video storage. You can't have too much hard disk space.

Tip

When calculating the necessary hard disc space, factor in the amount of "raw" video you have, not just the length of the final edited video. It's easy for your raw material to be ten times or more as long as your final product!

Finally, consider what type of monitor you'll be using. Here again, bigger is better—at least 20" diagonal. That's because you're displaying more than just your video onscreen; you also have to find screen space for all the components of your video-editing program. Go with the biggest widescreen monitor you can afford.

When a Semi-Pro Video Makes Sense

We've spent a lot of time discussing how to assemble the right equipment to shoot a semi-pro YouTube video. But just when does this type of video make sense for your business?

Video Blogs

In the previous chapter, we discussed using a webcam to create your video blog (called a *vlog*). Even though webcam video has the immediacy that defines such a vlog, the webcam's lower-quality picture and sound might work against any professional image you're trying to impart.

You can create much better looking, and better sounding, videos with a low-cost consumer camcorder, and still maintain the immediacy necessary for a legitimate vlog. The key here is to keep your "set"—what's in front of and behind the subject in the video—spare and functional. No elaborate decorations, no fancy lighting, just the subject speaking into a camcorder. The result is a clearer, less jerky picture than what you can accomplish with a webcam, but still with the personal one-to-one effect.

To shoot a video blog, all you need is a camcorder and a tripod. If you don't have a separate camera operator, make sure your camcorder has a wireless remote control so that you can turn it on and off from in front of the camera. You can shoot under natural light or augment the room light with a camcorder-mounted external light. It might be a good idea to use a lavalier microphone for better sound, if your camcorder has a mic input.

Tip

When you're shooting yourself with a camcorder, swivel the LCD viewfinder 180° so that you can watch yourself from in front of the camera while you're recording. (But make sure you look into the lens when you're recording, not into the viewfinder!)

Informational Videos

Informational videos—YouTube news reports, in other words—look more professional, and thus more authoritative, when shot with a camcorder versus the less professional look of a webcam video. You don't have to venture into a professional recording studio to record this type of video; you can record in any empty room or office, as long you have the space and a good strong lock on the door.

Although you might think you need professional video production for this type of video, complete with flattering lighting and a makeup person, the reality is that you can achieve similar results with a well-conceived semi-pro production. The key here is to act like it's a professional production, which also helps to improve your overall production values. Invest in some external lighting (which improves the video's look), hook up a wireless lavalier microphone (which improves the video's sound), and have an assistant dab some pancake on the newsreader's shiny forehead (which improves the subject's look). Mount the camcorder on a tripod, have enough staffers nearby to handle any contingencies, and use a laptop computer near the camera lens as a teleprompter. The newsreader should feel pampered enough, and the resulting video quality should be good enough, to please everyone involved.

Product Demonstrations and Overviews

You also don't need a fancy video recording studio to shoot effective product demonstrations. All you need is a quality consumer-grade camcorder, an adequate lighting setup, a boom or lavalier mic, and the patience to shoot the same sequence from multiple angles. The equipment should give you a quality video, and the multiple shots give you choices to use when you edit the video.

One of the common pitfalls of semi-pro product demonstrations is the sound. It's easy enough to get a quality picture (assuming that you're not shooting under straight room lighting), but the sound trips up a lot of inexperienced producers. The mistake is to think the camcorder's built-in microphone can do the job, which it probably can't; it captures all the sounds in the room, including the ancillary sounds of the crew and of the product itself. You'll get much better sound by using multiple external microphones: a lavalier mic to isolate the demonstrator's voice, and a boom mic to capture product sounds. You can mix the two soundtracks for optimal effect when you edit the video.

On-the-Scene Reports

Let's not forget the portable nature of a camcorder: A handheld model can shoot practically anywhere. This, of course, makes a camcorder ideal for shooting outside the office, in just about any location.

Consider, for example, shooting an on-the-road video, with a cameraman accompanying the host to various locations. Perhaps you need an outdoor demonstration of your product, or want to file a report from a trade show or conference, or document a visit to a remote office. You can shoot any of these videos with a simple camcorder, no optional equipment necessary—although an external mic and camera light might be useful if the situation allows.

Shooting a Semi-Pro Video

What's the best way to shoot a semi-pro video? It depends on your situation, but basic techniques hold in any instance.

Shooting in the Office

When you're shooting indoors in familiar surroundings, you have a nice home court advantage—and a lot of control over the situation. You can take advantage of this situation to shoot extremely high quality videos. All you need is the right equipment, a little preparation, and a lot of patience.

As to equipment, here's what I recommend:

- Mid-level HD camcorder with external microphone input
- Tripod
- Lavalier or boom microphone
- External video light—either a camera-mounted light or a set of separate photofloods

Set up your equipment in front of the subject. Set the subject in front of a plain, nondistracting background; if you can, choose a background color that contrasts with the subject's clothing or the color of the product you're shooting. Mic the subject with a lavalier mic or, if you have a dedicated sound person, use a boom mic positioned above and to the front of the subject.

If your subject is reading from a script, enter the script into a notebook computer or iPad and position the device either just below or to the side of the camera lens. I like to use Microsoft Word as a makeshift teleprompter, but other programs work just as well. Make sure the display font is large enough for the subject to comfortably read it from across the room, and that you have someone to scroll down the text in the program as the subject reads it.

After everything is set up (and take your time doing this; rushing things can create unsatisfactory results), run through the shoot a few times for practice. When everyone—including both the subject and the cameraman—is ready, shoot the video for real. If something goes wrong, stop the shoot and do another take. In fact, you should shoot several takes and use the best of the bunch in your final video.

You might also want to shoot the video again from another angle, or with close-ups on the product or the demonstrator's hands or whatever. This gives you a library of shots you can use during the editing process; cutting away to a close-up, for example, helps to increase the visual interest of the video. The key is to give yourself enough options to best edit the final video. Don't paint yourself into a box with a single take of a static shot.

Shooting Outside the Office

When you're shooting a video in the field, you're operating under less than ideal conditions. That isn't necessarily a bad thing, but it is something you need to be prepared for.

The first thing you need to know is that you probably can't use all your fancy equipment. In the worst case scenario, all you'll have is your camcorder, which means using available light and recording audio directly into the camcorder's built-in microphone. You might, under certain conditions, be able to use a camera-mounted video light or an external microphone. (In outdoor shots, I recommend a wireless lavalier microphone to cut down on background and wind noise; also, a wireless mic means you'll never trip over a mic wire.) But if all you get to use is the camcorder itself, be prepared to work under those conditions.

Working in the field means making the most of what you have available. Examine your surroundings to find an appropriate background for your subject. Unlike an in-office shot, going with a plain background might not be the best approach; you might want to capture some of the local flavor in your video, which means shooting with some sort of identifying landmark in the background. Make sure the background doesn't distract from the subject, and that you properly frame the subject and the background.

You also need to consider the lighting—both the type of lighting and its originating direction. Indirect lighting is better than direct lighting, which is often harsh and unflattering, and side lighting is better than overhead lighting. You definitely don't want the light to shine directly on the subject's face; it will make him squint. Light directly behind the subject is also bad because you get a backlight effect that puts the subject's face in shadow. The best light comes from the side and is slightly diffused—like what you get on a cloudy day. (Alternately, use a reflector to bounce sunlight onto the subject from below or from the side.)

 Tip

If you're shooting outdoors, try to shoot in the early morning or late afternoon—those so-called "golden hours" when the sun is low on the horizon and has a warmish cast.

Finally, if you have a tripod handy, use it—unless you want the "you are there" type of shaky cam effect. Get everything set up, do a run through or two if time and conditions permit, and then start shooting!

Transferring Videos to Your PC for Editing

After you shoot your video, you need to transfer it to a PC for editing and eventual uploading to YouTube.

If you have a digital camcorder, connecting your camcorder to your PC is a snap. All you need is the appropriate cable (typically a USB cable) to connect between your camcorder and your PC. Connect one end of the cable to your PC and another to your camcorder.

After your camcorder is connected to your PC, transferring a video is typically as easy as putting your camcorder into file transfer mode. Each video you record is stored in a separate digital file. When you transfer the movie, you're actually copying the digital file from your camcorder to your PC, just as you would any other digital file from any storage device. After you've copied the file to your PC's hard drive, you can edit the it or upload it to YouTube.

 Note

If you have an older VHS, VHS-C, SVHS, 8mm, or Hi8 recorder, the connection isn't as simple. That's because you have to convert the analog video from your camcorder to the digital format used by your PC. You'll need to purchase and connect some sort of analog-to-digital video capture device, then follow that device's instructions to make the conversion.

Tips for Shooting an Effective Semi-Pro Video

Do you want to shoot a better semi-pro video, one that truly looks professional? Then pay attention to the following tips—they'll help you avoid producing amateurish videos with your new equipment.

Shoot Digitally

This one should go without saying, but I'll say it anyway. I don't care if you are on a tight budget, and your uncle or the guy down the hall or whoever has an old camcorder he's willing to let you borrow at no cost. You don't want to shoot on analog tape; the best results come from keeping an all-digital chain. That means using a newer digital video camcorder, period. It doesn't matter whether you shoot to hard disk or flash storage, what does matter is that the video is digital.

Keep the Proper Resolution in Mind

If your camcorder is capable of shooting high definition widescreen video, do so. In fact, shoot at the highest resolution your camcorder offers. If you have a choice between 720p or 1080p, go with 1080p. There's no downside to shooting at the highest possible resolution.

 Note

This is different advice than what I gave in the first edition of this book, when YouTube only accepted 320 × 240 resolution files. With YouTube going full high def, you need to adapt your recording strategy accordingly.

Use a Tripod

One of the easiest ways to turn a good video into a mediocre one is to shoot it without a tripod. I know, handheld cameras are designed to be handheld, but that doesn't mean they should be. When you hold a camera in your hand, it *moves*; it's impossible for you to hold the camera perfectly still for the three minutes or so of the entire video. The result is a jerky, jumpy picture that looks more like a home movie than a professional video production. That's not what you want.

You obtain better results when you invest in a tripod. Mount the camera on the tripod and it won't move around anymore. Your picture stays stable and clear, with a much more professional look. A tripod is the first and best investment you can make in your video production capabilities!

Lighting Matters

I've already said it multiple times in this chapter, but it bears repeating: Shooting in available light seldom achieves acceptable results. You can dramatically improve the look of your videos by adding light—augmenting the available light with some sort of external light. This can be a camera-mounted video light, freestanding photofloods, or a full-blown video lighting kit. The key is to get more—and better—light into the shot.

Better lighting, by the way, isn't just to get rid of lingering shadows. Most indoor lighting isn't quite white; the color of white varies from light source to light source. Some types of lighting produce a cooler (bluer) white and others produce a warmer (redder) white. And when the light itself is colored, it affects all the other colors in the shot.

For example, candlelight casts a very warm light, almost orange. Incandescent bulbs are also slightly warm, whereas florescent bulbs are cooler—to the point of having a slightly greenish cast. In contrast, studio lighting has a more neutral cast, which is what you want for your videos.

 Note

You might be able to compensate for different types of lighting in your camcorder. Look for a white balance or color correction control, and follow your camcorder's directions for setting a true white level.

Use an External Microphone

All camcorders have a built-in microphone. With most lower-end camcorders, that's the only option you have; you have to use the camcorder's mic for all your audio needs. In contrast, higher-end camcorders come with an external microphone jack to which you can connect most any type of external mic. This is a good thing.

There are two bad things about using a camcorder's internal microphone. First, it's typically not a high quality mic; the sound quality is mediocre at best. Second, the microphone is on the camcorder, not on the subject—who is often on the other side of the room. That means the subject has to yell just to be picked up by the mic, which also picks up any other sounds between the subject and the camcorder—not the best situation for capturing quality audio.

It's far, far better to mic the subject directly, using a handheld mic, lavalier mic, or even a boom mic. The keys are to get the mic closer to the subject and to isolate the subject from all other background sounds. You want to clearly hear what the subject is saying, and only what the subject is saying—and the only way to do that is with an external microphone.

Watch the Background

Did you ever notice the background in a professionally shot video? Probably not, and that speaks to the care in which it was chosen. You're not supposed to notice the background; your attention is supposed to focus on the main subject.

The point is that you need to pay particular attention to what's behind the subject in your shot. Don't just point your camera at an executive sitting behind her desk without also examining what's behind that executive. If the background is too busy, it distracts from the subject; the viewer's eyes drift to the background instead of to the person who's talking.

What kinds of backgrounds do you want to avoid? The list includes things such as open windows (especially with people walking by outside!), busy wallpaper, cluttered bookshelves, and just general clutter. It's much better to shoot in front of a plain wall, if you have no other choice.

Even better is to use some sort of professional background. Any good photography store sells seamless background paper, as well as cloth and muslin backgrounds with various unobtrusive patterns. If you do a lot of corporate videos, consider creating your own unique patterned background that incorporates your company's logo, either large or in a smaller repeating pattern.

A Little Movement Is Good...

Not all semi-pro videos need to be static. One of the advantages of using a camcorder is that, unlike a webcam, you can move it. Get your subject out of her chair and capture her walking across the room, or moving back and forth between props. Use the camera in a handheld fashion or, even better, turn it on the tripod to follow the speaker's movement. Even in a small YouTube window, it's okay to have a little action in the shot.

...But Too Much Movement Is Bad

With that said, one sure way to make your video look amateurish is to show off your camera technique by zooming in and out, panning back and forth, and otherwise moving your camera too much. Although some camera movement is good, too much is bad. Don't overuse the zoom and pan; it just makes your video difficult to watch.

This is particularly so when your video plays in a small video window in a web browser, as it does on YouTube. On the Web, extraneous motion is your enemy. Even well-crafted motion can sometimes detract from the message. When creating video for the Web, you want to eliminate all unnecessary motion from both the camera and from the subject.

Worse is high-motion action, such as when capturing sporting events. When each new frame of your video holds substantially different information from the previous frame, you end up unnecessarily increasing the size of your video file. In addition, someone viewing your video on a slow Internet connection might see the action as jerky and disconnected, which is not the effect you want.

For this reason, many video producers try to keep their subjects as stationary as possible in the frame. They also try to keep camera movement to a minimum—no unnecessary zooming, panning, or tilting when a static shot works just as well.

Shoot from Different Angles

Another way to introduce visual interest in your videos is to cut between multiple shots. You might show the presenter speaking directly to the camera, and then cut to a short shot of the presenter from the side. This sort of rapid cutting is simply more interesting than a static front-on shot held for three minutes.

You can accomplish this in a number of ways. The easiest way is simply to shoot the video twice: once from the first angle and once from a second angle. You can then intercut shots from both takes in the editing process.

Another approach is to shoot the video only once, but using two cameras, each at a different position. Again, you can intercut shots from both videos during the editing process. The advantage of the two-camera approach is that the two videos are perfectly in sync, which is unlikely using a single-camera approach.

Close-Ups Are Good

While we're talking about using different shots in a video, consider the use of close-ups as one of your alternatives. Let's say you're shooting a product demonstration, which you shoot from an appropriate distance to capture both the presenter and the product. At some point, the presenter presses a particular button on the product, which is difficult to see from several feet away. The solution is to shoot a separate close-up shot of the presenter's finger on the button. You can then cut to this shot at the appropriate point in the video; doing so not only adds visual interest, it better demonstrates that facet of the product.

Don't Center the Subject

When shooting a video for YouTube, it's tempting to place your subject dead center in the video frame. Avoid the temptation, especially when shooting in widescreen.

A much better compositional approach is to utilize a technique called the *rule of thirds*. With the rule of thirds, you divide the frame into three vertical strips and three horizontal strips, as with a game of tic-tac-toe. You do this by drawing two equidistant vertical lines and two equidistant horizontal lines, as shown in Figure 9.9. This creates nine segments in the frame.

Figure 9.9 *Composing your shot via the rule of thirds.*

You want to avoid placing the main subject dead center in any of the nine segments. Instead, you want to position the focal point on or close to one of the four points where the vertical and horizontal lines intersect—the small circles in Figure 9.9. Alternatively, for a little more flexibility, you can position the focal point on one of the grid's horizontal or vertical lines. Which intersection point you choose is entirely up to you; the key is to achieve an interesting composition in a widescreen picture, like the one in Figure 9.10.

Figure 9.10 *A well-composed widescreen shot.*

Tip

When you position your subject at one of the rule of thirds intersection points, have your subject look either directly into the camera lens or slightly into the center of the frame. The alternative is to have your subject staring out of the frame, which is a trifle disconcerting.

Shoot to Edit

We'll get into video editing in Chapter 11, "Editing and Enhancing Your Video." But for better editing, you need to do a little preparation in advance.

The easiest way to make your videos easier to edit is by shooting to edit, which means thinking about your final production before and during the shoot. This lets you capture appropriate shots during the process, and keeps the shoot somewhat efficient by shooting only what you need. Not only do you speed up the shooting process, you also can edit much faster when you get to that phase of the operation.

 Tip

Consider creating a shot list—literally, a list of each shot you make—so you can remember exactly what you captured. A shot list, created in advance, is also helpful when working with a crew, because it lets them know what's coming up.

Use a Teleprompter

Unless your subject is a natural extemporaneous speaker, and few people are, he'll probably speak from some sort of script. That's fine, as long as he can actually read the thing without having to hold a distracting piece of paper in front of him.

The solution to this problem is to use a teleprompter or some semblance of one. A *teleprompter* is simply a device that displays the script, in very large type, on a screen mounted next to the camera lens. The speaker can read the script while appearing to look directly into the camera. It's what all the pros and politicians use.

 Note

Although I use the term *teleprompter* in a generic fashion, there is an actual device called a TelePrompTer, manufactured by the TelePrompTer Company, which first developed the device in the 1950s.

Although you could purchase an expensive professional teleprompter device, a better semi-pro solution is to turn a notebook computer or iPad into an impromptu teleprompter. There are a number of ways to do this, but all involve inputting the speech into a software program that displays the text in very large type on the notebook screen. Position the notebook or tablet next to or directly below the camera lens, and you're good to go.

If you're looking for a dedicated teleprompter program, consider Prompt! (www.movieclip.biz/prompt.html), which imports text from other programs and converts it into a format ideal for teleprompting. You can also simulate a teleprompter by using speaker notes and Presenter mode in Microsoft PowerPoint, or just scrolling through your script in Microsoft Word.

For a speaker, working with a teleprompter takes a bit of practice; using one for the first time can be tricky. The presenter sees only a few lines of the speech at a time, and there's no way to back up when he passes a particular point. And he's wedded to the speech as written; going off-topic can really confuse the teleprompter operator, who must follow along and manually scroll through the speech, line by line. The operator follows the pace of the speech so that the scrolling text follows the speaker as he delivers it. If the speaker slows down, the operator slows down the scroll so that the words scroll slower on screen. If the speaker speeds up, the scrolling speeds up. And if the speaker goes off-topic, the operator doesn't know what to do, which means it's time for another take.

Therefore, it helps to rehearse with the teleprompter ahead of time so that the speaker can get used to reading and speaking at the same time. Fortunately, that's not as hard as it sounds. The key is for the speaker to always speak at his own pace, and trust the teleprompter to follow him. The speaker should never let the scrolling words dictate how fast he talks.

Dress Appropriately

We finish these tips with a word about how the subject of your video should be dressed. The key word is *appropriately* because there's no single right or wrong for every possible type of video.

If your company appeals to young people with a hip and trendy image, don't dress the speaker in a Brooks Brothers suit and tie; khakis and a polo shirt (or jeans and a t-shirt, depending) might be more appropriate. Likewise, you probably don't want to shoot a video for an investment bank using a spokesmodel in a bikini. That wouldn't be appropriate.

You should also consider how the chosen clothing looks onscreen. Avoid clothing with tight or busy patterns; plain shirts are better than striped ones. Don't let the color or brightness of the presenter's clothing conflict with or blend in too much with the shot's background color or pattern. You want the subject to stand out from the background, but not glaringly so.

Here are some additional tips on choosing the most appropriate clothing for your subject:

- Choose clothing that reflects the subject's taste and personality, as well as the image you want to convey for your company or product. Unless you're deliberately striving for a particular effect, avoid clothing that isn't natural for the subject.

- Simplicity is best; go with solid colors or simple patterns. Avoid wild checks, stripes, and busy patterns that tend to draw attention to themselves or that "scream" on camera.

- Clothing should complement the subject's face, not be in conflict with it, which again argues for simplicity.

- The subject should dress comfortably, especially if it's going to be a long shooting session. Although a suit and tie are *de rigueur* for many corporate videos, more casual videos might call for turtlenecks, V-necks, open-collared shirts, and sweaters.

- For fancier videos, it's a good idea for the subject to have at least one change of clothes. This provides some flexibility and offers more choices when it comes to choosing the final shot.

- Women should generally avoid showing bare arms; it's better to wear long-sleeved shirts and blouses instead. (And the no-bare-arms rule goes double for men!)

- Similarly, women in full-length shots should almost always wear slacks, a long skirt, or dark stockings. It's not a good idea to show a lot of skin that draws attention away from the subject's face.

- In terms of color, darker colors are generally better than lighter ones. The best colors are medium shades of blue, green, rust, and burgundy.

- White, yellow, pink, and similar colors tend to overpower the subject's face and make her look pale.

- You should avoid bright reds and oranges. They draw attention away from the subject's face and from any product he's demonstrating!

But these are just general guidelines, not hard and fast rules. Go for what works best in your particular shot. Remember to envision the shot as it will look in a web browser!

The Big Picture

For most small and medium-sized businesses, and even many large ones, shooting semi-pro videos is the best way to create content for YouTube. All you need is a low cost consumer camcorder and a few accessories, and you can create all different types of videos with surprisingly professional results. In fact, most of the videos featured in the profile sections of this book came about in this fashion, to remarkable effect.

What do you need to create a professional-looking video on a limited budget? Not much: just a camcorder, a tripod, and perhaps some sort of auxiliary lighting and external microphone. Of course, you also need a computer and video-editing software to edit the videos you shoot. But that's not a large investment, and you can achieve impressive results with this approach. It's certainly preferable to investing in expensive professional production—at least in the early stages of your YouTube experience.

10

Shooting Professional Videos

Most YouTube videos, even those produced by businesses, come from standard consumer-grade equipment in the comfort of someone's living room, office, or conference room. In the past, at least, few YouTubers, even businesses, went to the trouble and expense of enlisting professional video makers to produce their videos; the expense was too great and the return too small.

This is starting to change, however, especially with larger businesses with big brands to promote. YouTube is becoming a big business, and making a larger investment to produce a more professional image sometimes pays off. It's a different model than what we're used to on YouTube, but it's not as rare as it used to be.

Of course, you pay more for these higher-quality results. A professionally produced video can cost $5,000 to $50,000 or even more, depending on the length and complexity of the shoot, and the amount of editing necessary to create the final cut. But if the video presents the image you want to portray on YouTube, it might be the only way to go.

Why Create a Professional Video for YouTube?

When the vast majority of YouTube videos come from consumer camcorders or webcams, why go to the expense of creating an expensive professionally produced video? There are some good reasons to do so, and some equally good reasons not to.

Advantages of Professional Videos

One of the main reasons to produce a professional video is that it looks professional. Let's face it: The average YouTube video looks amateurish, which is what you expect when amateurs are doing the shooting using consumer-grade equipment. That's fine for many businesses, but if you're in charge of marketing for a large multinational corporation, you might not want your YouTube presence to look as if your cousin Billy Bob did the filming in his basement.

This is why you see companies such as Apple, Ford, Nike, Samsung, Southwest Airlines, and Xerox spending big bucks to create videos for their YouTube channels. Their videos might lack the immediacy of webcam-produced video blogs, but they pack the much more powerful punch that their brands demand. In fact, many of their YouTube videos resemble traditional commercials—or, in many cases, extended versions of commercials.

 Tip

On YouTube, you're not limited to 30-second spots, as you are with traditional broadcast commercials. You can take advantage of the longer length to present a more detailed message.

When you go the pro video route, you get more than just a better-looking video. In most cases, you get a better produced video, all the way around. When you hire a professional video production company, they'll provide expertise to help you develop your concept, write your script, coach your on-air talent (or even provide their own professional on-air talent), create great-looking sets, and do everything else it takes to create a professional video, from start to finish. You get the complete package, if you want it.

So, if you represent a big company with a big message and a big budget, going with a professionally produced video makes a lot of sense. In effect, this is what your customers expect; anything less would invite cognitive dissonance into your brand message.

Disadvantages of Professional Videos

Of course, the primary disadvantage of going the professional route is that YouTube users might reject your message as being too commercial. It's a double-edged sword; you have a commercial message to impart, but the YouTube community is resolutely anti-commercial in nature. Unless your video is extremely entertaining or equally informative, you could end up receiving more negative comments than positive ones.

In addition, a pro-quality video might be overkill for YouTube, especially when it comes to video quality and production values. Your video, no matter how much money you spend on it, is still seen in the same web browsers as basement-quality webcam videos. The typical YouTube viewer, watching in his web browser, might not even see the better lighting, quality makeup, and appealing backdrops. A lot of money can get lost in the resolution.

 Note

A few years ago I hosted a series of videos for a major website (not YouTube). The website spent some big bucks to rent a studio, hire a crew, and execute the shoot—money that definitely wasn't seen onscreen. At one point, the wardrobe person asked what kind of shoes I'd be wearing—even though the shot was from the waist up! And even if it were a full-length shot, no one could see what was on my feet in a small onscreen video window. It was a lot of money wasted on a small video.

And that money is the real killer for a lot of businesses. Expect to pay in the range of $1,000 to $3,000 per minute of finished video. In most instances, you're looking at a minimum of $5,000 for a two- or three-minute video, with big shoots (requiring lots of studio time and personnel) costing three or four times that much. It's not cheap.

Bottom line, a professional video costs a lot more money than one you create yourself. Ask yourself whether you'll see the results of that expense. In addition, ask yourself whether your target audience in the YouTube community responds well to this type of video.

 Caution

A lot of video production companies are smelling the money to be had from producing YouTube videos, and aggressively going after new business. Beware of any firm that promises you they can create a viral video (no one knows when a video will go viral), or guarantees a certain number of views, or otherwise tries to sell you a bill of goods. The only thing a video production firm can do is produce a video, to one quality standard or another. No firm can guarantee results from their work.

What Makes a Professional Video Professional

To the untrained eye, there might be little difference between a well-done semi-pro video and a professionally produced video. But professionals can tell the difference; it's a matter of trained professionals using quality equipment to produce superior results.

Shooting can be either on location (typically in your offices) or in a video production studio. Both have their advantages.

Shooting in the Studio

Shooting in the studio has the advantage of more equipment and props being at hand. This is especially important in lighting and sound, which can be much better controlled in a studio environment.

When you first visit the studio, its size is likely to impress you. Most production studios are built around large sound stages, big spaces in which all manner of props and backdrops are used. For example, you might see some sort of curved seamless background wall, or perhaps a large curtain or roll of seamless background paper, in front of which the subject stands. This background is typically a neutral color; technicians shine colored lights on the background if a colored background is necessary.

You'll see one or more rows of spotlights on the ceiling, as well as various auxiliary lights mounted on stands. You'll also see various baffles, diffusers, and reflectors—all to better direct the right lighting to the right spots in the frame.

You'll shoot the video in front of the chosen background, lit by the appropriate studio lights. One or more DV or Betacam cameras, mounted on tripods or tracks (for moving shoots), are typically used to shoot the scene. If more than one camera is used, they're synchronized via time codes to make for easier editing between shots.

Sound can be recorded in a number of different ways. Some studios prefer to mic each subject individually, typically with wireless lavalier microphones hidden somewhere on the subject's person. Other studios prefer the old-school approach, using a boom microphone held over the heads of the subjects, just out of camera range. In both cases, a separate soundman is typically responsible for getting the best possible sound.

If the subject is reading from a script, and he probably is, you'll find a teleprompter mounted on top of each camera. The script for the video is entered into the teleprompter system via keyboard, and the teleprompter operator controls the scrolling speed of the script.

In addition to the camera operators, soundmen, and teleprompter operator, the crew might also include one or more lighting specialists, makeup and wardrobe people, various assistants and gofers, and, of course, a director. For a typical shoot, this means a crew of anywhere from a half-dozen to a dozen people—a lot more people than are typically involved with a semi-pro video.

Figure 10.1 shows how this all looks in a real-world setting. This photograph shows your humble author in a (non-YouTube) video shoot in a professional studio. I'm standing in front of a curved seamless background, surrounded by various lights, diffusers, and baffles. The camera is mounted on a four-wheeled trolley that travels on a set of train-type tracks; one person pushes the trolley for moving shots. It's very bright, and very busy, and very exciting, especially if it's your first time in the studio. In fact, it's so busy that it's sometimes hard to keep your concentration!

Figure 10.1 *A video shoot in a professional studio—look at all that equipment!*

Shooting in the Field

As you can see, shooting in the studio is a big production with a correspondingly big expense. A better approach, for some videos, is to use a remote production crew to shoot in the field—that is, at your location, rather than in the studio. A location shoot is typically less involved and often less expensive than renting a production studio with full crew.

A location shoot can be as simple as one guy with a camera. Of course, the camera is a pro-grade DV or Betacam model, and the cameraman carries a set of portable lights and a wireless lavalier microphone. He mics the subject, sets up and aims the lights, mounts the camera on a tripod, and starts shooting.

 Note

> In some instances, a mobile camera operator might be accompanied by an assistant to help set up the equipment.

The results of a location shoot, depending on the environment, can be as professional as that created in a studio. In most instances, however, a remote shoot has a slightly different look and feel, somewhat akin to that of a remote TV news report—more immediate, less polished.

Even though a location shoot uses less equipment and a smaller crew, it still can be more involved than a typical semi-pro shoot. Expect the camera operator to be very demanding, being critical about shadows, background noise, and slips of the tongue; multiple takes are obligatory. Just because you're shooting on location doesn't mean that standards are relaxed.

 Tip

> One of the chief advantages of a location shoot is that you don't have to take your company's personnel out of the office for an entire day. The video crew arrives, sets up their stuff, and then calls in the "talent" for the shoot. This can be an important factor, especially when your "talent" consists of busy upper management.

Preparing for a Professional Video Shoot

If you're in charge of creating a professional video, you need to do a few things to prepare your "talent" for the shoot. It isn't as simple as showing up and smiling; there's a lot of upfront work necessary before the cameras start rolling.

 Note

> In industry parlance, the *talent* is the person who appears on camera.

Make Friends with Makeup

This is a big deal, especially for guys. One of the primary reasons that professionals look so good onscreen is because they wear the right makeup. Makeup artists make big bucks in Hollywood and New York; the right makeup can make normal people look like stars, whereas the wrong makeup (or no makeup at all) can make even the most beautiful, blemish-free people look average on camera.

So, even if your talent is nonprofessional, you still have to work through the makeup angle. If your stars want to look good on camera, especially when shooting close-ups in high definition, they have to wear the proper makeup. And make sure your people know that this applies not just to women, but also to any males in front of the camera—it's an important issue.

One problem in producing your own videos is that you probably don't know beans about makeup. This is another area where a pro video shoot differs from an amateur shoot; when you hire a video production firm, a makeup person should be included as part of the deal. The makeup should be tonal to get rid of glare on the face; if the subject's hands are visible in the video, tone them, too.

Learn Your Shooting Angles

You've heard Hollywood types tell photographers to shoot them only from their good side. That might sound vain, and probably is, but there's also a bit of truth to it. Most people look better when shot from one side than the other. A skilled cameraman or director knows this and positions the camera accordingly.

In addition, you don't always want to face the camera head-on. A better shot often results from the subject's body turned to the left or right of the camera, with the head turned to face the camera. This slight body angle is more visually interesting, and avoids a boring "talking head" appearance.

Wait for the Lighting

One of the things you have to get used to on a professional video shoot is the waiting; there's a lot of it. You might spend a full eight-hour day just to get three minutes of finished video. Although some of that time comes from multiple takes (the talent almost never gets it perfect in one take), much of the time is spent waiting for the technicians to get the lighting right.

Lighting is important in a professional video. That's why they use more than just one light in the studio; there's typically a bank of lights above the stage and even more sitting around the side on stands. The director wants to light the subject (and every other important item in the shot) as flatteringly as possible, which takes time. One light aimed here, another aimed there, maybe a diffuser added in front of this one and a reflector to the side of that one—it's all very involved.

Lighting experts talk about direct lighting and indirect lighting, fill lights and bounce lights, main lights and hair lights. You don't have to know what all these things are—only that they're all important and take time to get in just the right position. The subject of a video has to be prepared to stand in one spot for long periods, being as patient as possible while technicians adjust all the various lights and accessories. Then, and only then, can the shoot proceed.

Prepare for Multiple Takes

Few professional videos happen in a single take. Most subjects require multiple takes to get one perfect reading, and even then the director might want yet another take as a safety. In addition, it's likely that the video consists of several different shots, intercut in the editing room. That probably involves delivering the same reading multiple times, with the camera moved to a different angle for each shot. Editors intercut the subsidiary shots into the master shot for more visual variety.

The key here is for the talent to deliver his or her lines not just perfectly, but *identically* across multiple takes. That's why most directors prefer the talent to read from a teleprompter script, rather than speaking extemporaneously. If the talent is improvising on each take, it makes it next to impossible to match shots from multiple takes into a cohesive whole. The best on-air talent nails a perfect and consistent reading take after take after mother-lovin' take.

If this sounds boring, it is; it's also a special skill that not everyone has. Those infomercial hosts and newsreaders might not have a spontaneous cell in their brains, but they do have the ability to speak clearly and consistently from a script. It's harder than you think.

The Big Picture

Most businesses don't go to the effort and expense of producing professional-quality videos for YouTube, and for good reason. Not only are professional videos considerably more expensive than the semi-pro type you can shoot on your own, but they're often too slick for the savvy YouTube audience. Tread carefully into these waters.

That said, more and more YouTube videos are being shot by professional video production houses. If you choose to go the professional route, go into it with your eyes wide open. Expect to spend a minimum of $5,000 or so, and to spend a full day in the studio shooting—a little less in terms of both money and time if you shoot on location in your own offices. And there's a lot of prep work involved in writing a script, arranging makeup, and the like. It's a fun experience, but it is an experience. Make sure everyone involved is properly prepared.

11

Editing and Enhancing Your Videos

Few videos are YouTube-ready out of the box, even those produced by professionals. No, you probably want to cut out the boring parts, trim the whole thing down to no more than two or three minutes (less is probably better), and convert the video to a YouTube-friendly file. You might even want to add titles, onscreen graphics, scene transitions, and other special effects.

Does that sound like a lot of work? It doesn't have to be— assuming that you have a well-powered personal computer and the right video-editing software.

Choosing a Video-Editing Program

In the not-so-distant past, if you wanted to edit a video, you had to use an expensive dedicated video-editing console, such as the ones found in local and network television studios. Not so today—any moderately powered personal computer, equipped with the right software, does the job quite nicely and at a much lower cost. Today's video-editing software lets you cut and rearrange scenes, add fancy transitions between scenes, add titles (and subtitles), and even add your own music soundtrack. The results are amazing!

There are four tiers of video-editing programs available, easily identifiable by price. The first-tier programs are free, the second-tier programs cost around $100, the third-tier programs run between $200 and $600, and the top tier costs $800 or more. We examine each tier separately.

Tier One: Free Programs

The first tier of video-editing programs is one of the most popular—because the software is free! In reality, these programs come bundled with your computer's operating system, which means there's one version for Windows and another for the Mac.

For the typical YouTube video producer, these programs do a good job. They include basic editing features, as well as scene transitions, titles, and other similar capabilities. They're not quite as high powered or flexible as the higher-priced programs, but how much power and flexibility do you need when creating videos for YouTube?

 Note

You might also have received a video-editing program when you purchased a camcorder. Some manufacturers offer their own video-editing programs or "lite" versions of other popular programs.

Windows Live Movie Maker

If your computer is running Microsoft Windows, you have access to an easy-to-use video-editing program. In Windows XP and Windows Vista, Windows Movie Maker was included free with the operating system. In Windows 7, you can download the latest version of this program, now called Windows Live Movie Maker, as part of Microsoft's free Windows Live Essentials suite of supplemental applications for Windows.

Note

To download Windows Live Movie Maker (free, remember), go to the
Windows Live Essentials website (explore.live.com/windows-live-essentials/).

Like more expensive programs, Windows Live Movie Maker enables you to import videos in a variety of formats, edit your videos on a scene-by-scene basis, and add elements such as scene transitions, static or animated titles and credits, secondary audio tracks, and other special effects. The latest version of this program also handles HD video, in either 720p or 1080p formats.

As shown in Figure 11.1, Windows Live Movie Maker makes it easy to add titles, credits, and onscreen text overlays. You can save your video in Windows Media (WMV) format, burn it to DVD, or publish it directly to YouTube.

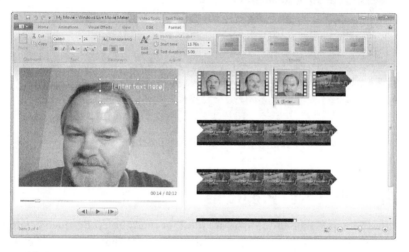

Figure 11.1   *Windows Live Movie Maker—a free video editor ideal for YouTube use.*

In short, Windows Live Movie Maker is an easy-to-use, completely free program and is available to anyone running Microsoft Windows. It's an ideal solution for those with modest editing needs—like most YouTube content creators.

Apple iMovie

Windows Movie Maker is exclusively for Windows users, but if you're a Macintosh user, you have a similar preinstalled solution. Apple includes its iLife software with all Macs, and the iLife suite includes the iMovie video-editing program. Like Windows Movie Maker, iMovie is a surprisingly full-featured video-editing program, quite easy to use, and completely free.

iMovie includes a variety of useful features, including transitions, titles, and special effects. Also useful are the powerful color correction tools, a tool for cropping and zooming video clips, and the ability to rotate videos.

To create a project, simply drag a clip (scene) into the project area, as shown in Figure 11.2. You can then drag and drop transitions, effects, titles, and even an optional audio soundtrack into the project as desired. You can upload completed videos directly to YouTube from the iMovie interface.

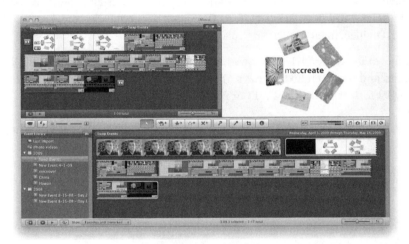

Figure 11.2   *iMovie—Apple's free video-editing program.*

Tier Two: Mid-Level Programs

Windows Movie Maker and iMovie are ideal for many YouTube video creators, but they're not the most sophisticated programs around. (What do you expect at no charge?) If you find yourself wanting more or different special effects, or greater control over your video editing, it's time to invest in a freestanding video-editing program.

This second tier of video-editing programs consists of a multitude of relatively inexpensive programs. Prices on these programs run from about $50 to $200—certainly affordable for most businesses.

Adobe Premiere Elements

Adobe is the premier producer of digital photography and video-editing programs, and the company's main video-editing product is Adobe Premiere. The company makes two versions of Premiere: the full-featured Premiere Studio CS, which we discuss later in this chapter, and the more affordably priced Premiere Elements, which is a Windows-only program.

Premiere Elements got its name because it includes key elements from the more expensive Premiere Studio CS product. It's the product of choice for many amateur video makers, priced at just $99.99. You can learn more about the program at www.adobe.com/products/premiereel/.

The latest version (8) of Premiere Elements, shown in Figure 11.3, includes a sleek interface that includes a video preview window, a task panel that includes various content and effects controls, and a timeline/sceneline along the bottom. Predesigned themes let you jump-start the video-editing process.

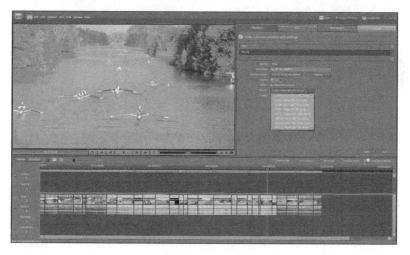

Figure 11.3   *Adobe Premiere Elements—an affordable video-editing solution.*

You can create multiple video and audio tracks for your video. This lets you easily transition from one clip to another or mix background music and sound effects into your video. Naturally, the program includes a variety of animated titles and transitions. The program features automatic formatting and uploading for YouTube.

Apple Final Cut Express

Let's start by discussing Apple's Final Cut Express. This is a slightly stripped-down version of the company's full-featured Final Cut Pro software, and a big step up from the free iMovie program. It's available for $199 from www.apple.com/finalcutexpress/. As you might suspect, this is a Mac-only program.

As you can see in Figure 11.4, Final Cut Express offers an assortment of sophisti-cated transitions, filters, and effects, including dynamic animated text. You can also use multiple audio tracks, utilize automatic audio levels, and employ various advanced audio filters.

Figure 11.4   *Final Cut Express—big-time video editing at a small-time price.*

The program works with both standard and high definition video from any digital camcorder. You can mix and match video formats in the program's timeline, using traditional drag-and-drop editing. You have a comprehensive set of editing options, including insert, overwrite, fit-to-fill, and such; you can fine-tune your edits with a variety of trim options, such as ripple, roll, slip, slide, extend, and shorten. Final Cut Express even lets you create professional-quality *L cuts*, where the audio and video start at different times.

ArcSoft ShowBiz DVD 2

ShowBiz DVD 2 from ArcSoft is an easy-to-use program that includes video editing and DVD creation. It's a Windows-only program, and is available from www.arcsoft.com for $99.99.

The video-editing part of the program features the obligatory Storyboard view for arranging various video clips, as well as a more advanced Timeline view that gives you more control over your clips, audio tracks, transitions, and special effects. You can also use the program to create photo slideshow videos.

CyberLink PowerDirector

CyberLink's PowerDirector is another easy-to-use video-editing/DVD creation program. It's a Windows-only program, and is available from www.cyberlink.com in two versions: Ultra ($99.95) and Deluxe ($69.95).

Like most of these programs, PowerDirector provides a selection of transitions, titles, and special effects. You also get some neat enhancement tools to fix and improve less-than-perfect videos. It imports high definition video and publishes videos direct to YouTube.

MoviePlus

MoviePlus offers digital video editing and DVD creation. It's a Windows-only program, and is available from www.serif.com/movieplus/ for $79.99.

The program's feature set is similar to other competing programs. It imports high definition video and includes a variety of transitions and special effects; it also lets you easily create photo slideshow videos.

Nero Vision Xtra

Nero Vision Xtra offers the expected video-editing features, a user-friendly interface, and high definition video support. It provides easy exporting and uploading to YouTube, and can also save videos to DVD or Blu-ray disc. This is a Windows-only program that sells for $59.99 from www.nero.com.

Pinnacle Studio

Pinnacle offers two different versions of its Pinnacle Studio video-editing program: Pinnacle Studio HD ($49.99) and Pinnacle Studio Ultimate ($99.99). Both versions of this Windows-only program enable you to combine video clips with still photos and MP3 audio tracks and then add your own transitions and effects. The Ultimate version adds a full complement of professional audio- and video-editing tools. You can find more information at www.pinnaclesys.com.

 Tip

Even though Pinnacle Studio Ultimate is at the high-end of the mid-level programs, the quality and quantity of the special effects offered make it the program of choice for many budget-conscious video makers.

Roxio Creator

Roxio Creator offers easy-to-use operation and basic editing and effects, for $99.99. Like many of these programs, Creator is a combination video editor and CD/DVD creator. It features easy importing of camcorder video, scene- and timeline-based editing, and a variety of transitions and other special effects. It also supports high definition video and Dolby Digital sound. More information on this Windows-only program is available at www.roxio.com.

Sony Vegas Movie Studio HD

Sony's Vegas Movie Studio HD is a surprisingly powerful video-editing program. Priced at $44.95, you can purchase this Windows-only software at www.sonycreativesoftware.com/products/vegasfamily.asp.

 Note

> Vegas Movie Studio HD is also available in a $94.95 Platinum Edition that adds a variety of color correction tools and other special effects.

Vegas Movie Studio HD is a combination video editor and DVD-authoring program. The video-editing component includes more than 185 professional transitions and nearly 300 customizable special effects—including a green screen feature and something called the "Ken Burns Effect," which makes for more interesting photo slideshow videos. Editing is via a familiar drag-and-drop interface.

 Note

> Ken Burns is the PBS documentary filmmaker known for his panning and scanning and zooming of archival photographs.

Ulead VideoStudio

Another popular video-editing/DVD-authoring program is Ulead VideoStudio. This Windows-only program is available from www.ulead.com/vs/ for $99.99.

VideoStudio features a variety of auto color and tone filters, as well as DeBlock and DeSnow filters to clean up the recorded video. You also get complete HD workflow, as well as DVD and Blu-ray disc burning.

Tier Three: High-End Programs

If you want true professional-quality editing and effects, and money is no object, these final three programs are worth considering. These are true pro-level video-editing programs, with much more sophisticated features and functionality than the other programs previously discussed—including multi-track editing, advanced audio editing, and a greater number of more sophisticated titles, transitions, and special effects.

Adobe Premiere Pro CS

For many video creators, the ultimate video-editing suite is Adobe Premiere Pro CS. At $799, the program isn't cheap; for the price, however, you get a variety of different software programs that help you create truly professional videos. (More information is available at www.adobe.com/products/premiere/; the program is available in both Windows and Mac versions.)

Figure 11.5 gives you a flavor of what Adobe Premiere Pro CS offers. The interface changes a bit depending on what type of editing you're doing at the time, but you have the expected timeline editor, video window, and a bevy of available editing, audio, and video effects.

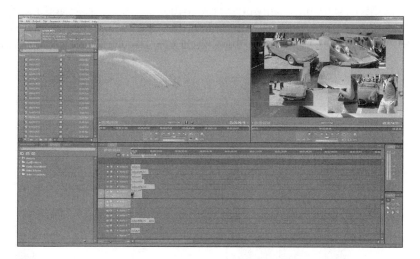

Figure 11.5   *Adobe Premiere Pro CS—a pro-level video-editing suite.*

Adobe Premiere Pro CS works seamlessly with professional video equipment from Panasonic and Sony, with native editing for both companies' proprietary media formats. You can generate a variety of high quality video effects, including slow motion and other time-remapping effects. Also available are professional-caliber color correction, lighting effects, audio filters, and more. The program also makes it easy to edit footage from multicamera shoots.

Naturally, Premiere Pro works with both standard and high definition video. It integrates seamlessly with other Adobe applications, including Photoshop and After Effects.

Apple Final Cut Studio

Adobe's chief competitor in the high-end video-editing space is Apple Final Cut Studio, a Mac-only suite that retails for $999. The suite includes the Final Cut Pro video editor, along with Color (professional color grading), Motion (3D motion graphics), Soundtrack Pro (audio post production), Compressor (encoding for different video formats), and DVD Studio Pro (DVD authoring). You can find more information www.apple.com/finalcutstudio/.

Apple claims more than one million users of its Final Cut software; it's definitely the first choice of professional video editors worldwide. Final Cut Studio works with virtually any video format, including high definition and professional formats. You can easily combine clips of different formats on the program's timeline.

As you can see in Figure 11.6, Final Cut Studio offers a wide variety of sophisticated video special effects—including the ability to create 3D multiplane environments. Even better than all the cool transitions and special effects is the Color component, which enables you to create a consistent look and feel for shots from different sources; this elevates the quality of any production to a truly professional level. Also useful in this regard is the program's SmoothCam feature that automatically stabilizes shaky shots while preserving the original camera moves.

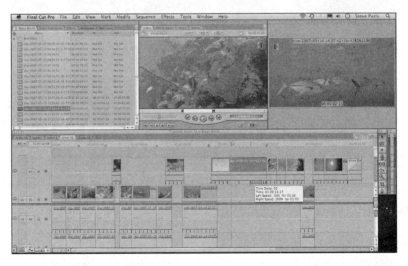

Figure 11.6 *Apple Final Cut Studio.*

Sony Vegas Pro

Like the other high-end programs, Sony's Vegas Pro is actually a suite of related products. For $599.95, you get the Vegas video editor, the DVD Architect DVD-authoring program, and Dolby Digital (AC-3)–encoding software. More information

on this Windows-only solution is available at www.sonycreativesoftware.com/
products/vegasfamily.asp.

Vegas Pro's editing tools for both standard and high definition video utilize both
mouse and keyboard trimming. You get ProType Titling technology, tools to edit
multi-camera shoots, auto-frame quantization, and other pro-level tools. On the
audio front, Vegas Pro lets you use unlimited audio tracks with punch-in recording,
5.1-channel surround mixing, and real-time automation for various audio effects,
including equalization (EQ), reverb, delay, and more. As you can see in Figure 11.7,
all these tools are combined in a busy but easily navigable interface—just what
you'd expect from a semi-pro level program like this.

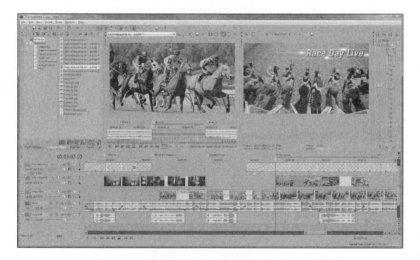

Figure 11.7   *Vegas Pro—a sophisticated interface for a powerful video-editing
program.*

This is a very powerful program, offering many of the professional editing func-
tions and effects as found on the top-tier programs, but at a slightly lower price.

Using a Video-Editing Program

Whether you use a free video-editing program or one that costs a cool grand, you
use the program to do pretty much the same tasks: edit together multiple scenes,
add titles and transitions before and between scenes, and apply any desired special
effects. If the program allows it, you can also choose to clean up your audio and
video, using various color correction and noise reduction tools.

How do you perform these essential tasks? Obviously, the specific steps vary from program to program, but the general approach remains the same. Read on to learn more.

Note

For the examples in this section, we use Windows Live Movie Maker, the free video-editing program available for users of Windows 7. Similar features are available in other programs, and work in similar ways.

Editing Together Different Shots

Unless you shot your video in a single continuous take, you probably have multiple takes and shots to work with. To create an interesting video, you need to edit these various clips together into a cohesive whole so that the video flows from shot to shot and scene to scene.

In most video-editing programs, you have the ability to work in some sort of clip view. This involves dragging and dropping individual clips onto the program's storyboard. As you can see in Figure 11.8, the storyboard is a filmstrip-type area in the interface. You can easily change the order of clips on the filmstrip, and delete clips that you don't want in the final video. Just keep rearranging clips until your video is in the order that you want.

Figure 11.8 *Arrange multiple video clips into a single storyboard.*

The key to effective editing is to tell a cohesive story. Don't jump around from topic to topic; more important, don't jump around temporally. Tell a linear story from start to finish; don't make the viewer work hard to figure out what's going on. Make sure one shot leads logically and directly to the next without any glaring gaps. If you're not sure whether the scene order works, just watch the video from start to finish—if you can't follow the threads, re-edit!

Inserting Transitions Between Scenes

There are numerous ways to move from one clip or shot to another within a video. The most direct approach is to use a *jump cut* where one scene abruptly cuts to the next, with no fancy transition. Although this can sometimes be jarring, it's a very commonly used technique.

Another approach is to ease the flow from scene to scene by using a transition of some sort. This might be a fade, a wipe, or something fancier, such as some sort of revolving or rotating effect. The key is to match the transition with the onscreen action; for example, if one scene ends with the subject punching forward into the camera, cutting to the next scene via some sort of shatter or "breaking glass" transition might work well.

 Caution

Avoid overusing some of the fancier transitions. The more animated the transition, the more attention it draws to itself—and away from the video.

In most programs, you add a transition by dragging the icon for that transition onto either a clip in the storyboard or a specific area between clips. Figure 11.9 shows just some of the transitions available in the Windows Movie Maker program.

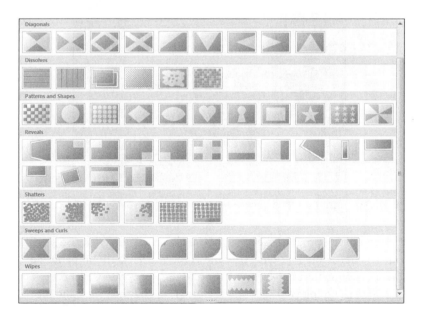

Figure 11.9 *Add transition effects between video clips.*

When deciding what transitions to use, less is more. That is, fancy transitions tend to draw attention to themselves; kind of like, "Hey! Look at this gee-whiz transition effect!" So, it's best to avoid spins and whirls and shatters and the like. Simple old school transitions, such as fades, dissolves, and iris ins/outs are best, even if you think they're a tad boring. Ultimately, the transition should go unnoticed by the viewer; what's important is moving seamlessly from one scene to the next.

In addition, know that transitions are less effective in the small YouTube video window, solely due to the size of the thing. Fancy transitions can also "choke" video playback, especially for viewers with slower Internet connections. So, especially where YouTube is concerned, simpler transitions are definitely better.

Inserting Titles and Credits

Just as important as scene transitions are the titles and credits you add before and after the main body of your video. The main title, like the one shown in Figure 11.10, introduces the video to YouTube viewers. The credits provide more information, direct the viewer to your website, and provide proper credit to the individuals that worked to create the video.

Figure 11.10   *Insert a title sequence before the start of your main video.*

Most video-editing programs let you choose from various styles of titles and credits. You can choose the font type, size, and color; the background pattern or color; and the transition effect between the title and the main video. In most instances, this is as easy as typing your text into the program and then selecting the desired style or theme.

Creating Other Onscreen Graphics

Titles and credits don't have to be the only onscreen text in your video. You can also superimpose other text and graphics on your picture, anywhere in the course of the video.

For example, Figure 11.11 shows a subtitle added to a piece of video. You can typically choose from a number of different colors, themes, and effects for these onscreen graphics.

Figure 11.11   *Add onscreen graphics to identify what's happening onscreen.*

Adding Background Music

Many video-editing programs let you enhance the video you shoot with background music. This is typically added as a separate track to the program's timeline or storyboard; just drag and drop the chosen music file (typically in MP3 format) into the proper position. You can then adjust the sound level of the music track to best blend the background music with the foreground speaking.

When choosing background music, make sure the music you choose is the right length for the accompanying video—you don't want the music to end before the video or scene is over. The background music should complement the onscreen action, not overpower it in terms of volume level, lyrical content, and beat/feel. For example, you don't want to accompany an emotional confessional video with an up-tempo hip-hop beat. Select carefully and sympathetically, and remember that it's the main content that matters, not the music in the background.

Caution

Make sure you have permission to use the chosen background music. Most music you hear on the radio or CD has a copyright, and you cannot use it for any purpose without express permission. For this reason, you might want to use the public domain music supplied with many video-editing programs—no copyright problems!

Getting Creative with Other Special Effects

Most video-editing programs let you add a plethora of other special effects. For example, you might be able to decolorize the entire video, add an old-timey sepia tone effect, or make the video look like well-worn film stock. Some programs even let you play around with the video's time perspective by speeding up the video or slowing it down into slow motion.

 Tip

For most business-oriented videos, you want to keep it simple—keep the fancy special effects to a minimum.

You typically add special effects one scene at a time. In most programs, that means dragging and dropping a special effects icon onto a specific clip in the program's storyboard or timeline. The program adds the effect to that clip as it processes the video. To apply the same effect to multiple clips, just do more drag and dropping.

Although some special effects can be useful in special situations, most business videos need a straight-ahead approach that argues against the more creative of these effects. Remember, you want the viewer to pay attention to your video's content, not to the way it looks or the special effects you use. Use special effects minimally to keep them special.

Converting and Saving Video Files

When you've finished all your editing and applied all your transitions and special effects, it's time to save your work. In most video-editing programs this is a two-step process: First you save the project, and then you process or publish the final video. This second step involves a lot of computer processing because it compiles all the clips and effects you select into a single video file.

When compiling your final video, save it at the highest possible resolution in one of the approved file formats discussed in Chapter 7, "Understanding Audio/Video

Technology." These specs ensure the best quality playback on the YouTube site—after YouTube converts your file to its own Flash format, of course.

 Note

> Videos all converted and edited? Learn how to upload your videos in Chapter 13, "Uploading Your Videos to YouTube."

The Big Picture

Unless you want the raw look and feel of an unedited webcam video, you'll probably need to do some editing of the video you shoot with your camcorder or webcam. This necessitates the use of a video-editing program on a personal computer.

Although you can use a free program such as Windows Movie Maker or Apple iMovie, or a high-end program such as Adobe Premiere Pro CS3 or Apple Final Cut Studio, most video creators get the best results from a low-cost program such as Adobe Premiere Elements or Sony Vegas Movie Studio HD. These programs let you do sophisticated editing and add pro-level special effects and transitions; the results are close to what you see on local newscasts and network television programs. The key is to pick a program that offers the features you need, with an easy-to-use interface, and then to learn all the ins and outs of that program.

Of course, just because a video-editing program can do all sorts of fancy stuff doesn't mean that you need to use every one of the program's bells and whistles. Most videos benefit from minimal editing; too many special effects draw attention to themselves. The key is to edit your video to tell a logical, straightforward story, using available effects to move the story forward rather than to impress the viewer with how sophisticated you are.

12

Tips for Producing More Effective YouTube Videos

So, you've decided to make YouTube part of your company's marketing mix and you've even decided what type of video to produce. How do you go about making a must-see video, one that draws viewers and generates sales for your business?

There's no one-size-fits-all approach to producing effective YouTube videos. But I can impart lots of tips that can guide you in the right direction. Read on to learn how to make better-looking, better-performing YouTube videos—and drive customers to your accompanying website.

Tips for Creating Better-Looking Videos

When shooting a video for YouTube, it's important to get the file format and technical details right. It's also important to get the visual details right—to create a video that is visually and stylistically interesting to YouTube viewers.

What works well on a big movie screen works less well on a smaller home television screen. Similarly, what looks good on a TV-sized screen doesn't look nearly as good when viewed in a small window in a web browser. If you want to create an effective YouTube video, you have to produce for the medium, exploiting those elements that make YouTube unique.

Shoot for the Smaller Screen

Given that most YouTube viewers will be viewing your video in a small window in their web browser, you must create a video that looks good at this small size, viewed on a typical computer screen. What does this mean in terms of visual style?

Put simply, when viewing videos in a small onscreen window, detail gets lost. Don't expect a video crowded with multiple objects to look good in YouTube's default player window; in fact, smaller objects in the frame might simply disappear in the background blur.

The best YouTube videos are those that exploit YouTube's standard display. Don't put small, complex objects on screen; use a large, simple subject instead. What works best? A simple talking head, positioned front and center in the frame. No fancy background, no fiddly details, just the speaker's face big in the frame.

That goes even when you're shooting in high definition. You can shoot an epic with a cast of thousands, and an HD picture will accurately reproduce the entire cast, but those thousands will look like little dots in a small browser window. It's a matter of size. The best YouTube videos are visually simple, with a single main subject filling up most of the small video window. Get up close, and frame the subject so that he or it fills most of the screen.

When using a webcam, filling the screen means getting up close to the lens. When using a camcorder, you should zoom into the main subject, and remove any unnecessary people or objects from the frame. Close-ups are good; crowd shots aren't.

You also want to make sure the scene you're shooting has adequate lighting. Too many YouTube videos come out way too dark, which makes them hard to view. This is especially important when you're shooting with a webcam; even though a webcam might claim to work under normal room light, you're better off investing in a set of affordable photo floodlights or a separate speed light.

Accentuate the Contrast

As noted previously, visual contrast is highly desirable with small-footprint videos. Put a pale or white-clad subject in front of a black background, or a black-clad subject in front of a white one. And consider using brightly colored backgrounds, which pop in YouTube thumbnails. Believe it or not, hot pink really grabs the attention of casual viewers!

 Caution

Contrast is good, but too much contrast can play nasty tricks with many webcams and camcorders. A bright white background can cause many cameras to darken the foreground subject, either reducing detail or casting the subject entirely into darkness. For this reason, always test your shooting environment before finalizing your video—including watching a test video on your computer screen.

Slow and Steady Wins the Race

YouTube is streaming video, which means that a video streams from the YouTube site to a viewer's computer in real time. Streaming typically works well if a viewer has a fast broadband Internet connection, and less well if he doesn't.

To that end, know that streaming video doesn't always reproduce rapid movement well. Move the camera too fast, or have your subject move too fast in the frame, and viewers are likely to see motion smears, pixilation, and other unacceptable video effects. Keep things slow and simple for best results.

Invest in Quality Equipment

To make a quality video, you need a quality video camera. That doesn't necessarily mean a professional camera; a high-quality consumer-grade camcorder will do a good job. Make sure you have a digital camcorder, rather than an older analog one, so that your video is completely digital from start to finish. Look for a camcorder that works well under low-light conditions, has a quality lens with a nice zoom factor, and that lets you connect an external microphone. Personally, I prefer hard disk camcorders because they make it very easy to transfer video from the camcorder to your computer for editing; it's a simple matter of transferring files from one hard disk to another, without having to play back a tape in real time. And the bigger the camera's charge-coupled device (CCD), the better the picture quality.

Note

Speaking of editing, you'll also need to invest in a fast computer and quality video-editing software. Learn more in Chapter 11, "Editing and Enhancing Your Videos."

Shoot Like a Pro

When you're shooting your video, embrace professional production techniques—even if you're just using a consumer-grade camcorder. Here are the things you need to keep in mind:

- Make sure the subject is well lit; use an external lighting kit.

- Make sure the speaker can be heard; use an external microphone, if your camera has an auxiliary mic input.

- Monitor the audio with a set of headphones while rehearsing and recording; don't assume the camcorder is recording good sound just because the level meters are bouncing.

- Minimize background and crowd noise; keep it quiet on the set.

- Keep the camera steady; use a tripod.

- Don't move the camera around too much.

- Don't zoom in and out too much.

In other words, do everything you can to keep the focus on the main subject. Don't let the camerawork distract the viewer!

Use Two Cameras

Here's another way to add a professional sheen to your videos. Instead of shooting with a single camera directly in front of the subject, shoot with two cameras, shooting the subject from two different angles. This enables you to cut between shots in the editing process, adding visual variety to the video.

In addition, having two different angles to choose from makes it easier to edit the speaker, if you need to. Editing in different shots from different angles makes the fact that you're editing less apparent; the cut isn't as jarring or noticeable when you switch from one angle to another.

Look Professional—Or Not

If you're representing a professional business, your videos need to look professional. The standard look of personal YouTube videos—an unshaven twenty-something in a t-shirt, staring intently at a web camera—just doesn't give off the professional vibe that most businesses want. Whether your video's cast is one or thousands, make sure that anyone on camera is well dressed and well groomed, that everyone is well lit and well mic'd, and that the whole production has a professional sheen.

Unless, that is, you want to give out a hip young vibe. In that instance, take off the suits and ties and emulate the personal look that's become ubiquitous on YouTube. In other words, make sure your video has a look and feel that matches your company's message.

Don't Just Recycle Old Videos—Re-Edit Them, Too

Many businesses get started on YouTube by uploading existing company videos. This isn't a horrible idea, especially as a first effort. It's a low-cost, low-effort way to get your feet wet in the YouTube pond. However, your results will suffer if you just upload old videos without changes. You'll do better if you bring an older video up-to-date in its content and appearance, even if that means re-editing the video or shooting new scenes.

Consider Creating a Slideshow

If you don't need full-motion video or don't have access to a video camera, consider putting together a slideshow of still photographs. Just compile the photos into a slideshow, add background music or a voiceover, and upload the whole thing to YouTube. Likewise, some topics benefit from PowerPoint presentations, which you can also convert to video for uploading to YouTube.

Hire a Pro

Don't have the skills or equipment to create a video in-house? Hire an outside firm to produce the video for you. Every town has one or more video production companies that do this sort of thing. There's no need to reinvent the wheel; let the pros teach you the right way to do things.

 Tip

If your budget is tight, consider contacting the film or marketing department of a local college to recruit lower-cost student talent.

Break the Rules

Don't confuse these tips for creating better-looking videos with hard and fast rules. It's okay to think outside the box and do things a little different. For example, if you want to create a hip-looking video for a younger audience, it's permissible to take the camera off the tripod and go for a "shaky-cam" effect. Do whatever it takes to achieve the effect you want.

Tips for Improving Your Video Content

Even the best-looking video will fail miserably if the content isn't compelling—and compelling content can compensate for poor production values. Remember that what you're shooting is more important than how you're shooting it; it's the content, stupid!

When creating content for YouTube, you want to give viewers a reason to come back for future viewings and to share your video with others. It's this sharing that makes for a viral video—compelling content begs to be more widely viewed.

Be Entertaining

The first rule of YouTube content is the most obvious: Your video must be entertaining. Produce a boring video, and no one will watch it. People like to be entertained. Give the people what they want.

It doesn't matter what product you're selling or what your message is. Find a way to make your product, service, brand, or company entertaining. Not necessarily funny (although that helps—as you'll learn shortly), but entertaining—at least enough to keep viewers watching for the entire length of the video.

 Note

Trust me on this one. There is absolutely no way on this planet to make a recycled corporate PowerPoint presentation entertaining.

Be Informative

Being entertaining is essential, but so is being informative. A good video needs some meat to it; ask yourself, "Where's the beef?"

The typical name for this combination of education and entertainment is *edutainment*. That is, useful information presented in an entertaining manner. People might come for the entertainment, but they stay for the information.

Go for the Funny

Remember when I said that your video needs to be entertaining? Well, in many instances, the best way to be entertaining is to be funny. People like to laugh—and they remember the funny videos they view on YouTube.

It's a fact; the majority of top-rated videos on YouTube are funny ones. It's easier for a humorous video to go viral than it is for a deadly serious one to get the same exposure.

That means, of course, that you can't take yourself, your product, or your company too seriously. Your company needs a sense of humor and has to be able to laugh at itself. When you laugh at yourself, your audience will laugh with you, which establishes an emotional connection with your customer.

Keep It Short

One way to kill your video's entertainment value is to make it too long. Viewers today, and especially online, have a very short attention span. The YouTube audience is the post-MTV generation, which means even a three-minute video has trouble holding the viewers' attention.

It's imperative, then, that you keep your videos short enough so that viewers don't tune out mid-way through. How short is short? It depends on who you ask; some experts say five minutes at the top end, some say one minute or less, some even say 20 seconds is ideal. My recommendation is to keep your video no longer than two or three minutes—and the shorter, the better. Videos longer than three minutes or so typically don't get big viewership.

That doesn't mean you have to produce a video that's exactly three minutes long. As I said, shorter is better. If you can say what you want to say in 60 seconds, great. If you need the full three minutes, take it. But take into account viewers' short attention spans, and present your message quickly and efficiently.

 Tip

Some topics might require more than a few minutes to present. That's especially the case with some complicated step-by-step how-to videos; you just can't get through the steps in a minute or two. If this is the case, you can produce a longer video (YouTube accepts videos up to 15 minutes long), or you can break your video into several shorter segments. So instead of a single 12-minute long how-to, you might do four 3-minute long videos—Part 1, Part 2, Part 3, and Part 4.

Keep It Simple

You don't have to spend a lot of money on a YouTube video for it to be effective. In fact, it's easy for a company to spend too much money on its videos; the result is typically an overproduced monstrosity that looks horrible online. In many cases, a single person talking directly to a camera is all you need.

Stay Focused

Part of keeping it simple is focusing on a single message. Remember, you have only a few minutes at most to communicate to YouTube viewers. Don't spend that time trying to show your entire product line, or even multiple features of a sophisticated product. Home in on a single product and communicate its strongest feature or benefit. One video per product or feature should be your rule.

Communicate a Clear Message

Whether you produce a talking-head video or one with a cast of thousands, make sure the message of your video is clear. Viewers have to come away with a clear idea of what you're selling and why they need it. Don't let the production get in the way of the message.

One way to do this is to test your video by showing it to a few people—family, friends, colleagues, whatever. Ask them to give you a single-sentence description of what they've just seen. If they can't repeat your message simply and succinctly, then you haven't communicated your message well—and you have more work to do.

Avoid the Hard Sell

Even though your message should be clear, you don't have to hit the viewers over the head with it. On YouTube, the soft sell works better than the hard sell. That's why a how-to video showing your product in use typically works better than a straight-ahead product demonstration; the former is a soft sell that communicates a subtle message to the viewers—who will typically turn off a harder message.

In other words, infomercials and edutainment are better than straight advertisements. In fact, if a video feels like an ad, most YouTube viewers will avoid it like the plague.

 Tip

If you're showing your product in a video, make sure you show it well. You need to clearly demonstrate your product throughout the course of the video; fortunately, video is uniquely suited for this sort of detailed product demonstration.

Keep It Fresh

The video you create today will be forgotten a month or two from now. With users posting thousands of new videos on YouTube every day, your video will quickly become yesterday's news. This requires you to update your company's video library continually; you need to either replace or refresh older videos on a regular basis. If you go more than a few months without posting a new video, your company's channel will lose viewership.

Design for Remixing

Here's a tip for advanced video marketers. The Internet and YouTube encourage interactivity; passive viewership is rapidly becoming a thing of the past. To that end, consider the act of remixing when creating your videos. That is, design a video that viewers can edit, adding their own dialog and music, or even cutting and pasting elements in a different order. When you encourage viewer interaction, you make a stronger connection with potential customers; you make them feel as if they're part of the process, and thus uniquely invested in your success.

Tips for Generating Sales

Creating a highly viewed video is great, but it's ultimately meaningless unless you can convert those viewers into paying customers. How, then, do you turn views into sales? Here are a few tips that will help in the process.

Include Your Website's Address in the Video

The key to marketing on YouTube is to lead viewers from your video on the YouTube site to your company's website—where you can then directly sell your products and services. How can you accomplish that?

Unfortunately, YouTube doesn't allow live links from a video to a third-party website. You can, however, include your website address in the body of the video and hope that viewers will remember it or write it down for future reference.

There's no point being subtle about this. Because people have trouble remembering things such as 800-numbers and URLs (*uniform resource locators*, also known as website addresses), you need to include your address early and often in the video. I recommend starting your video with some sort of title screen with the URL overlaid, as shown in Figure 12.1. You should also end the video with a similar screen with the URL displayed. Make sure the URL is big and easily readable; high contrast colors, such as white text on a black background (or vice versa), provide the best results.

Figure 12.1 *A title screen with the company's URL prominently displayed.*

 Note

> Naturally, if your business is telephone-based instead of Internet-based,
> you can substitute your 800-number for the website address—or list them
> both, if you prefer.

You might even want to include your URL onscreen during the main part of your
video. Use your video-editing program to overlay the URL, as shown in Figure 12.2.
The URL shouldn't interfere with the main content, of course, but you should be
able to overlay it in a nonintrusive way.

Figure 12.2 *A URL superimposed on the bottom of the video screen.*

Note

How do you create title screens and overly text on a video? By using a video-editing program, as discussed in Chapter 11.

Include Your URL in the Accompanying Text

You can't live link from within a YouTube video; unfortunately, you also can't include a link to your website in the description that accompanies the video. You can, however, include your URL in the text description, but not as a live link. So, when you write the description for your video, make sure you include your URL or 800-number in the text.

Link from Your Channel Page

Although you can't include a live link in your video or its accompanying text, you can include a direct link to your website on your YouTube channel page. Anyone clicking your username will see your channel page with the link to your website in the Profile section, as shown in Figure 12.3. When viewers click the website link, they're taken directly to your site—where you can sell them more of what you have to offer.

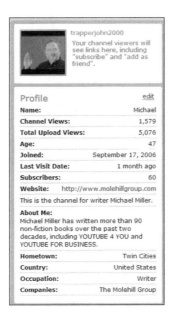

Figure 12.3 *The Profile section of a typical YouTube channel page, complete with a live link to an accompanying website.*

Note

Learn more about channel pages in Chapter 16, "Establishing Your YouTube Channel."

The Big Picture

What's the takeaway from all the tips presented in this chapter? The big picture is that you need to create professional-looking videos that are both entertaining and informative, and then make it easy for viewers to go to your website for more information or to purchase what you have to sell. Your videos can be funny or educational (or both), but they most definitely should be short; YouTubers have a notoriously short attention span. And, whatever type of video you produce, you should design it to be visually appealing in the small YouTube video window. There's no point including a cast of thousands when everyone has to fit in a space only a few inches across!

13

Uploading Your Videos to YouTube

You've determined how YouTube fits into your online marketing mix. You've decided what type of YouTube video to produce. You've even made the video, edited it, and converted it to the proper video format. Now it's time to upload your video to the YouTube site and put your message in front of millions of YouTube viewers.

Uploading Videos from Your Computer

Let's start at the top. Assuming that you shot your video with a camcorder, you've since transferred the video from your camcorder to your computer's hard disk, where you performed any necessary editing. The final video file you create is what you upload to YouTube.

Selecting a File to Upload

To upload a video file, it must be in a YouTube-approved format, be less than 15 minutes long, and be smaller than 2GB in size. If your video meets these requirements, you're ready to upload.

 Caution

Videos you upload cannot contain any copyrighted content, including commercial music playing in the background. In addition, videos should not contain offensive or adult content.

 Note

Learn more about YouTube-approved video formats in Chapter 7, "Understanding Audio/Video Technology."

To upload a video, start by clicking the Upload link near the top right corner of any YouTube page, as shown in Figure 13.1. This displays the Video File Upload page, shown in Figure 13.2; click the Upload Video button to proceed.

 Note

If you're capturing a video "live" from a webcam, click the Record from Webcam link instead. Learn more in Chapter 8, "Shooting Webcam Videos."

Figure 13.1   *Click the Upload link to begin the upload process.*

Figure 13.2   *Click the Upload Video button to select a file to upload.*

You now see the Select File(s) to Upload window. Navigate to and select the desired video file you want to upload and then click the Open button. YouTube begins to upload the selected file—which, depending on the file size, might take a bit of time.

 Note

It can take several minutes to upload a large video, especially over a slow Internet connection. There is additional processing time involved after the upload is complete, while YouTube converts the uploaded video to its own format and adds it to the YouTube database.

Entering Information About Your Video

As your file uploads, YouTube displays the Video File Upload page, shown in Figure 13.3. The upload progress is displayed at the top of this page.

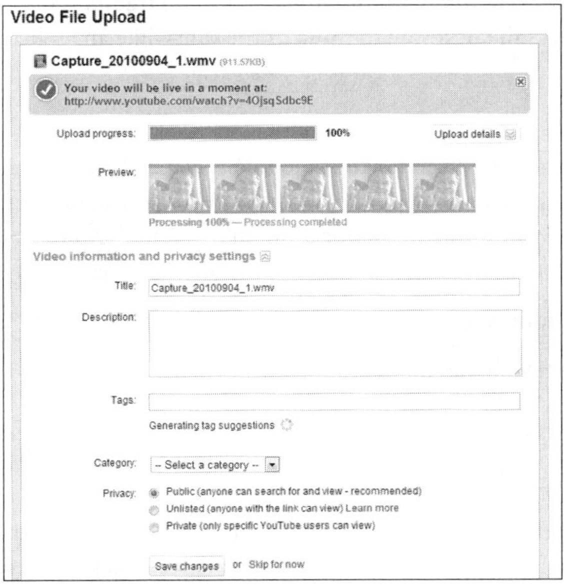

Figure 13.3   *Entering information about your video.*

The bulk of this page, however, is dedicated to information about your video—which you need to enter. When you're done entering the desired information, click the Save Changes button.

Let's look at each type of information requested by YouTube.

Thumbnail

YouTube displays a thumbnail image for each video on its site; viewers see this thumbnail in YouTube's video search results, on a producer's channel page, and elsewhere on the site. You need to choose the image you want displayed as your video's thumbnail.

After most of your video has been uploaded, YouTube will select five images from your video that can be assigned as the thumbnail. Click the image you want to use as the thumbnail image.

 Caution

Potential thumbnail images might not be displayed until the video is almost finished uploading.

Title

The first piece of text you need to enter is the title of this video. The title should be descriptive without being overly long, as catchy as a traditional advertising headline. In fact, that's the best way to think of the title—like an ad headline.

Description

You now enter a description for the video. This can and should be longer and more complete than the shorter title. The description is also where you include the information that drives viewers to ask for more information or purchase what you're selling. That means including all or some of the following:

- Website address (URL)
- Toll-free telephone number
- Email address
- Mailing address (postal)

Although subtlety is important within the video itself, don't be quite so subtle when soliciting customers. Include all the information necessary for viewers to contact you about your product or service; don't be shy about asking for further contact.

Tags

Next, you need to enter one or more tags for the video, separating each tag by a space. A *tag* is another name for a keyword, and just as important as any keyword on your website or in your online advertising.

As such, a YouTube tag is a word or phrase that viewers enter when searching the YouTube site. The tags you enter should be keywords that viewers might enter if they're looking for products or services like yours.

You can use as many tags as necessary to capture all possible search words. Your tags should include your company name, the topic of the video, and any other descriptive words or phrases.

Category

Next, select a category for your video from the pull-down list. From the following list, pick the category that best fits your video:

- Autos & Vehicles
- Comedy
- Education
- Entertainment
- Film & Animation
- Gaming
- Howto & Style
- Music
- News & Politics
- Nonprofits & Activism
- People & Blogs
- Pets & Animals
- Science & Technology
- Sports
- Travel & Events

Privacy

Finally, you need to determine who should see your video, which you do in the Privacy section. You have three options:

- Public—Anyone on YouTube can search for and view the video.

- Unlisted—Only people who know the link can view the video.

- Private—Only those people you invite can view the video.

Make your selection from this list.

 Tip

Most videos for businesses should be set for public access, unless you have a private presentation or real estate walk-through you want to share with only selected clients.

 Note

Videos you upload are not immediately available for viewing on YouTube. They must first be processed and approved by the site, which can take anywhere from a few minutes to a few hours.

Sharing Options

At the bottom of the Video File Upload page is the Sharing Options section. Here is where, after the video is uploaded and processed, you find the URL of the video and the HTML code you need to embed this video in another web page.

 Note

Learn more about sharing and embedding videos in Chapter 18, "Incorporating YouTube Videos on Your Own Website."

Editing Video Information

After you uploaded your video to YouTube, you can edit all information about your video. All you have to do is click the down arrow next to your name at the top of any YouTube page, then select My Videos. This displays a list of all the videos you've uploaded, as shown in Figure 13.4. From there, click the Edit button beside the video you want to edit.

Figure 13.4   *Click the Edit button to edit information for a specific video.*

The fun begins when YouTube displays the edit page for the selected video. As you can see in Figure 13.5, this page contains a viewing window for the video, along with a Video Information section that includes all the information you previously entered for the video. You can edit all the fields listed here, including the video's title, description, category, tags, and the like. You can even choose a different thumbnail, if you wish. Click the Save Changes button at the bottom when you're done editing the info.

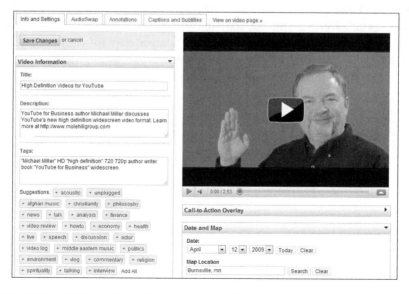

Figure 13.5   *Editing information about your video.*

Removing a Video from YouTube

When a video has run its course, you can remove it from the YouTube site; otherwise, it stays online forever (or until YouTube goes out of business, whichever comes first).

To remove a video from YouTube, click the down arrow next to your name at the top of any YouTube page and then select My Videos. When the list of your videos appears, check those videos you want to remove and then click the Delete button. It's that simple.

 Caution

Think twice before you click the Delete button. YouTube permanently deletes all the videos you remove. You have to re-upload the video if you click the Delete button by mistake.

The Big Picture

Assuming that you prepared your video properly, uploading a video file to YouTube is a simple task. The hardest part is filling in all the blanks. It's important to write a catchy title and detailed description, as well as to choose tags and keywords that viewers might use to search for your video.

When you upload your video to YouTube, approach it in the same way you would create a print advertisement. You have to create a compelling headline (title) and a "why to buy" and "how to buy" description. Then you have to select the best place to market your ad/video (category), and the best keywords to get your video notice (tags). This isn't a job to do at the last minute without any preparation; you want your best marketing people working on the textual part of your YouTube videos.

14

Annotating and Linking Your Videos

Want to make your video a bit more interactive? Then consider adding annotations to your videos, so that viewers can click on the video to view additional information, links to other videos, and the like.

Understanding Annotations

A YouTube annotation is like an overlay put on top of a normal video. The overlay can be a speech bubble, such as those used on pop-up video programs, or a note containing a link to another YouTube video or user channel. Viewers see your annotations when they click a specific area on the video screen. These overlays can also be used to pause the video playback.

You can add annotations to any video you've uploaded. You specify where the annotation appears in the video playback, what area of the screen is clickable, and what happens when that area is clicked.

YouTube lets you add four types of annotations, the first three of which are shown in Figure 14.1:

- **Speech bubble**, a cartoon-like text box.

- **Note**, a simple text box.

- **Spotlight**, a text box that appears only when the user moves his mouse over the overlay area.

- **Pause**, an area which, when clicked, pauses the video. (There is no text associated with this type of annotation.)

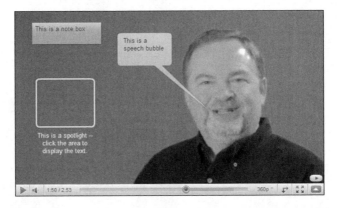

Figure 14.1   *A video annotated with a pop-up speech bubble, a note, and a spotlight area.*

 Note

Unlike spotlights, both speech bubbles and notes appear automatically at the selected point in the video. No involvement from the viewer is needed.

All three types of annotations can include both text and clickable links. You can link your annotations to other YouTube videos, playlists, channels, groups, and search queries. What you can't do is link to any pages not on the YouTube site—such as your own web page. You have to satisfy yourself with linking to your other videos or to your channel page.

 Note

> If you want to link to your own website, you have to promote the video and add a Call-to-Action Overlay, as discussed in Chapter 23, "Using Call-to-Action Overlays on Your Videos."

The overlay for the annotation can be any size and placed anywhere on the video window. You can place multiple annotations on screen at the same time or you can use them at different times throughout the video.

Uses for Video Annotations

Annotations are a great way to stuff more information into a YouTube video. How exactly can you use annotations? Here are some ideas:

- Expand on the information presented verbally in the video—give the viewer something to read that provides more depth.

- Detail the steps in a how-to video. Instead of just saying "Step 1, do this," you can display that text onscreen in an annotation. This makes it easy for the viewer to pause the video and either digest or write down the details in the step. For example, if you're presenting a cooking how-to, you might list the ingredients for each step in annotations.

- Add interesting but non-essential information, like in those pop-up videos VH1 used to show. Interesting stuff for anyone who cares to click it.

- Link to the next video in a series. If you have a long how-to, for example, you can break it into multiple parts and use annotations to link from one part to another.

- Link to a related video. If you have another video that provides useful background information for the current video, link to it. For example, if you're annotating a video about changing the oil in a car, you might link to a related video that talks about the different types of motor oil. Figure 14.2 shows just such a supplemental video link, along with an information box, in a video by Catspit Productions (www.youtube.com/user/CatspitProductions/).

Figure 14.2 *Two different types of annotations used in a YouTube video.*

- Link to your channel page. Why not? Your channel is your home on YouTube, you might as well direct viewers there.

- Display your contact information. You can use an annotation to display your toll-free phone number or the URL for your own web page; just put the contact information right on screen. Know, however, that while you can display your URL, you can't actually link to it; annotation links are only for pages on the YouTube site.

That's just a start. I'm sure you can think of other uses for these onscreen annotations. Just be sure not to overdo it; you don't want to distract viewers with too many pop-up boxes obscuring your video.

Annotating a Video

Adding annotations to any existing video is relatively easy. You start by clicking the down-arrow next to your user name at the top of any YouTube page, then selecting My Videos. When the My Uploaded Videos page appears, click the down arrow next to the video you want to annotate and then select Annotations. This displays the Annotations page for that video, as shown in Figure 14.3.

Play or fast forward the video to the point where you want the annotation to begin and then click the Add button for the type of annotation you want to add. You can select from Add Speech Bubble, Add Note, Add Spotlight, or Add Pause Annotation.

The overlay for the annotation now appears onscreen, as shown in Figure 14.4, along with four editing buttons—Change Annotation Type, Add Annotation Link, Change Annotation Color, and Delete. Use your mouse to drag the overlay into the desired position or to resize the overlay as necessary and then enter the desired text into the annotation's text box.

Figure 14.3   *The Annotations page for a YouTube video.*

Figure 14.4   *Creating a video annotation.*

If you want the annotation to include a clickable link to another video or to your channel page, click the Add Annotation Link button to display the Add Link box, shown in Figure 14.5; pull down the Link Type list and select the type of link; enter the URL for the link into the link box; and then click the Save button.

Add link

Link Type	Video	
Paste a link to a Video		
Please enter a valid URL	Cancel	Save

Figure 14.5   *Inserting a link into an annotation.*

Tip

To change the color of the annotation, click the Change Annotation Color button and select a text and background color combination.

To establish the start and stop points for this annotation, drag the right and left positioning cursors (located above the video's playback slider) into the desired positions, as shown in Figure 14.6. Alternatively, you can enter the precise start and stop times into the panel to the right of the video window, as shown in Figure 14.7.

Figure 14.6   *Defining the length of an annotation.*

Figure 14.7   *Entering precise timing for an annotation.*

You can insert multiple annotations into the video, if you like. When you're done adding annotations, click the Publish button.

Watching an Annotated Video

Watching an annotated video is like watching any YouTube video. At a given point in the video, the annotations will appear onscreen. Spotlight annotations, of course, are visible only when you hover your cursor over that area of the screen. If an annotation contains a link, viewers can click that link to go to the given video or channel.

The Big Picture

Annotations let you display more information onscreen for any YouTube video. You can add note boxes and speech bubbles, and even include links to other YouTube videos or your channel page. It's easy to add annotations to any existing video—in fact, you can add more than one annotation if you like.

15

Managing Comments

One of the fun things about marketing via YouTube is that you get to immediately see the comments and responses from people who view your videos. Although this can be fun, it isn't always pleasant, which is why YouTube lets you manage these comments.

Enabling Comments—and Other User Response Features

Viewers can leave both text comments and video responses to your videos—if you let them. At your discretion, you can allow, disallow, or allow with prior approval either comments or video responses for any individual video you upload. (This means you can allow comments for one video and disallow comments for another.)

To control comments and video responses, click the down arrow next to your name at the top of any YouTube page, then select My Videos; this displays a list of all your videos. Then click the Edit button for the video you want to control. When the edit page for this video appears, scroll down to the Broadcasting and Sharing Options section, shown in Figure 15.1. We'll skip the Privacy section, which we've previously discussed, and focus on the remaining half-dozen options.

Figure 15.1 *Enabling or disabling comments and video responses.*

 Note

You might need to expand some of the items in this section to edit them. Click the right arrow to expand a section; click the down arrow to contract an expanded section.

Comments

By default, anyone viewing your video can leave text comments about the video, like those shown in Figure 15.2. You can disable comments, however, or choose to moderate comments before they appear publicly. The options you have for accepting comments include the following:

- **Allow Comments Automatically**—Viewers can submit text comments, which appear immediately on your video page.

- **Allow Friend Comments Automatically, All Others with Approval Only**—Viewers can submit text comments, but you have to approve each comment before it appears on your video page—unless the viewer is part of your preapproved Friends list.

- **Allow All Comments with Approval Only**—All comments, even those from friends, have to be preapproved.

- **Don't Allow Comments**—The Comments section does not appear on the page for this video.

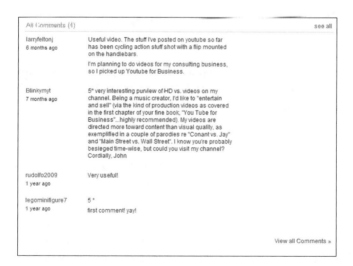

Figure 15.2 *Viewer comments beneath a YouTube video.*

Should you allow comments on your videos? I think so; even negative comments provide valuable feedback from consumers. However, not all companies are culturally suited to deal with potentially negative comments, or simply don't have the resources to monitor and respond to comments. We'll discuss this more in the "Dealing with Negative Comments" section, later in this chapter.

Comment Voting

This feature lets viewers give up or down votes on comments left by other viewers. Select Yes to allow comment voting or No to disallow it.

Video Responses

When you enable this option, viewers can make and upload their own videos in response to your video. You can choose from the following options:

- **Yes, Allow Video Responses to Be Added Automatically**—Viewers can upload their video responses, which appear immediately on your video page.

- **Yes, Allow Video Responses After I Approve Them**—Any video responses have to be approved by you before they appear on your video page.

- **No, Don't Allow Video Responses**—The video response option does not appear on your video page.

Ratings

In lieu of (or in addition to) detailed text comments, you can also allow your video to be rated by viewers. Viewers rate videos by giving either a thumbs up (positive) or thumbs down (negative) vote.

 Tip

To view the overall rating for your video, go to that video's page and scroll to the options box below the video player; the rating displays there.

Of course, you have the option of not allowing viewers to rate your video. This might be desirable if you don't want your business's videos perceived in a negative fashion. On the other hand, if you have a popular video, you probably want to enable ratings—highly rated videos rank higher in YouTube search results than do poorly rated ones.

Your option in regard to ratings is simple: Check Yes to allow ratings or No to disallow them.

Embedding

YouTube makes it easy for any user to embed your video in his or her own website or blog. If you want wider exposure for your video, check Yes to display the embeddable

HTML code. If, on the other hand, your lawyers tell you that you need to keep complete control over where and how users view your video, click No to hide the embeddable code.

 Tip

I can think of no good reason not to allow embedding, unless you have a legal staff paranoid about copyright and fair usage. If you want to create a truly viral video, you have to allow fans to embed the video across the Web.

Syndication

You can achieve even wider viewership by making your video accessible to viewers on mobile phones and TV. YouTube dubs this added exposure *syndication*, and you can turn it on or off for any specific video.

Approving Comments and Video Responses

If you choose the "with approval" option for comments or video responses, you have to manually approve any comments or responses viewers post to this video. When a viewer posts a comment or response, YouTube sends you an email like the one in Figure 15.3.

Figure 15.3 *YouTube sends an email notification when you receive a comment or response to your video.*

Thus notified, go to the YouTube site click the down arrow next to your name at the top of any page, and select Inbox. When the Messages page opens, click the Comments link along the left side. As you can see in Figure 15.4, this displays a list of all pending comments/responses in your inbox.

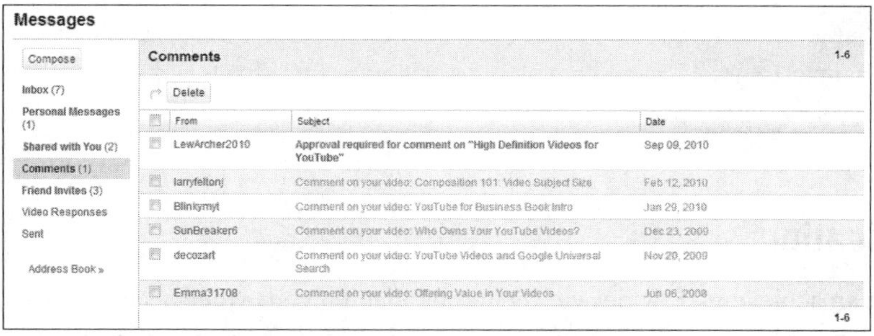

Figure 15.4   *Pending comments and responses in your YouTube inbox.*

Click the message link to display the comment, as shown in Figure 15.5.

Figure 15.5   *Responding to a viewer comment.*

To approve a comment or response to your video, and display that comment publicly on your video page, click the Approve button. To not approve (and not display) a comment, click the Ignore link.

Dealing with Negative Comments

When you let viewers comment on your videos, you're opening a Pandora's Box. Yes, you'll receive some useful comments from satisfied viewers, but you'll also receive some negative comments—some of which might be downright nasty.

Some companies want to see only positive comments, which is fine but not necessarily realistic; you'll never have 100% approval of anything you do. Other companies are more open minded and don't mind the negative comments; they feel it presents a forthright, warts-and-all image to the market.

There's no right or wrong here. Just know that if you enable comments, you *will* receive some negative ones. How you respond to those negative comments depends on your how your company deals with criticism.

Removing Viewer Comments and Responses

One way to deal with negative comments is simply to remove them. All you have to do is go to the edit page for that video and highlight the comment you want to remove. This displays a number of new buttons, as shown in Figure 15.6; the one you're interested in is the Remove (trashcan) button. Just click the Remove button and the comment disappears. Voila!

Figure 15.6   *Removing an unwanted comment—click the Remove button.*

Blocking Specific Viewers from Leaving Comments

Every now and then, you'll run into a virtual stalker, a disgruntled customer (or perhaps a competitor) who delights in leaving negative comments on all your videos. Although you can manually remove all of this user's comments, a better approach is to keep him from leaving those comments in the first place.

To this end, YouTube enables you to block individual members from leaving comments and responses (and from flooding your YouTube inbox with negative messages). To block a user, all you have to do is click that member's name to access his channel page, scroll to the information box above the user's Profile, and click the Block User link. This blocks the user from commenting on your videos and contacting you.

 Tip

You can also block a user directly from the video page. Just click the Block User button by that user's comments.

Responding to Negative Comments

Another way to deal with negative comments is to deal with them head on—by responding directly to the comments. YouTube lets you add your own responses to any comments left about your videos; this can be a good forum for exchanging views and opinions with your customer base.

If you decide to respond to a negative comment, a few things to keep in mind. First, speed is of the essence. There's no point responding to comments made a month or two ago; you need to jump in while the conversation is fresh. This shows that you take viewer comments seriously enough to respond quickly.

You also need to respond positively, even to the most negative comments. Don't be defensive, and certainly don't be offensive; don't resort to name-calling or other insults. You need to be the adult in what might otherwise be a childish situation. Be professional, be calm, be cool, be collected. Don't let yourself get angry.

But don't be so calm cool and collected that you come off as being a PR flack. Yes, you probably should toe the company line, but you also have to genuinely respond to comments, on a personal basis. Admit to mistakes, if there are any. Offer help or advice, if any is to be given. Be sympathetic. Apologize. (You'd be surprised how far a genuine "I'm sorry for your problems" will go.)

There's a certain amount of acceptance involved in all this. You simply can't control what people say about you, no matter how much you (or upper management) might like to. You're always going to have some people saying bad things about your company, your products, and even your people. You can't take it personally. You have to accept that negative comments exist, and learn to live with it. A thick skin is a must, but it also helps to develop an understanding of how people use the Internet to amplify their petty (and more-than-petty) complaints. Remember, as a company, you are a lot bigger than any single complaint or complainer.

 Caution

> In some cases, your best recourse might be *not* to respond to a negative comment. When you enter your reply, you run the risk of fanning the fires of a burgeoning flame war, from which neither the disgruntled viewer nor you might come off looking good. Sometimes the better course of valor is to just walk away—and respond with silence only.

Fortunately, it's easy enough to respond to comments on YouTube. Just go to the video page and scroll down to the comments section under the video window; you should see a list of all viewer comments. Highlight the comment to which you want to reply, and then click the Reply button. This displays a reply box, as shown in Figure 15.7. Enter your reply into this box, and then click the Post button. Your reply displays directly beneath the comment in question.

Figure 15.7   *Replying to a viewer's comments.*

The Big Picture

You need to determine, early on, how you want to respond to the inevitable negative comments posted about your videos. You can choose to ignore the negative comments, reply to them, or just delete them. You can also choose to skip the issue entirely by not enabling the comments feature for your videos. If your company is particularly thin-skinned or you think your videos might generate particularly controversial responses, this might be the way to go. Otherwise, consider all comments—positive or negative—as valuable feedback, and learn how to engage even negative viewers in a positive fashion

16

Establishing Your YouTube Channel

Your presence on YouTube is more than just your videos. You have a home based on YouTube that you can use to establish and promote your overall brand. This home page is called your channel, and it's the gateway to all the videos you upload.

Understanding YouTube Channels

Every user on YouTube has his or her own channel, which is just a fancy name for what you might otherwise call a profile page. A YouTube channel is like a broadcast or cable television channel, in that it's where all your programming (all your uploaded videos) appears.

As soon as you post your first video, YouTube automatically creates your channel. At that point, users can access your channel to see all the videos you've uploaded; users can also subscribe to your channel to be notified when you upload new videos to the YouTube site.

Because your channel page is your de facto home on YouTube, it's this URL that you want to publicize. Yes, each video you upload has its own unique URL, but the one address that stays constant is the one for your channel page. When you're referencing your YouTube videos, in general, in other media, display the URL for your YouTube channel page. Viewers can access all your other videos from there.

Viewing a Channel Page

YouTube viewers access your channel page to learn more about you and to connect with your business. A viewer accesses your channel by clicking your business's name wherever it appears on the YouTube site.

Although each profile page is unique, all pages contain the same major elements, as shown in Figure 16.1:

- Information about the user, including a link to subscribe to this channel
- Videos uploaded by this user
- Links to connect to the user, via email, comments, and so on—including a link to the user's non-YouTube website
- Links to the user's favorite videos, playlists, groups, friends, and the like
- Subscribers to the user's channel
- Comments on this user's channel
- The user's favorite videos
- Channels the user is watching

If a viewer likes what he sees on your channel page, he can subscribe to that channel. When a viewer subscribes to your channel, he is automatically notified (via email) when you upload new videos.

Figure 16.1   *A typical YouTube channel page.*

 Note

To subscribe to your channel, all a viewer has to do is go to your channel page and click the Subscribe button.

Personalizing Your Channel Page

Because a YouTube channel page is really a profile page, you want to customize your page to reflect your business's image and brand. It's easy to do.

As for creating your channel page, there's nothing to do; YouTube creates a profile page for you when you subscribe to the site. The default channel page is a little bland, however, which is why you should customize it.

To personalize your channel page, click the down arrow next to your user name at the top of any YouTube page, then select My Channel. This displays your current channel page, with a group of editing buttons aligned along the top. Click each button to edit specific things about your channel page: Settings, Themes and Colors, Modules, and Videos and Playlists.

Tip

Another way to brand your channel page is to upload your company logo as your personal profile picture. This picture displays next to your user name on the channel page, which is a great place to display your logo.

Editing Channel Settings

When you click the Settings tab, you see a new Settings panel at the top of your Channel page, as shown in Figure 16.2. This panel lets you edit your channel page's title, as well as the tags you assign to your channel. Make the appropriate changes and click the Save Changes button when done.

Figure 16.2   *Editing the title and tags for a channel.*

What settings can you edit? Here's the list:

- Title

- Channel Type (YouTuber, Director, Musician, Comedian, Guru, Reporter)

- Make Channel Visible (Yes/No)

- Channel Tags (keywords)

- Let Others Find My Channel on YouTube If They Have My Email Address (Yes/No)

Editing Channel Themes and Colors

When you want to change the look and feel of your channel page, click the Themes and Colors tab. This expands the top of the channel page to display the Themes and Colors pane, shown in Figure 16.3. Click a color theme to switch your channel to that theme.

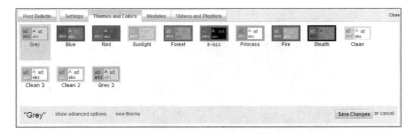

Figure 16.3   *Changing your channel's color scheme.*

If you want even more personalization, click the Show Advanced Options link. This expands the Themes and Colors pane even further, as shown in Figure 16.4, with options to control the color of various page elements.

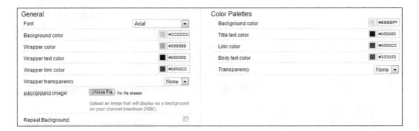

Figure 16.4   *Fine-tuning colors for individual page elements.*

This expanded pane also enables you to add your own background image to your channel page, which is a nice way to display your product or company logo. All you have to do is click the Choose File button in the Background Image section to select a JPG image for the background. You can opt to display the image once on your page (default), or repeat the image through a longer page (check the Repeat Background option).

For example, some firms like to repeat their logo as a background image, like the one from Drum Workshop (www.youtube.com/user/DrumWorkshopInc/) shown in Figure 16.5. Other companies take a more cosmetic approach, as with the tasteful-yet-branded background image on Pepsi's channel page (www.youtube.com/user/pepsi/), shown in Figure 16.6.

When you're done making changes, click the Save Changes button.

Figure 16.5 *A repeating logo in the background of Drum Workshop's channel page.*

Figure 16.6 *A well-branded background image on Pepsi's channel page.*

Editing Channel Modules

You can also control what content displays on your channel page. Click the Modules tab to display the Modules pane, shown in Figure 16.7. You can choose to display any or all of the following content modules:

- Comments

- Friends

- Groups

- Moderator

- Other Channels

- Recent Activity

- Subscribers

- Subscriptions

Figure 16.7   *Selecting the content modules for your channel page.*

Click the Save Changes button when done.

 Note

Your custom content modules supplement the default content displayed on all channel pages: user information, Uploads, Favorites, and a big featured video.

Choosing Videos and Playlists

You can also customize your own content that is displayed on your channel page. In particular, you can choose which video you want displayed in the large "featured video" window in your channel.

Click the Videos and Playlists tab to display the lists of content shown in Figure 16.8. From here you can choose to display My Uploaded Videos, My Favorites, or Playlists; you can also display an All button that displays all this content at once.

Figure 16.8   *Selecting which video content you display in your channel.*

This pane also lets you choose between the default Player view or a Grid view, which is a little less appealing. You can also determine your featured content set, as well as which video is your Featured Video; you can opt to automatically play this video when your channel page is opened, if you wish.

Click the Save Changes button when done.

Establishing a Brand Channel

YouTube's basic channel pages are fine and, as you've seen, somewhat customizable. But there's even more customization to be had, in the form of a YouTube *brand channel*.

Understanding Brand Channels

You've probably noticed some channel pages that have more visible branding, typically in the form of the company's logo or other graphic as a banner along the top of the page. This banner is often clickable (back to the company's main website), sometimes with multiple clickable links or buttons.

For example, Figure 16.9 shows a simple banner ad at the top of the channel page for TOMS Shoes (www.youttube.com/user/tomsshoes/); clicking the banner opens TOMS' regular website. Figure 16.10 shows how Ford (www.youtube.com/user/ford/) uses this banner space, by essentially turning it into a brand graphic (though still clickable). Figure 16.11 shows an even more sophisticated channel page from Kmart (www.youtube.com/user/kmart/), complete with links to the company's store finder and weekly ads.

Figure 16.9   *A channel page with banner ad from TOMS Shoes.*

Figure 16.10   *A banner used to brand Ford's channel page.*

Figure 16.11   *A channel page banner with multiple links from Kmart.*

This type of fancy channel page is called a *brand channel*, and it's available to high-volume YouTube/AdWords advertisers. You have to apply to get a brand channel; YouTube will accept your application if you're a big enough advertiser.

Benefits of a Brand Channel

Why bother with a brand channel? Primarily because you get a much better-looking and better-branded channel page. In essence, a brand channel affords several advantages to marketers, including the following:

- Channel banner (960 × 150 pixels) at the top of the channel page; this banner can be clickable.

- Side column image (300 × 250 pixels) that appears on the left side of the channel page, below the channel information module, such as the one for Coca Cola (www.youtube.com/user/CocaCola/) in Figure 16.12; this image can be clickable.

Figure 16.12   *A clickable side column image on Coca Cola's channel page.*

 Tip

Clickable channel banners or side column images can be used to lead to all sorts of other content. For example, Coca Cola's side column image includes clickable links to Coke's accounts on Facebook, Twitter, and other social media sites.

- Autoplay of a featured video on the channel page.

- Ability to add up to two self-hosted channel gadgets, to add more functionality to your channel page.

Note

A *gadget* is a small application, typically written in Flash or HTML/Ajax, that adds specific functionality to a web page.

- Video page banner (300 × 45 pixels) displayed above the video player on all your video pages, like the Sony (www.youtube.com/user/sonyelectronics/) logo shown in Figure 16.13.

- Custom thumbnail image, provided by you, for each video you upload.

- Ability to use demographic filters to restrict access to your channel.

- Additional tracking capabilities within Google Analytics.

Figure 16.13 *A brand logo banner displayed on a Sony video page.*

The result is a much more customizable page, in terms of both look and feel and content, as well as better-branded video pages. Done right, a brand channel page can seem much more like a traditional company or product web page than a typical YouTube channel.

Applying for a Brand Channel

If any or all of this sounds good to you, how do you apply for a brand channel? First, you need to have a regular YouTube account. Second, you need to be signed up for Google AdWords PPC advertising, or be ready to sign up—and make a big advertising commitment.

Next, you need to contact YouTube and ask for your regular YouTube account to be converted to a brand channel account. You do this by going to www.youtube.com/t/advertising and clicking the Contact Us link. This displays the contact form shown in Figure 16.14; fill out the requested information (including your estimated YouTube advertising budget), select Brand Channel from the pull-down list, and click Submit.

Figure 16.14   *Applying for a YouTube brand channel.*

YouTube will not approve every request. They're looking for marketers willing to make a large advertising commitment—and I do mean large. YouTube requires spending of at least $250,000 across both YouTube and AdWords, with at least $100,000 of that on YouTube only. That's a big commitment, and a major roadblock for setting up brand channels for many smaller marketers.

If you are approved, it can take up to two weeks for the conversion to take place. You will then have access to all the new brand channel features.

The Big Picture

Your channel page is your gateway to all your YouTube videos. As such, it's important to customize and brand this page to best present your company, your brand, and your products. You can customize the look and feel of your channel page, as well as the content that appears on this page.

If you want enhanced customization, including a clickable banner and the ability to add your own custom content, you can apply to convert your normal channel page to a YouTube brand channel. These special channels are available only to major YouTube/AdWords advertisers, but afford much greater branding and customization.

17

Leveraging the YouTube Community

YouTube is more than just a source of videos; it's a community. The community aspects of the site help you build viewership and a customer base, and establish your own unique business presence. That's right, being successful on YouTube isn't just about creating a great video; you also have to take advantage of the social nature of the YouTube site to build a community of friends and subscribers.

Working the YouTube Community

With all the focus on YouTube as a video viewing site, it's easy to forget that YouTube is actually a video sharing *community*. As such, YouTube thrives on social networking—and your channel and videos get more viewers if you fully participate in the YouTube community. You can't just post some videos and expect to get viewers automatically; you have to make your presence known to inform viewers of the videos you've posted.

In reality, this means being an active viewer as well as a poster. You can't just sit back and wait for customers to come to you; you become a member of the community when you view and subscribe to a lot of other channels. And you become even more noticed when you leave comments with those videos and users that best serve your needs.

Social marketing on YouTube is no different social marketing on Facebook or MySpace; it requires active participation. As you should know by now, social media is a two-way street. You can't just ask for attention, you have to provide something in return.

In most instances, that something is your own input—comments on other users' videos or channel pages, subscribing to channel pages, and the like. You have to become an active member of the YouTube community to be taken seriously.

Of course, this means connecting and contributing on a fairly regular basis. You—either you personally or someone specifically assigned to your YouTube marketing efforts—needs to connect often and personally. You don't want to be anonymous in these conversations; it's better for users to connect with "Phil from Jascorp" than with "Jascorp Marketing."

Connecting with the YouTube community involves both your company presence and your presence on other pages on the site. Yes, you need to establish a YouTube channel page, but you also need to view and comment on other YouTube videos. You have to get out there and participate; you can't wait for your customers to come to you.

For example, if work for a home and garden retailer, subscribe to your suppliers' YouTube channels, if they have them. Seek out videos that have to do with gardening and landscaping topics and comment on them, as well as subscribe to their producers' channels. Build a network of people interested in what you do, and establish ongoing contacts with them.

Caution

When you're participating in the YouTube community, you can't be blatantly promoting your business. It's no good to leave a comment along the likes of "Great video! Look for our new widget in stores near you." That's self-serving and doesn't do anybody any good. Instead, you need to contribute relevant and useful comments; you have to advance the conversation, not hijack it.

How does this work in reality? It takes time and effort. You want to search the YouTube site for videos like yours, or users who have something in common with your business. After you find a sympathetic user, view his videos and leave some comments. You might want to mention that you have similar videos in your channel and encourage friends of this user to head over to your channel to see more. At the very least, you want to spark interest in your videos from the person whose videos you're viewing. If you view his videos, he'll view yours, and hopefully tell other viewers about what he's seen.

What goes around comes around; the more comments you leave, the more people see your name and channel and the more views your videos receive. To get people interested in your channel, you have to show interest in theirs.

Posting Bulletins to Your Channel's Subscribers

One type of community available on YouTube revolves around your YouTube channel. Everyone who subscribes to your channel becomes a member of your own community, and YouTube makes it relatively easy to communicate with (and promote to) those subscribers.

The best way to get a message to your subscribers is to post a *bulletin* to your channel. This is a short update that you enter on your channel page that then appears not only in your channel but also on each of your subscribers' home pages, in the Recent Activity module. (Figure 17.1 shows a bulletin on a home page.)

Bulletins can be text only or include a link to a YouTube video. To post a bulletin, click the down arrow next to your user name at the top of any YouTube page, then select My Channel. When your channel page appears, click the Post Bulletin tab; this opens the new pane shown in Figure 17.2.

You can now enter the text of your bulletin into the large Enter Message text box. If you want to include a video in the bulletin, enter the link to the video into the Enter Your YouTube Video URL box. A preview of your in-progress bulletin appears in the box on the right side of the pane. When you're ready to post the bulletin, click the Post Bulletin button.

Figure 17.1   *A bulletin posted on a channel page.*

Figure 17.2   *Posting a bulletin.*

Working with Friends and Contacts

Another way to work the YouTube community is to add people to your YouTube Friends list, and use that list to promote new videos. YouTube Friends are just like friends on Facebook, MySpace, and other social networks; they're people with whom you can easily communicate and share things on the YouTube site.

You can think of YouTube's Friends list as a kind of high-tech customer mailing list. When you have something portentous to announce to your customers (such as a new video or a product introduction), you can send out a message to your list. Unlike traditional customer mailings, however, sending electronic messages to your YouTube friends list is completely free.

Adding a Friend to Your List

Adding an existing YouTube member to your friends list is relatively easy. Just go to that member's channel/profile page, scroll to the Connect With box, shown in Figure 17.3, and click the Add as Friend link. YouTube now sends an invitation to this person to be your friend; if he accepts, YouTube adds him to your Friends list.

Figure 17.3   *Adding an existing YouTube member to your Friends list.*

Sending Messages to Your Friends

When you want to send a message to someone in your Friends list, click the down arrow next to your user name at the top of any YouTube page and select Inbox. When the Messages page appears, click the Address Book link in the left sidebar.

This displays the All Contacts page, shown in Figure 17.4, which lists all your YouTube Friends. Check the box next to those people you wish to send the message and then click the Compose button.

Figure 17.4   *Viewing all your YouTube contacts.*

You now see the Compose page, shown in Figure 17.5. Enter a subject for your message and the text of the message itself. If you want to attach a YouTube video to this message, pull down the Attach a Video list and choose a video from your favorites. Click the Send Message button to send the message on its way.

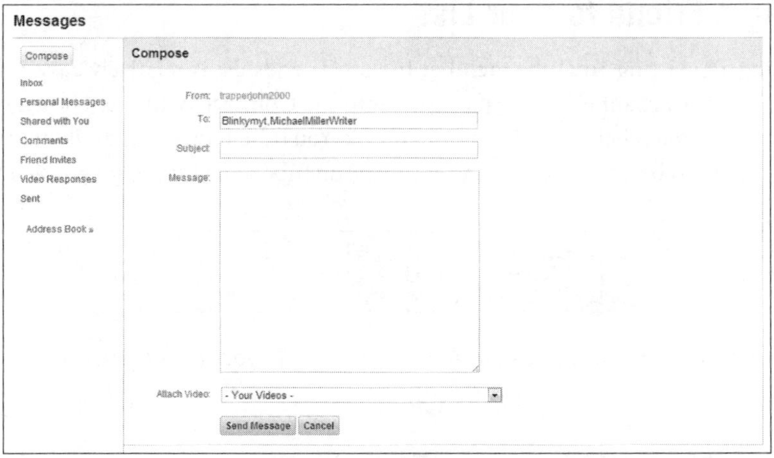

Figure 17.5 *Sending a message.*

 Tip

You're not limited to sending messages to only existing friends and contacts. To send a message to any YouTube user, go to your inbox and click the Compose button; from there you can enter any member's username for the message you compose.

Reading Messages from Other Users

YouTube also lets you receive messages from your viewers and customers; these messages end up in your YouTube inbox. To access your inbox, click the down arrow next to your user name at the top of any YouTube page and select Inbox. As you can see in Figure 17.6, your inbox lists all email messages you've received. You can view other types of messages by clicking the Personal Messages, Shared with You, Comments, Friend Invites, Video Responses, and Sent links.

To read a message, just click it in your inbox; the message displays onscreen. You can delete the message, mark it as spam, or send a reply to the message by using the Your Reply box and the Send Message button.

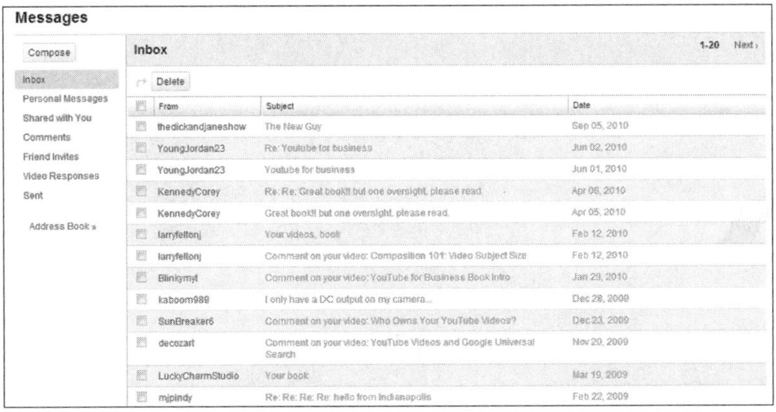

Figure 17.6 *Waiting messages in your YouTube inbox.*

The Big Picture

Taking advantage of the YouTube community is essential to promoting your business or online content. It's through these community ties that you drive viewers to your videos and then on to your own website.

Of course, participating in the YouTube community requires a real commitment; it's not something you can do halfway or hire someone to do. (YouTubers can spot a "hired gun" from a mile away.) You have to take the time to learn the YouTube community and actively participate in it. That means viewing lots of videos, entering lots of thoughtful comments, and joining lots of groups. It can be a full-time job.

18

Incorporating YouTube Videos on Your Own Website

YouTube is a great place to display your company's videos. But you can display the videos you create for YouTube on your own website or blog, too. And the great thing is, you don't have to host them—YouTube does all the hosting and handles all the traffic for you!

With that in mind, let's look at the various ways to incorporate your YouTube videos into your company's website or blog. It's easy!

Why You Should Let YouTube Host Your Videos

If you produce a lot of videos for YouTube, there's no reason not to display those videos on your own website or blog, too. The more eyeballs the better, after all.

Now, it's probably easy enough to pipe a copy of each video over to your tech guys and let them create a video viewing page on your site. They can figure out how best to host and serve the videos, and you're ready to go.

However, it costs space and money to store a video on your own web server. If you're a small business, you can quickly eat through the storage space included with your hosting plan, and have to pay extra for additional storage. (Videos are big files, after all.) In addition, some hosting plans charge extra if your bandwidth usage goes above a certain number each month, and videos use a lot of bandwidth.

You see where we're going here. The more videos you create, the more storage space you use, and the more that's going to cost you. Likewise, the more videos that are viewed—or the more viewers a given video attracts—the more bandwidth you use, and that's going to cost you, too. In fact, if you're fortunate enough to have a video that goes viral, with hundreds of thousands of viewers, it could bankrupt you—or clog your available bandwidth.

You don't have that problem if you let YouTube host and serve your videos. All you have to do is insert a bit of code for each video onto your site's video viewing page, and the videos show up on the page just as if you were hosting them—but you're not. The video files themselves are stored on YouTube's servers, using YouTube's bandwidth whenever they're viewed. You don't have to devote any disk storage or bandwidth to serve the videos, which relieves a big load on your end.

The best thing is, YouTube does this all for free. YouTube doesn't charge a single penny to host or serve your videos. It doesn't matter how many videos you upload or how many people view them, you don't pay a thing. And that's a good thing, especially for small or cash-strapped businsses.

Adding YouTube Video Links to a Web Page

Now, not all companies want to include videos on their official websites. Instead, you might want to reference your YouTube videos without displaying them.

The easiest way to do this is via a link to a specific video on the YouTube site. Every YouTube video has its own unique web address (URL). You can copy and paste that URL into a page on your company's website, email messages, blog postings, and the like.

Linking to an Individual Video

As just mentioned, every video on YouTube has its own unique web address. When you navigate to a video page, its URL is in the Address box in your web browser.

You could copy the URL from your browser's address bar, but there's an easier way to do it. Go to the video's page and click the Share button beneath the video. When the Share panel expands, as shown in Figure 18.1, the URL is displayed. You can copy the URL as-is, or if you want a shorter URL, check the Short URL option and then copy that.

Figure 18.1   *Generating the URL for a YouTube video.*

 Tip

By default, YouTube generates the URL for the standard definition version of a video. If the video is in high definition, you can check the HD URL box to generate a link to the HD version.

You can then paste the video's URL into the underlying HTML code for your web page or blog, surrounded by the appropriate link tag. The resulting code should look something like this, although on a single line:

```
Click <a href="http//:www.youtube.com/watch?v=12345">here</a>
to view my YouTube video.
```

Naturally, replace the href link with the URL of the video you're linking to. When visitors click the link in the text, they go to that video's YouTube page.

 Tip

To insert a YouTube video link into an email message or blog post, simply copy the URL from the video page and paste it into the body of the message.

Linking to Your YouTube Channel

YouTube also lets you link to your YouTube channel page. Just use this URL within your link code:

```
http://www.youtube.com/user/username
```

Just replace *username* with your YouTube username.

Embedding YouTube Videos in a Web Page

Linking to your YouTube videos is good, but embedding one or more of your videos on your own website is even better. It's an easy process to embed *any* public YouTube video on your site, even those you didn't upload.

YouTube automatically creates an embed code for every public video on its site (as well as your own private videos), and lists this code on the video page itself. You display the embed code by clicking the Embed button beneath the video player.

As you can see in Figure 18.2, you have some options when it comes to embedding a video. The options you choose are reflected in the code that YouTube generates.

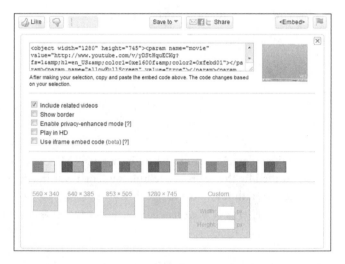

Figure 18.2 *Generating the embed code for a YouTube video.*

What can you customize in an embedded video? Here's the list:

- **Include related videos.** By default, YouTube will display a list of "related videos" when your video is done playing. If you'd rather not display these videos (which can interfere with your branding—or even come for your competitors!), uncheck this option.

- **Show border.** By default, YouTube creates a borderless player. If you want a border around the embedded player on your page, check this option.

- **Enable privacy-enhanced mode.** By default, YouTube creates and stores a cookie on that user's computer when someone watches a video. If you'd rather not infringe quite so much on your visitors' privacy, check this option to instruct YouTube not to store personally-identifiable information.

 Note

Enabling privacy-enhanced mode doesn't mean YouTube won't store *any* cookies for viewers of that video. YouTube might still set cookies for that video, but not store information that identifies the video's viewer.

- **Play in HD**—If you're embedding a high definition video, checking this option creates a larger video player and initiates playback in HD mode. Note, however, that this will be a very large playback window, and might not fit on all web pages.

- **Use iframe embed code**—This generates a different, more versatile embed code. The iframe code can play back in either Flash or HTML5, depending on the viewing environment, which will make some embedded videos viewable on mobile devices. (At present, this feature was still in the testing phase.)

- **Color scheme**—By default, the embedded viewer uses the standard grayish color scheme. If you want a more colorful player window, choose a different color scheme.

- **Size**—You can choose the size of video player you want embedded on your page. Select the size that fits best.

For example, Figure 18.3 shows a video player embedded with the standard options (gray color scheme, small size, no border, and so on). Figure 18.4 shows the same player embedded at a larger size with a red color scheme and colored border.

You'll need to copy this entire code (it's longer than the embed box itself) and then paste it into the HTML code on your website. Just insert the embed code into your web page's HTML where you want the video player window to display. What you get is a special click-to-play YouTube video player window in line on your web page or blog. The video itself remains stored on and served from YouTube's servers; only the code resides on your website. When a site visitor clicks the video, YouTube's servers deliver it to your viewer's web browser, just as if your own server sent it.

Figure 18.3   *A video player embedded with standard options.*

Figure 18.4   *A bigger video player embedded with a red color scheme and colored border.*

 Tip

If you're a website developer, YouTube offers a set of tools, called the GoogleData Application Programming Interface (GData API), which lets you develop web-based applications using YouTube videos. Learn more at code.google.com/apis/youtube/.

The Big Picture

YouTube videos aren't just for YouTube viewers. You can offer your YouTube videos to visitors to your website or blog, either by including a link to your videos or by embedding specific videos on your web pages. YouTube makes it easy to do, just by including a short piece of HTML code. You can even customize the video player window to better match the look and feel of your company's web pages.

The nice thing about all this is that YouTube does all the hosting for you. If you run a small business and have only a limited amount of storage space and bandwidth for your website, you won't tap out your resources if your video becomes a hit. YouTube hosts the video and provides all the bandwidth necessary to view it—no matter how many viewers your video attracts. Viewers will think they're viewing the video on your website, but in reality YouTube is doing all the heavy lifting!

19

Tracking Performance

Posting a video to YouTube is just the start of the market-
ing process. You need to judge how effective that video
is—how many viewers it attracts and how many sales
result from those viewers.

Fortunately, YouTube provides a number of metrics you
can use to track the performance of each video you post.
Read on to learn more.

Why Tracking Is Important

Why should you bother tracking the performance of your YouTube videos? For the same reasons you track the performance of other parts of your marketing mix—to fine-tune your activities to have bigger impact, to measure the effectiveness of your efforts, and to learn from your efforts when planning future activities.

Let's look at each reason individually.

Fine-Tuning Your Efforts

You don't have to wait until the end of a campaign to track its performance. In fact, it's a good idea to look at what's happening while it's happening, so that you can make any mid-course corrections that might be necessary.

Let's say, for example, that you've launched a series of YouTube videos but discover, after the first few weeks, that viewership is much less than what you anticipated. Why is this? What do you do about it? Can you tweak upcoming videos to make them more attractive to potential viewers? These are all questions you can answer *now*, without having to wait until the end of the campaign. Track the performance and make necessary changes along the way—this is how you get the most out of any marketing campaign.

Measuring Effectiveness

At the conclusion of the campaign, you need to measure just how effective it was. Did the campaign meet your goals? Did you achieve the viewership you wanted? Was there the expected increase in sales? And if not, why not?

You need to apply the same sort of scrutiny to your YouTube activities as you do to any marketing campaign. This means setting goals beforehand, and then measuring the actual performance against those goals. Just as important, you need to analyze the results to see why your videos under- or over-performed against expectations. Set a goal, measure performance, and then analyze that performance—that's Marketing 101.

Planning Future Activities

Finally, you need to learn from your YouTube activities. If your first campaign bombed, figure out why and apply that knowledge to your next campaign. If the campaign was a success, determine what contributed to that success so you can replicate it in future efforts. Each activity you engage in should be a learning experience that informs the next activity, and the one after that. Don't repeat your mistakes—and don't abandon your successes.

Tracking Views, Ratings, and Comments

Some of the most important metrics can be found directly under the video player on each video page, as shown in Figure 19.1. Just go to the page for the video you want to track, and look at the key metrics there—views, likes/dislikes, and comments.

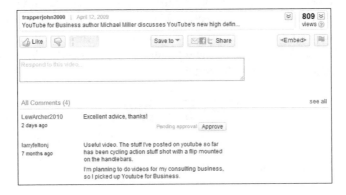

Figure 19.1   *Viewing views, ratings, and comments.*

Measuring Views

The most important metric is the *views* number—literally, how many times your video was viewed. This number appears directly beneath the video player on the video page.

When it comes to judging this basic performance, how many views is a good number? That's hard to say. Certainly, if your video gets a million views overnight, you're doing something right—that's pure viral status. But, for certain types of videos and businesses, a total of 100 views might be good. (For example, if you're selling high-priced real estate.) You have to judge performance based on your own parameters, and with realistic expectations.

 Tip

It's particularly useful to compare views for all the videos in your library. Although raw numbers might not tell you much, comparative numbers tell you which of your videos are performing best and which might need to be replaced.

In my mind, however, raw views is a false measurement. Just because your video has a lot of viewers doesn't mean that it has accomplished the goals you set out to achieve. A video with 100,000 views is nice, but it means nothing if you wanted to boost your sales and it didn't do that. Entertaining YouTube viewers is one thing, generating sales (or establishing brand image or whatever) is quite another.

Judging Likes and Dislikes

Viewers can rate a video using a thumbs up/thumbs down system—up if they like it, down if they don't. The likes versus dislikes are graphed on the third button from the left underneath the video; hover over this button to view the graph in color, as shown in Figure 19.2, along with the total number of likes and dislikes. Obviously, the more liked your video is, the better.

Figure 19.2   *Viewing likes and dislikes.*

Reviewing Comments

Another important metric is represented by those comments left by a video's viewers. These comments don't constitute a hard metric, of course, but do represent a source of useful feedback from those who watch your videos. The number of comments indicate the degree to which the video engaged viewers; the content of the comments will tell you what viewers liked or disliked about what they saw.

 Note

Learn more about viewer comments in Chapter 15, "Managing Comments."

Tracking Basic Metrics

There's a lot more you can learn about who has watched your videos. These additional metrics are provided via YouTube's Insight tracking tool. You use Insight to track viewership of your videos, as well as reveal other important statistics.

To view basic Insight metrics, click the down-arrow next to the Views metric underneath a given video. This displays the Insight panel for that video, shown in Figure 19.3.

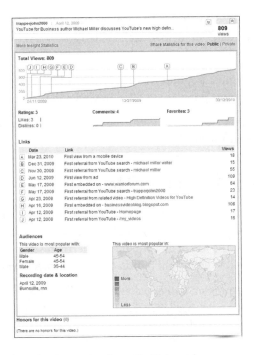

Figure 19.3   *Tracking basic metrics for a YouTube video.*

This panel displays a variety of basic performance metrics:

- **Total Views**. Insight displays the number of views in total, as well as (in graph format) over time. The graph also has several key landmarks noted, as lettered points on the graph. Each letter corresponds to an event in the Links section, further down the panel.

- **Ratings.** The total number of ratings (both likes and dislikes) your video has received. The number of likes versus dislikes is detailed under the total number.

- **Comments**. The total number of comment this video has received. The graph beneath this number reflects comments over time.

- **Favorites**. The number of times this video has been added to a viewer's favorites list. The graph beneath this number reflects favorites over time.

- **Links**. These are actually milestones for your video, along the lines of "First view from a mobile device," "First view from ad," "First referral from YouTube search," and so forth.

- **Audiences**. This section provides a general demographic breakdown of who your video is most popular with—what genders and age groups.

- **Recording date & location**. This isn't demographic information per se, but rather the date you uploaded the video and where you uploaded it from.

- **This video is most popular in.** This is a world map. Countries where your video is most popular are filled in with a darker color.

- **Honors for this video.** If your video has won any YouTube honors, they're listed just beneath the Insight panel.

Tracking More Advanced Metrics

If you want more detailed performance metrics, YouTube has them. The best way to access Insight's advanced metrics for any given video is to click the down arrow next to your name at the top of any YouTube page, then select My Videos. When the next page appears, click the Insight button for the video you want to analyze.

The Insight page features six individual tabs, each focusing on a particular type of data. The tabs for this video are located at the bottom left of the page, as shown in Figure 19.4. We'll look at each in turn.

Figure 19.4   *The tabs on YouTube's Insight page.*

 Caution

Don't confuse the tabs for the selected video with the tabs in the All Videos section, which display combined metrics for all the videos in your channel.

Views

The Views tab presents a graphical display of the number of views for your video, both over time and by region.

You use the graph and map at the top of the page, shown in Figure 19.5, to designate the time period and region(s) analyzed. Drag the sliders beneath the top left graph to expand or contract the time period; click one or more areas on the map to determine from which regions you wish to include data.

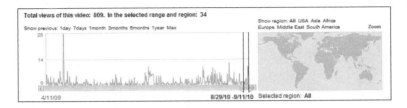

Figure 19.5   *Selecting which time period and region(s) to analyze.*

 Note

The time and region controls are the same for all insight pages.

Down in the main part of the page, shown in Figure 19.6, the Views graph displays the number of views your video received over the designated period. By default, it shows views per day (Daily Views); however, you can pull down the list above the graph and select Regional Popularity, which alters the graph to show views by region, along with a regional table beneath the graph.

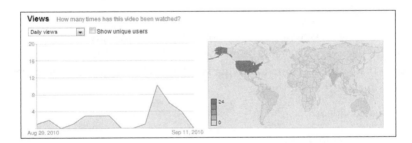

Figure 19.6   *Displaying views over time and by region.*

The right graph is a map of the world, with the number of views for your video displayed in different colors for each region. When you click a country or region on the map, the view count for that area appears in Views graph.

 Note

YouTube's view count data includes views of the video on the YouTube site as well as views from other sites on which the video is embedded.

Discovery

Insight's Discovery tab, shown in Figure 19.7, tells you how viewers discovered your video. This is a great way to determine where to put your promotional efforts.

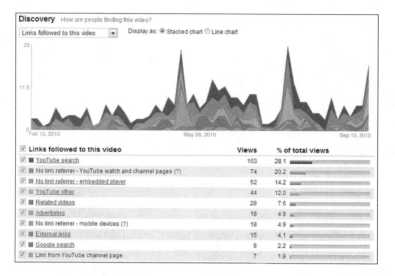

Figure 19.7 *Using the Discovery tab to determine how viewers are finding your videos.*

The stacked chart displays views per day, with each color representing a different method of discovery. The table below the chart details the different methods of discovery—that is, the top sources driving viewers to your video. These discovery methods include the following:

- Related videos
- YouTube search
- Google search
- Advertising
- Embedded players (your video embedded on other sites)
- Link from YouTube channel page
- Other links on the YouTube site
- External links

Click a particular discovery method in the table and you'll see a list of specific items related to that method. For example, if you click the YouTube Search link, you receive a list of the top search queries that found your video; further click a query link to see all the results for that query, and where your video appears on the results list.

 Tip

If you'd prefer to see the location of where the video was viewed—YouTube watch page, YouTube channel page, embedded player, or mobile device— pull down the list above the chart and select Location of Player When Viewed.

Of all these more advanced metrics, I think Discovery might be the most important. It's key to determine how viewers find your videos; until you know this information, it's impossible to determine how to promote your YouTube videos.

For example, if you find that the majority of viewers discover a video by searching on Google, you know that you need to optimize future videos for Google search. In this instance, you're further empowered by Insight's listing of what keywords your viewers searched for. With this knowledge in hand, you can make sure to include the most popular keywords in the descriptions of subsequent YouTube videos.

Alternatively, you can use the Discovery tool to determine why a particular video performs less well than others. Look at how viewers did (or, more importantly, didn't) find a less viewed video, and you'll find out areas where you need to improve. If, for example, a video didn't pull well via Google search, you know that you need to pay more attention to keywords in future video descriptions.

The key is to determine how viewers find out about your videos—and then exploit that information.

Demographics

The Demographics tab, shown in Figure 19.8, tells you the age and gender breakdown of the video's audience. The left hand bar graph displays age ranges; select Male or Female to see age ranges by gender. The pie chart on the right shows the gender breakdown.

 Note

YouTube only knows demographic information for videos viewed on its own site, not for videos embedded on other sites. That's because it gets its demographic information directly from its own subscribers; the information is only as accurate as what YouTube's members supply.

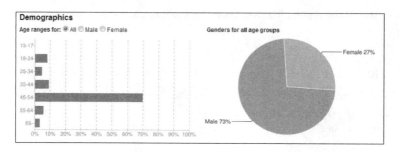

Figure 19.8   *Using the Demographics tab to look at age and gender data.*

Community

The Community tab, shown in Figure 19.9, measures so-called community engagements—ratings, comments, and number of times your video was chosen as a viewer favorite. Pull down the list above the left hand chart to select different engagement metrics.

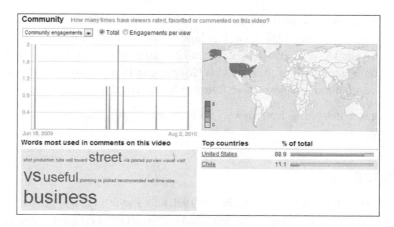

Figure 19.9   *Using the Community tab to evaluate viewer engagement with your video.*

Also of interest is the list of words beneath the graph. This displays, in graphic format, those words most used in the comments about this video. The larger the words, the more often they were used.

Hot Spots

The Hot Spots tab, shown in Figure 19.10, is an interesting one. The graph on the left analyzes how popular your video is over the course of the video—that is, at what point(s) viewers lost interest while watching. You can watch or scroll through the video using the player window on the right, so you can see what exactly it is in the video that people are either liking or not.

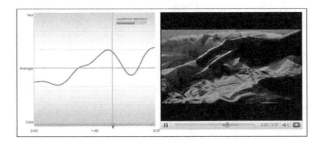

Figure 19.10 *Using the Hot Spots tab to analyze the most and least popular moments in a video.*

Call-to-Action

This tab is only visible when you've promoted a video and added a Call-to-Action Overlay. The graph on the left displays the number of clicks the overlay received during the selected time frame; the table under the graph displays the most clicked URLs in your overlays. You can also pull down the list above the graph to display impressions and click-through-rate—which are also displayed underneath the map on the right.

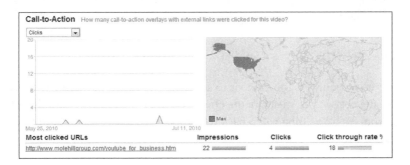

Figure 19.11 *Analyzing the performance of a video's Call-to-Action Overlay.*

 Note

Learn more about overlays in Chapter 23, "Using Call-to-Action Overlays on Your Videos."

Tracking Effectiveness

The number of views a video obtains isn't necessarily indicative of how effective it is. A video might gain a huge viewership but result in few sales or little brand awareness; conversely, a video with a small number of viewers might result in much higher sales or brand awareness.

Tracking the effectiveness of a video is more difficult than tracking simple viewership. No analytical tools measure this metric; in fact, it's more of a black art than it is a science. With that caveat, there are ways to get a general handle on how effective a video is.

Tracking Interactivity

One measure of effectiveness is how well the video involves the viewers—that is, how viewers interact with the video. You can deduce the level of interaction from the number of comments and video responses left by viewers. The more that the video draws in viewers, the more viewers leave personal comments and responses.

Think of it this way. If your video is just a light entertainment, viewers will likely not be inspired to leave comments. If, on the other hand, your video proves particularly useful or educational, viewers are more likely to leave comments to that effect. The more comments you get, the better the video is at involving the viewer.

On a meta level, you can track the effectiveness of all your videos in total by noting the number of subscribers you get to your YouTube channel. If your videos connect with viewers, they're more likely to subscribe to your channel to get notice of future videos. If your videos are less effective, viewers are less likely to subscribe.

Tracking Traffic

If you're using your YouTube videos to sell products or services directly from your website, the best way to measure the effectiveness of each video is simply to track traffic from each YouTube video back to your site. There are a number of ways to do this.

 Note

Most website-hosting services provide their own traffic analysis tools. You can also use a third-party tool, such as Google Analytics or Webmetrics, to do the tracking.

Just about any website analysis tool will show where your site traffic comes from—that is, the previous sites viewed by your site's visitors. By using this type of tool, it's easy enough to track the traffic from the YouTube site (www.youtube.com) to your site. If you see a spike in traffic from YouTube after you post a new video, it's a good bet that the traffic was driven by that video.

More sophisticated website analysis tools track traffic from specific pages on the originating site. This makes it even easier to determine which videos are driving the most traffic back to your site.

Alternatively, you can include a special code for each video you upload to YouTube. The easiest way to do this is to display a unique URL for your main site in each YouTube video; the URL should lead to a unique landing page on your website. For example, you might create a series of landing pages for each of your videos, with URLs such as www.yourwebsite.com/youtubepromo01/, www.yourwebsite.com/youtubepromo02/, www.yourwebsite.com/youtubepromo03/, and so on. This makes it easy to track hits on each specific landing page, providing a detailed analysis of the effectiveness of each originating video.

Tracking Conversions

Another way to measure video success is to determine what kind of response you want. Is the video designed to generate direct sales, either via your website or 800-number? Is the video designed to drive traffic to your website? Is the video designed to enhance or reinforce your company or brand image? Or is the video designed to reduce customer or technical support costs?

This is key—to measure the success of your YouTube video, you have to first determine what it is you hope to achieve. Then, and only then, can you measure the results:

- If your goal is to generate sales, then measure sales. Include your website URL and 800-number in the video, along with a promotion or order code, and then track sales that include that code.

- If your goal is to drive traffic to your website, then measure your traffic pre- and post-YouTube video. Use web analytics to determine where site traffic originates from; specifically track that traffic that came directly from the YouTube site.

- If your goal is to build your brand image, measurement is more difficult. You'll need to conduct some sort of market research after your YouTube campaign has had a chance to do its thing, and ask customers what they think of your brand—and where they heard about it.

- If your goal is to reduce customer or technical support costs, measure the number of support requests before and after uploading the YouTube video(s). The more effective the video, the lower the subsequent calls for support.

You get the point. Know what you want to achieve, and then measure that metric. You might find that a video that outperforms its siblings in terms of views doesn't actually deliver the conversions you were seeking—or vice versa.

Tracking Direct Sales

If you're in the business of selling stuff online, the ultimate measure of a video's effectiveness is how many sales directly result from the viewing of that video. Determining which sales result from which videos is a simple tracking issue. Assign each video a special tracking code, and include that code in the video's text description and onscreen information screen. Encourage customers to enter that tracking code on your product purchase or checkout page, and you'll know from which video the sale came.

What's a good conversion rate? That's entirely within your judgment; for some companies, converting 1 sale per 100 views is good performance, whereas other companies might be satisfied with a 1 in 10,000 conversion rate. It all depends on the type of product you sell.

In any instance, the total number of conversions might be less important than comparing the conversion rates of different videos. If one video has a 0.1% conversion rate and another a 0.5% rate, you know that second video is five times more effective than the first one. Knowing that, you can then analyze the *why* behind the numbers—what it was about that second video that drove more viewers to become paying customers.

With this knowledge in hand, you can better focus future videos to include the elements that made the second video more effective. And that's the key: To learn from what you've done to become more successful going forward.

The Big Picture

One of the great things about online videos is that it's easy to track how successful they are. YouTube includes a wealth of tools that tell you how many people view each video, how they found it, and how your videos compare to other videos on the site. You can supplement YouTube's statistics with data from your own website to judge which YouTube videos are driving the most traffic back to your site.

Ultimately, however, you want your YouTube videos to result in increased sales for your products and services. Tracking direct sales is easy enough (by embedding some sort of unique tracking code in each video), but almost impossible if your products are sold via traditional retail or wholesale channels. That said, you can get a hint of how well your videos work by talking directly with your customers via surveys and the like; you can gain much knowledge by simply asking your customers, "Have you seen our videos on YouTube?"

The point is to do more than just post videos on YouTube; you want to post *effective* videos. The only way to do that is to track each video's performance and learn from what you discover. Use all the tools at your disposal (from YouTube and other services) to gather all the data possible, and then determine what makes one video more effective than another. That knowledge is power—and the way to make YouTube an even more effective part of your marketing mix.

20

Marketing Your YouTube Videos

The best-made video on YouTube is a dismal failure if no one watches it. How do you attract viewers to your YouTube videos, and thus create more potential customers for your business?

With millions of videos posted on the YouTube site, it's tough to get your content noticed. Fortunately, there are many different ways you can promote your YouTube videos to attract new viewers. We discuss some of the more effective ones in this chapter.

Start with Great Content...

It goes without saying that all the promotion in the world won't attract viewers to a video that doesn't offer some distinct value. Viewers who follow the promotion to a lousy video simply click the Stop button when they begin to get bored, which happens soon enough. It all starts with great content, which can benefit from additional promotion.

Entertain, Inform, or Educate

The best YouTube videos offer something valuable to viewers. As I've noted earlier in this book, for a video to attract viewers, it has to do one of three things: entertain, inform, or educate the viewer. Here's what I mean:

- **Entertain**—Most videos on YouTube strive to be entertaining. Whether you're talking cute kittens, stupid human tricks, or wryly humorous vlog postings, the typical YouTube video contains some measure of entertainment value. This can also work for business videos; just as many of the most memorable television commercials are vastly entertaining (typically in a humorous vein), some of the most-viewed YouTube business videos are similarly entertaining. After all, people like to be entertained; if you can pull off such an entertaining video, it's bound to draw viewers.

- **Inform**—One other thing that attracts viewers is information—in particular, information that is specifically relevant and useful to the viewer. I'm talking about the latest news, tailor-made for the target YouTube customer. When your company video has information that matters to particular YouTube viewers, those people will watch it.

- **Educate**—In a similar fashion, anytime you can help someone learn how to do something that they need to do, you attract eyeballs. Show mechanically inept viewers how to change the oil in their cars, or teach would-be chefs how to prepare a gourmet meal, and the help you provide gains praise. Step-by-step instruction attracts large numbers of viewers in today's increasingly do-it-yourself world—as witnessed by the success of HGTV and the Food Network on cable television.

Pick one approach—entertainment, information, or education—and do it as best you can. Provide stellar content and you're well on your way to upping your video view count.

Target Your Content

Here's something else about the content of your videos: The more targeted it is, the faster it finds an audience. Yes, general videos would seem to appeal to a larger slice of the YouTube community. But general videos also get lost among the millions of other general videos; it's tough to stand out in a crowd this large.

A much better approach is to target a particular slice of the community—a distinct customer base. As in any other form of advertising, the more narrowly you target the message, the more appeal you have to those targeted consumers.

In addition, when you niche-target your content, you can more easily promote it via YouTube's community features, as well in the blogosphere and via social media such as Facebook and Twitter. When you narrowly identify the audience, it's a snap to locate the groups, blogs, forums, and other outlets that target the same audience. A broadly focused video is much more difficult to promote; there are just too many channels to choose from, none of which is an exact hit. In fact, a general interest video might reach an audience altogether different from the one you really want to reach. Why waste your time targeting viewers who will never be your customers? You can more effectively and efficiently promote a narrowly targeted video via channels narrowly targeted in the same way.

Write a Compelling Title

The title of your video is crucial to attracting viewers. Not only is your title searched by YouTube when users submit queries, it's also how most viewers determine what your video is about.

Yes, the full description is there to read, but most people skim rather than read—especially when they're browsing through a page full of search results. So your title has to not only include the most important keywords or tags, but also convey the content of the video.

This means, of course, that you have to create a concise, descriptive, and compelling title. It's copywriting at its finest, distilling the essence of what you have to offer in a very short line of copy; it takes a lot of work and no little experience to get right.

Pick the Best Thumbnail Image

Finally, remember what a typical YouTube search results page looks like—lots of video listings, each accompanied by a single thumbnail image, as shown in Figure 20.1. You need to attract viewers to your specific listing in the search results, which means presenting the most attractive and relevant thumbnail image possible.

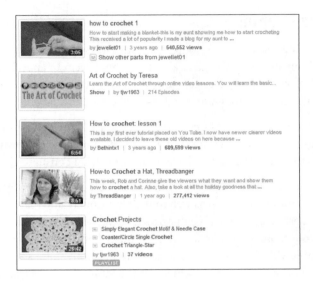

Figure 20.1   *Optimize your thumbnail image to stand out on search results pages.*

YouTube lets you choose from three possible images to use as your video's thumbnail image. It grabs the images from different points in your video. To choose a thumbnail image, go to your My Videos page and click the Edit button for the video you want to edit; when the next page appears, as shown in Figure 20.2, click the image you want to use as your thumbnail.

Figure 20.2   *Choosing an image to use for your video thumbnail.*

 Tip

You don't have to keep the same thumbnail image forever. Many marketers switch thumbnail images over the course of a video's YouTube life, thus freshening the video's appearance on search results pages.

The best thumbnails are clear, not blurry, and have a dominant subject—ideally a person's face or a close-up of the product you're selling. You can also stand out from the other listings with a brightly colored or high contrast image in your thumbnail—anything to make the thumbnail "pop" on the search results page.

Take Advantage of YouTube's Community Features

One of the best places to promote your YouTube video is on YouTube itself. When you make the YouTube community aware of what you're doing, other viewers do your promotion for you. Word-of-mouth marketing is alive and well on the YouTube site.

Sharing with Subscribers and Friends

Let's start with those users who subscribe to your video channel, as well as those who added you to their Friends list. How do you let these positively predisposed viewers know that you have a new video to watch?

Dealing with subscribers is easy: YouTube does the work for you. Whenever you post a new video to the YouTube site, YouTube automatically sends an email to all of your channel's subscribers informing them of the video. That's easy.

More work is necessary to notify your friends of your latest video. Go to the video page, select the Share tab (under the video player), and click the Email button. This opens a new message window, shown in Figure 20.3. To send a message to all your contacts or friends, click the Add All Contacts or Add All Friends link in the scrolling list. Enter your message (something along the lines of "Check out our latest video") in the Message box and click the Send button.

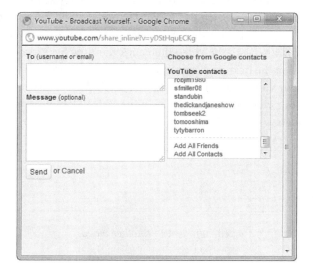

Figure 20.3 *Sending an email to your YouTube friends.*

Your friends receive an email message like the one in Figure 20.4. To view your video, all they have to do is click the video thumbnail or the link to the video; doing so takes them to the video page on the YouTube site, and you have one new viewer.

Figure 20.4   *The email that your friends receive.*

Guerilla Comments

Here's a neat little promotional trick that might work for some businesses. It's kind of a guerilla tactic, in that you piggyback on the success of someone else's video.

Here's how it works. You start by finding a video that's similar to yours, in terms of subject matter or audience appeal. You want to find a video that has a much larger viewership than yours; this won't work if you pick a lesser-viewed video.

The related video found and displayed, you now want to attach your video as a video comment to the more popular video. That's right, you "comment" on the other video by displaying the video you want to promote. To do this, click within the comments box beneath the video then click the Attach a Video link, as shown in Figure 20.5. When the next page appears, as shown in Figure 20.6, click Choose a Video, select your video from the list and then click the Use the Selected Video button. That's it; your video will now appear in the Video Comments section beneath the original video.

Figure 20.5   *Adding a video comment to another video.*

Figure 20.6   *Selecting the video to use as your video comment.*

As I said, this is definitely a guerilla marketing technique. It will get your video more exposure, but some YouTubers will be turned off by the blatant self-promotion. Attempt this one at your own risk.

Use Email Marketing

Of course, you're not limited to promoting your videos just to the YouTube community. You can also promote your videos to anyone else on or off the Web.

One of the best ways to do this is to create an email mailing list on your main website, typically populated with email addresses provided by your customers. When you post a new video to YouTube, send a mailing to the entire list, letting your customers know all about the video and including a link to the video on YouTube. You might be surprised at how effective this simple technique can be.

 Caution

Your email mailing list needs to be an opt-in list, or you might be accused of sending spam to your valued customers.

Reach Out to the Blogosphere

You can drive a lot of traffic to a YouTube video by getting that video mentioned on relevant blogs. It requires a bit of work to identify the blogs that might be interested in the content of your video, but then it's a simple matter of sending out a press release (via email) that describes the video and includes a link to the YouTube video page. You might even want to include your video's embed code in the introductory email, in case the blogger wants to actually embed your video in his blog.

 Tip

If you're so inclined, and have the time, you can reach out to individual bloggers via personal emails. This hands-on approach is much more effective than the blanket press release method.

In some instances, you might be able to pay bloggers to mention your videos. This pay per post (PPP) approach seems odious to some, but it's increasingly common in the blogosphere.

When a blogger links to or embeds your video in his blog, you just created a new stream of viewers for your video. A certain percentage of these new viewers link back to your corporate website, just as a certain percentage subscribe to your channel to view future videos—thus becoming future potential customers.

Post to Other Web Forums

Along the same lines, you should work the various websites, forums, and message boards that target the same audience as your videos. Participate in appropriate discussions on these forums so that you can throw in a mention of or link to your video without appearing particularly mercenary.

After you become a familiar face on a given forum, it's okay to start a new discussion when you have a new video to promote. Yes, this is a tedious and time-consuming approach, but it's quite effective; you're reaching out to some of the most influential members of the target community.

 Caution

In most web communities, don't even think about making a promotional post until you've established a presence in the community. Most communities are quite insular and uniformly dismissive of "carpetbaggers" operating purely in their own self-interest.

Work the Social Media

Another way to drive traffic to your videos is via a presence on Facebook, Twitter, and other social media sites. After you create your own personal or company page on these websites, you can then include YouTube videos as part of your status updates and tweets.

In fact, YouTube makes it easy to send videos to the most popular social media:

- Facebook
- Twitter
- MySpace
- Orkut
- hi5
- Bebo
- Google Buzz
- StumbleUpon

In addition, you can use this feature to send your videos directly to your Blogger-hosted blog.

To post a video to one of these social media sites, click the Share button under the video player on the video page and then click the appropriate social media button. This displays the list of compatible social media, as show in Figure 20.7.

Figure 20.7   *Sharing a video via social media.*

What happens next depends on the button you select. For example, when you click the Facebook button, you see the Post to Profile window shown in Figure 20.8. Enter a comment in the box and click the Share button, and your Facebook profile adds the video, as shown in Figure 20.9.

 Note

Whichever social media site you select, you might be prompted to sign into that account with the appropriate user name and password.

Figure 20.8   *Posting a video to your Facebook profile.*

Figure 20.9   *A Facebook profile with a YouTube video added.*

If you click the Twitter button, you see the Share This on Twitter window, shown in Figure 20.10. Edit the text of the tweet as you like, then click the Tweet button. Twitter generates the tweet, linking to a short URL for the video you selected. Your Twitter followers can click this link to view the video.

The takeaway here is that you should take advantage of all the features of the major social networking sites to promote your video with the widest possible network of online friends and acquaintances.

 Tip

You should also promote your video on social bookmarking sites, such as Digg (www.digg.com) and Delicious (www.delicious.com). When you post a link to your video on these sites, it will be discovered by a wide range of other users—thus broadening the viewership of your video.

Figure 20.10   *Sharing a video via Twitter.*

Run a Contest

Here's a method mentioned elsewhere in the book, but worth repeating here. One interesting way to draw viewers to your videos is to run a contest of some sort. Some of the most successful contests directly involve viewers with the company's videos by encouraging them to remix existing videos or create their own videos for the company or product.

Naturally, some customers will be attracted by any prizes you dole out, but most will visit your channel or group just to see what other YouTubers are posting; contest entries are bound to be entertaining in any number of ways. The most creative viewers will post entries to the contest—some of which might be good enough for you to use in other media. It's a win-win for you because you get a spike in viewership, attract new customers, and reinforce your bonds with your existing customer base.

Promote Traditionally

While our focus is primarily on the Web, we mustn't neglect more traditional forms of promotion—including old fashioned PR. This means issuing paper (and electronic) press releases, as well as picking up the phone (or firing up the email program) to hand-target individual publications and news outlets.

For example, if you have a video that has particular relevance to a particular industry, you can reach out to industry trade groups, publications, and the like with news about your video. Make sure you include a link to (or the URL for) the video in your press release, of course; any online news source can link directly from their coverage to the video on the YouTube site.

Likewise, if your video is of local or regional interest, reach out to your local news organizations—newspapers, television stations, radio stations, and their online arms. The best of all possible worlds comes when your video is not only mentioned on a local newscast, but also shown on air!

Upload to Other Video-Sharing Sites

You shouldn't limit your videos to only YouTube. There are lots of other video sharing sites on the Web that, although smaller than the YouTube community, can help expand the reach of your videos. You already have your video produced, after all; why not distribute it as widely as you can?

Granted, none of the following sites has near the traffic as does YouTube, but they're all free to use, so you might as well get to know them. These sites include the following:

- blip.tv (www.blip.tv)
- Dailymotio (www.dailymotion.com)
- Flixya (www.flixya.com)
- GUBA (www.guba.com)
- Metacafe (www.metacafe.com)
- Revver (www.revver.com)
- Veoh (www.veoh.com)
- Vimeo (www.vimeo.com)
- Yahoo! Video (video.yahoo.com)

Obviously, you should include your video on your own company website or blog. Your site has lots of visitors that might never visit the YouTube site; give them the opportunity to view your videos without leaving your official site!

 Note

Learn more about posting your video on your company's website in Chapter 18, "Incorporating YouTube Videos on Your Own Website."

Advertise Your Video

This is a relatively new option for producers of YouTube videos. YouTube now offers the option of advertising your video on the YouTube site to YouTube viewers. YouTube calls the ads Promoted Videos, and they work just like Google AdWords or any other pay-per-click (PPC) advertising program. This is such a big deal that I've devoted a whole chapter to the topic; flip ahead to read about it.

 Note

> Learn more about YouTube Promoted Videos in Chapter 22, "Advertising Your YouTube Videos."

The Big Picture

You can't just upload a video to the YouTube site and expect a thousand views overnight. It takes a lot of hard work and creativity to attract viewers to your videos; it doesn't happen by chance.

If you're lucky, all your effort results in an upsurge of viewers for your video. At this point, success begins to beget success. That is, the more viewers you attract, the more they talk about and recommend your video, thus further increasing the view count. You need viewers to create more viewers.

Then, if you're even luckier, your video's view count is high enough to become one of YouTube's top-rated videos. When this happens, your video appears on YouTube's Videos tab, which displays the daily most-viewed videos. This is when your video hits the big time; with this type of prominent exposure, you get even more views than you did before. As I said, success begets success.

From there, the next logical step is to go viral. This happens when your video's viewership expands beyond YouTube. Maybe a local television station picks up the video, or you get a mention on a major website, or CNN or MSNBC—or even David Letterman or *The Daily Show*—start showing the video on the home screen. If you're lucky enough for this to happen, get ready for a wild ride. Your view count could easily hit the seven figure mark, and you could get more buzz than you ever thought possible.

This, of course, is what we all strive for: massive exposure with minimal cost and effort. But both you and I know that the effort wasn't minimal; you have to work hard just to get basic exposure for your video, let alone go viral.

21

Optimizing Your Videos for Search

How do people find your videos on YouTube? Most people discover new videos by searching for them—or rather, by searching for a particular topic or type of video. Those videos that display high in the search results get the views.

This means that you need to optimize your videos to rank as high as possible in YouTube's search results. Video search optimization is similar to the search engine optimization (SEO) you perform on your website; it's all about figuring out what people are searching for, and inserting those keywords into the appropriate places.

How YouTube Searches for Videos

Online search is all about *keywords*. A keyword is a word or phrase entered as part of a search query; it's what people are searching for.

For example, if someone is looking for videos about sailboats, he might enter the keyword **sailboat**. If someone is looking for videos about meatloaf recipes, she might enter **meatloaf recipe**. If someone is interested in learning how to shoot a jump shot, he might enter **how to shoot jump shot.** You get the drift.

YouTube, then, tries to match the keywords entered by a user with those videos that best fit that query. In our first example, YouTube would display videos about sailboats; in the second, videos showing how to cook meatloaf; and in the third, videos that demonstrate how to shoot jump shots.

Just how does YouTube match queries to videos? Unfortunately, YouTube has no way of analyzing a video itself to determine its content; that technology does not yet exist. Instead, YouTube must rely on the description of the video to determine its content. That's right, YouTube analyzes the text you enter to figure out what your video is about—and match it to the appropriate search queries.

As to exactly where YouTube looks, the answer is "everywhere"—everywhere that contains text, that is. That means youneed to focus on three fields when uploading or editing your video: tags, title, and description. They all matter, to some degree, and will affect how your video is ranked when someone is searching for a related topic.

Choosing the Right Keywords

Whether we're talking tags, title, or description, you need to determine the right keywords to use, and then include those keywords in all three fields, as best you can. It all revolves around the keywords, however.

It's vital, then, that you learn how to create a list of keywords that best describe your video, in the way that users will think of and search for that video. It's a matter of learning how to *think like the customer*; you need to get inside the heads of potential viewers to determine which words they're using in their queries.

The art of determining which keywords to use is called *keyword research*, and it's a key part of SEO, whether you're optimizing your complete website or a single YouTube video. When you know which keywords and phrases that your target customers are likely to use, you can optimize the description of your video for those words and phrases; if you don't know how they're searching, you don't know what to optimize.

It's all a matter of determining how viewers search for the information they need. When you figure out the keywords they'll most likely search for, you have the most effective keywords for your video.

You have to learn how customers think, and how they search. When someone is in the market for a new car, and trolling YouTube for useful information, how are they likely to search? If they're just starting out, and don't know what models best fit their needs, you're likely to see queries that focus on particular features, such as **four wheel drive sedan** or **hard top convertible** or **fuel efficient SUV**. After customers narrow down their choices, they're more likely to search for information about specific models, such as **Ford pickup** or **BMW 3-series** or **Audi A5 convertible**. You have to pick your keywords to match the stage at which you're trying to reach these customers.

As such, you probably need to come up with a combination of both generic and specific keywords. For example, if your video talks about the differences between incandescent and fluorescent lighting, you should include generic tags such as **lighting**, **light bulb**, **energy efficient**, and the like, as well as more specific tags such as **incandescent**, **fluorescent**, and *your company name*. In this way, you attract viewers that are essentially browsing or just getting interested in the topic, as well as make yourself known to those viewers that have more specific needs in mind or are searching specifically for your company.

Optimizing Your Tags

After you come up with a list of keywords and phrases, just how do you use them? As noted earlier, there are three places where you can include keywords: your video's tags, title, and description.

Let's start with the Tag field first. What YouTube calls "tags" the rest of us call keywords; it's just another term for the same thing. So naturally you should enter your keywords into the Tags field when you first upload your video, or later via the editing function.

As you can see in Figure 21.1, the Tags box has plenty of room for all the keywords you might want to target. Enter individual words with spaces in between. To enter a multiple-word phrase, enclose the phrase within quotation marks, like this: **"multiple word phrase"**.

You'll also note that YouTube recommends additional tags, beneath the Tags box. These are based on the tags you've previously entered and the video's title and description. To add any of these suggestions to your official tags list, just click the tag.

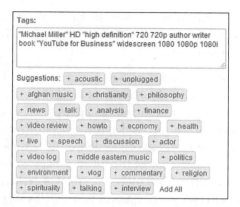

Figure 21.1 *Keywords entered into the Tags field for a YouTube video.*

The tags field is perhaps the most important for optimizing your video for search; it's where YouTube looks first. Without the right tags, great content will go unfound. Add the appropriate tags, however, and you make it easier for viewers to find your videos.

Optimizing Your Title

YouTube also looks within your video's title for keywords that match viewers' queries. It's more difficult to fit keywords into a title, however, because you're limited as to the title's length. Specifically, a title can include no more than 100 characters, so writing a title that is both descriptive and includes a number of keywords is challenging, to say the least.

But that's part and parcel of SEO, in all its forms—learning how to incorporate your most important keywords into various text elements, while maintaining the usefulness and integrity of those text elements. Yes, it's challenging, but it needs to be done.

This argues for taking some time to figure out the best titles for your videos. This isn't something you want to do on the fly; it's something that requires work.

The best titles describe the video's content in a way that appeals to the target audience. They also include a handful of the most important keywords, those words that target viewers are most likely to be searching for. Ideally, these keywords are also the best descriptors of your video's content.

What you don't want to do is randomly insert keywords into the video's title. One, that makes the title less descriptive, and thus less useful for prospective viewers. Two, it reeks of keyword stuffing, and YouTube won't reward that. Instead, work the keywords into your title in an organic fashion; if you can't do so, then don't include them.

Optimizing Your Description

Finally, we come to the text description of your video. Here is yet another opportunity to include keywords that viewers might be searching for.

Adding keywords to your video's description is much like performing SEO on your website's body copy. You have lots of space to work with, so you're not as limited as you are with the video's title. Yet you still need to incorporate keywords in an organic fashion; they have to feel natural, not artificial.

Fortunately, it's easier to work keywords into descriptive copy than it is into short titles. The extra length works wonders. Again, make sure that the keywords aren't just inserted randomly, or in a list at the end of the description; that's keyword stuffing, and that's a no-no. Instead, write your copy to include as many keywords as genuinely fit. If your keywords are indeed descriptive of your video's content, and not just chosen to attract a certain audience, then this shouldn't be a problem.

Optimizing Embeds and Links

In traditional website SEO, the number of inbound links to page will increase that page's ranking. The same thing goes for YouTube videos. The more web pages that link to your video, the more likely it is that your video will appear higher in YouTube's search results. Likewise, you can increase your search ranking by getting your video embedded in more external web pages.

That's right, links to and embeds of your video will affect its YouTube search rank. The challenge is, you have little control over how many sites link to or embed your video. That doesn't mean you have no influence, however.

First, the more unique and authoritative the content in your video, the more likely it will be linked to or embedded. It all comes down to quality content; you need to make your video as "linkworthy" as possible.

In addition, you will want to encourage viewers to link to your video. The more you spread word of your video, the more people who will be exposed to it. Have your PR department push your video to influential bloggers, encouraging links or embeds. Email related websites and encourage them to embed or link to the video. Encourage recipients of your email mailing list, readers of your company blog, fans of your Facebook page, and followers of your Twitter feed to do the same. Get the word out and encourage as many links and embeds as possible.

Optimizing Views

Here's another important factor in determining YouTube's search rank—the number of times your video has been viewed. Fair or not, YouTube will rank a popular video higher than a less popular one. This is just another good reason to try to push more people to view your video, even though it's admittedly a bit of a circular endeavor.

Optimizing Comments and Ratings

The final factor in YouTube's search rank are the comments and ratings your video receives. A video with more comments and ratings (assuming it's a net positive rating) will rank higher than one with fewer comments and ratings. For this reason, you need to activate comments and ratings for your videos, and then encourage viewers to voice their opinions.

The Big Picture

For your video to be found by the viewers you desire, it has to include those keywords that those viewers will be searching for. You should include these keywords in your video's tags, title, and description; all these fields are used by YouTube to determine your video's content. (Interestingly, YouTube can't determine the content just by viewing the video; technology of that sort is still years away.)

YouTube also looks at the number of pages that link to or embed your video; the number of comments and ratings your video receives; and the total number of views of your video. In other words, the more popular a video is, the higher it will rank in YouTube's search results—assuming it contains the appropriate keywords, of course.

22

Advertising Your YouTube Videos

How do you make your videos stand out from the millions of other videos on the YouTube site? Organic promotion for your videos, as we discussed in the previous chapter, is fine, but sometimes you might want or need to engage in more blatant promotion—the kind you have to pay for.

If you're jonesing to add another line to your advertising budget, good news: YouTube lets you advertise your videos on the YouTube site. These so-called Promoted Videos appear on YouTube search results pages, much like traditional PPC ads appear on the results pages for a Google search.

Understanding YouTube Promoted Videos

What, exactly, is a YouTube Promoted Video? It's an advertisement, pure and simple, for a specific YouTube video. Specifically it's a pay-per-click ad, where you're charged only when someone clicks the ad to view the video.

How PPC Advertising Works

Pay-per-click (PPC) advertising is the dominant form of advertising on the Internet. Unlike traditional cost-per-thousand (CPM) advertising, where you pay for impressions or views, PPC advertising charges advertisers only when an ad is clicked by a consumer; the advertiser does not pay for the placement of the ad itself.

The advantage of PPC advertising is that you're truly paying for results; it's definitely a performance-oriented approach. You don't pay if no one takes action on your ad. It's that simple—and that powerful.

Payment for PPC advertising is calculated on a cost-per-click (CPC) basis. The CPC is typically determined by how much the advertiser is willing to bid on a specific keyword. That is, you choose a keyword to associate with your ad; your ad is displayed on search results pages when a user searches for that keyword.

How often your ad is displayed, or how high up on the search results page, is a factor of how high you bid for the chosen keyword, in relation to how high competing advertisers also bid. If you bid more than your competitors, your ad will be seen more often and be more visible. If you're cheap about it (that is, if you get significantly outbid), your ad will be less visible.

As to that CPC bidding, how much you actually end up paying is a factor of what you bid versus what your competitors for that keyword bid. You don't necessarily pay the full bid price; if you outbid the competition, you'll only be charged slightly more than the next-highest bid. So if you bid $2.00 per click and the next-highest bid is $1.00 per click, you might only be charged $1.10 per click or so. In any case, you'll never be charged more than your specified bid amount.

And remember, you only pay when someone clicks your ad. Even if your ad is displayed to 100,000 viewers, if only one of those viewers clicks your ad, you pay just for that single click. (Of course, if you only get one click from 100,000 views, there's probably something wrong with your ad.)

Given that you never know in advance how many clicks an ad might receive, how do you know how much you'll spend for CPC advertising? That's simple; you establish a budget up front. The ad network (in this instance, YouTube) runs your ad until you've hit your budget level, then ceases all further display; you're never charged more than what you budgeted.

Most online ad networks, including YouTube, work with a daily CPC budget level. So, for example, if you set a $100 daily budget and bid $2.00 per click, your ad will run until you've received 50 clicks. (That's $100 total budget divided by $2 per click.)

PPC advertising is typically associated with the major search engines—Google, Yahoo!, and Bing. In fact, the largest PPC ad network is Google AdWords, which places PPC ads on Google's search results pages. Google also runs the PPC advertising on YouTube's site—which can also tie into AdWords advertising, if you already have an AdWords account.

 Note

> There is a noticeable similarity between YouTube Promoted Videos and Google AdWords. They're both part of the same Google empire, after all, and actually share much of the same backend.

How YouTube Promoted Videos Work

YouTube introduced its Promoted Videos program as a means for users to promote individual videos they've uploaded to the YouTube site. Each Promoted Videos ad promotes a specific video; to promote more than one video, you have to run multiple ads. Naturally, YouTube lets you run as many ads as you want, all at once.

Promoted Video ads appear on YouTube's search results pages. When someone searches for a particular topic, ads related to that topic appear in the Promoted Videos section on the right side of the page.

 Note

> Sometimes Promoted Videos also appear at the top of the search results page, in a shaded box.

As you can see in Figure 22.1, each Promoted Videos ad includes a title, a brief text description, and the producer's name, as well as a video thumbnail. When a user clicks on the title or thumbnail, he or she is taken to the advertiser's video page; when a user clicks the producer's name, he or she is taken to the user's channel page. In either instance, when a click is made, the advertiser is charged for that click.

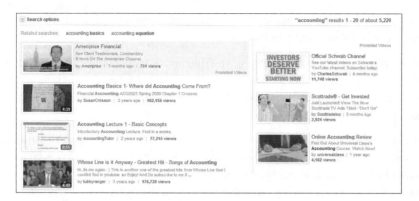

Figure 22.1 *Promoted videos at the top and right side of a YouTube search results page.*

Not surprisingly, YouTube's promoted videos work just like traditional text-based PPC ads, such as those in Google's AdWords program—with the addition of a video thumbnail to accompany the ad's text. This is a pay-per-click program, just like AdWords; you're charged only when someone clicks on your ad. You bid on specific keywords and pay a certain price per click.

And remember, you're advertising a video on the YouTube site. You're *not* advertising your own website, or your business—just the selected video. It's an ad for the video that appears in the Promoted Videos section, and it's the video that displays when someone clicks the ad. The Promoted Videos service, then, exists to help advertisers get more views for their YouTube videos—nothing more and nothing less.

Creating a Promoted Videos Campaign

You can set up advertising campaigns for any video you've uploaded to the YouTube site. In fact, you have to promote each video individually; you can set up separate campaigns for different videos, but you can't set up a generic campaign for all your videos.

Getting Started

To create a Promoted Videos ad, click the down-arrow next to your user name at the top of any YouTube page, then select My Videos. When the My Videos page appears, click the down arrow next to the video you want to advertise, then select promote. This displays the Choose Video page, shown in Figure 22.2; once again, select the video you want to advertise, then click the Next, I Agree button at the bottom of the page.

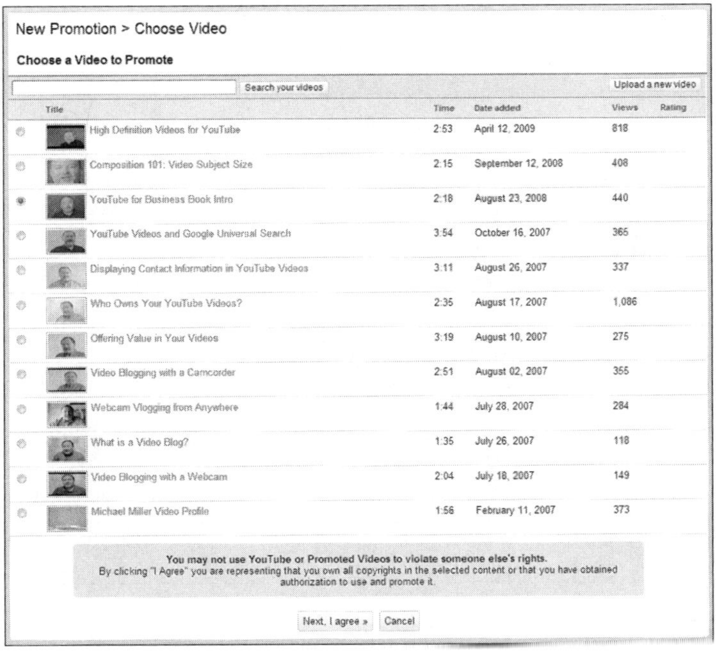

New Promotion > Choose Video

Choose a Video to Promote

	Title	Time	Date added	Views	Rating
○	High Definition Videos for YouTube	2:53	April 12, 2009	818	
○	Composition 101: Video Subject Size	2:15	September 12, 2008	408	
●	YouTube for Business Book Intro	2:18	August 23, 2008	440	
○	YouTube Videos and Google Universal Search	3:54	October 16, 2007	365	
○	Displaying Contact Information in YouTube Videos	3:11	August 26, 2007	337	
○	Who Owns Your YouTube Videos?	2:35	August 17, 2007	1,086	
○	Offering Value in Your Videos	3:19	August 10, 2007	275	
○	Video Blogging with a Camcorder	2:51	August 02, 2007	355	
○	Webcam Vlogging from Anywhere	1:44	July 28, 2007	284	
○	What is a Video Blog?	1:35	July 26, 2007	118	
○	Video Blogging with a Webcam	2:04	July 18, 2007	149	
○	Michael Miller Video Profile	1:56	February 11, 2007	373	

You may not use YouTube or Promoted Videos to violate someone else's rights. By clicking "I Agree" you are representing that you own all copyrights in the selected content or that you have obtained authorization to use and promote it.

[Next, I agree »]   [Cancel]

Figure 22.2 *Choosing a video to promote.*

Creating an Account and Setting a Budget

The first time you choose to advertise, you're prompted to create a Google account and enter a payment method (credit card), as shown in Figure 22.3. You're charged a one-time $5 activation fee, just to ward off posers. Enter the asked-for information, then click the Add Billing button.

You're now asked to set your daily budget, as shown in Figure 22.4. Remember, this is how much money, maximum, you're willing to spend *per day*; it can be as little or as much as you wish. You're probably used to monthly budgets, so you'll have to adjust your normal calculations. Enter your budget and then click the OK, I Want to Use This Budget button.

After you've set up your account and set your budget, you need to return to your My Videos page and select the video you want to advertise, again. (YouTube doesn't seem to remember that this is what you wanted to do, in the first place.) Of course, if you've already set up your account and budget, you skip that entire process when you start to create an ad.

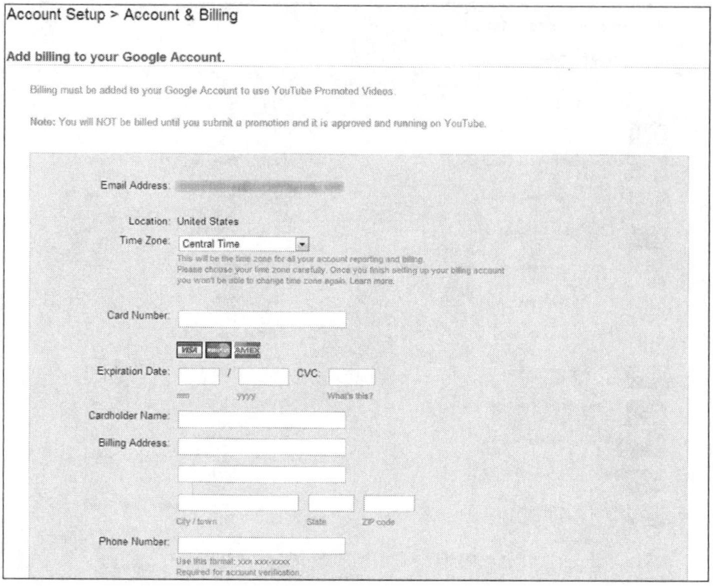

Figure 22.3   *Entering payment information.*

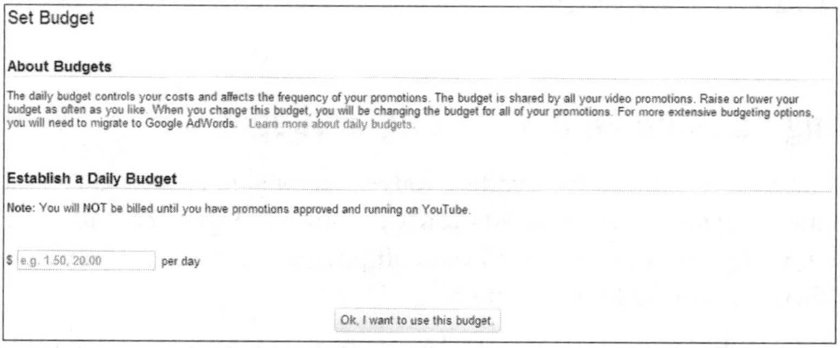

Figure 22.4   *Setting your daily budget.*

Writing Your Ad

You're now shown the Write Your Promotion page, shown in Figure 22.5. Not surprisingly, this is where you actually create the ad. Enter a title (25 characters max) and two lines of descriptive text (35 characters per line) into the appropriate boxes. You also get to select which thumbnail image accompanies the ad; choose from one of the three that YouTube presents. A preview for the ad you create is displayed on the right side of the page. If you like what you see, click the Next button.

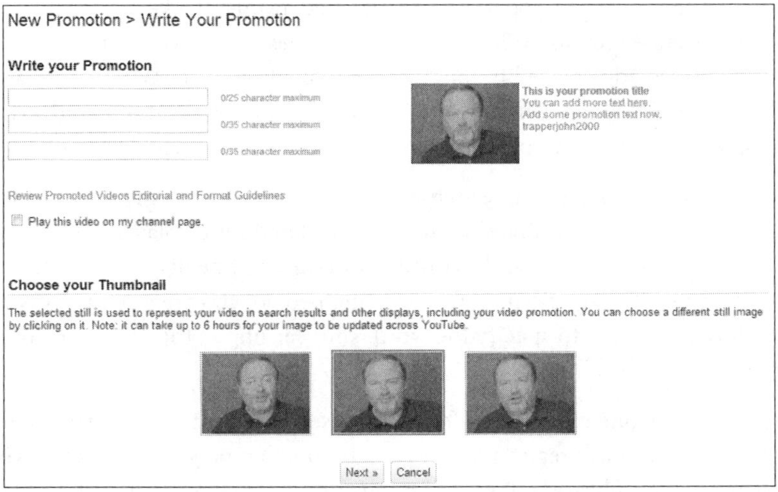

Figure 22.5   *Creating your Promoted Videos ad.*

Choosing Keywords

You now get to choose the keywords that trigger the display of your ad—the keywords on which you'll be bidding. As you can see in Figure 22.6, you can enter as many keywords (individual words or phrases) as you like, one per line. You can also let YouTube automatically generate keywords for you, per the characteristics you choose.

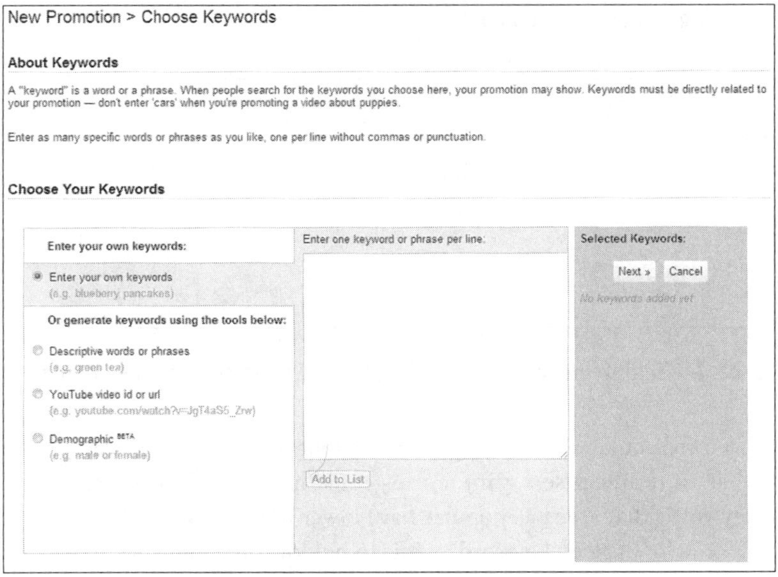

Figure 22.6   *Entering keywords.*

Remember, the keywords you select are matched against the keywords that YouTube's users search for. When someone searches for one of your keywords, your Promoted Video ad is placed in the running to be displayed. (Whether it's actually displayed or not depends on how much you bid per click, what other advertisers are bidding on that same keyword, and other factors, as previously discussed.)

So, for example, if someone is searching for the word "shirt," only advertisers who bid on the word "shirt" will have their ads considered for display. If you haven't specified "shirt" as one of your keywords, your ad won't be displayed on this person's search results page. So if you're targeting people who are looking for videos about shirts, you want to specify the word "shirt" as one of the keywords for your campaign.

Similarly, if someone is searching for the phrase "polo shirt," only advertisers that specify that phrase will register as a match. If your campaign includes the word "shirt" but not the phrase "polo shirt," it won't be a match for that particular query. You need to specify the entire key phrase as part of your campaign.

As I said, you can enter as many keywords as you like, then click the Add to List button. This adds the keywords to your list; click the Next button to proceed.

Setting CPC

After you assemble the list of keywords you want to associate with your PPC ads, you need to determine how much you should bid on those keywords. When you get to the Set CPC page, shown in Figure 22.7, enter your maximum CPC—the most you're willing to pay for each click.

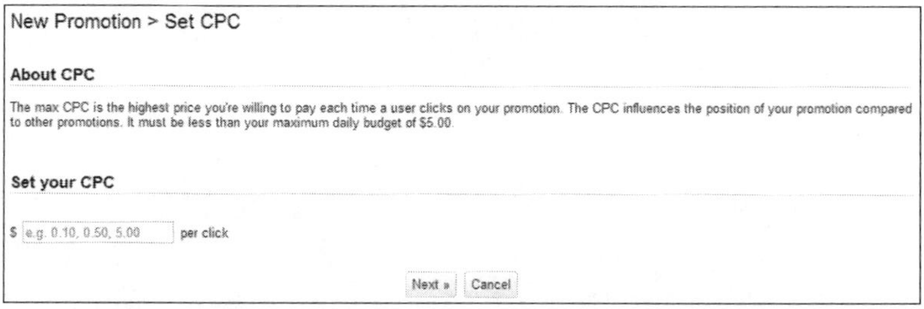

New Promotion > Set CPC

About CPC

The max CPC is the highest price you're willing to pay each time a user clicks on your promotion. The CPC influences the position of your promotion compared to other promotions. It must be less than your maximum daily budget of $5.00.

Set your CPC

$ [e.g. 0.10, 0.50, 5.00]   per click

Next »   Cancel

Figure 22.7   *Setting the maximum CPC for your Promoted Videos campaign.*

In reality, different keywords will go for different rates. It's logical, really. Those keywords that more advertisers want to use get bid higher, and have higher CPC rates; those keywords that aren't as popular have lower CPC rates. So it's just as easy to bid high on a low-priced keyword as it is to bid low on a high-priced one.

If you bid way too low, your ad simply won't appear for a given keyword. And if you consistently bid too low on keywords, you won't generate enough traffic to make your campaign profitable—and thus reduce your campaign's return on investment (ROI).

On the other hand, if you consistently bid too high on keywords, you'll spend more advertising funds than you need to—and also reduce your ROI. That's why you need to figure out how to bid the right amount—neither too high or too low—to strike the right balance between traffic and cost; this will maximize your ROI for a given campaign.

This means you need to go through a little trial-and-error, and be prepared to adjust your bids over the course of a campaign. If you find yourself being constantly outbid on a desired keyword, you'll need to raise your maximum CPC for that keyword. If, on the other hand, your ad gets displayed too many times for your daily budget (that is, if you run through your budget before each day is half over), you can lower your maximum CPC for that keyword, so you don't overpay.

In any case, after you've set your maximum CPC, click the Next button.

Confirming the Promotion

YouTube now displays the Confirm Promotion page, shown in Figure 22.8. If you like what you see, click the Okay, Run My Promotion button. This gets the campaign started.

Figure 22.8   *Confirming a Promoted Videos campaign.*

Using the Promoted Videos Dashboard

You track the performance of and manage your promoted videos from the Promoted Videos Dashboard, located at http://ads.youtube.com. As you can see in

Figure 22.9, this Dashboard displays key information about your current campaigns.

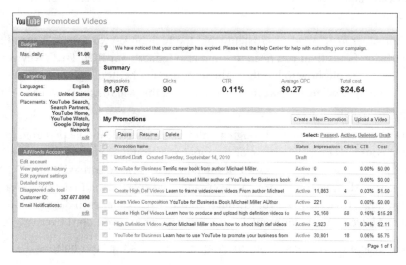

Figure 22.9   *The Promoted Videos Dashboard.*

Examining Key Metrics

The Promoted Videos Dashboard displays key metrics for all your campaigns in total. Here's what's tracked:

- **Impressions**: The number of times your Promoted Videos ads were displayed.
- **Clicks**: The total number of clicks your Promoted Videos ads received.
- **CTR**: The click-through-rate, calculated as clicks divided by impressions.
- **Average CPC**: The average cost for each click made on your ads.
- **Total cost**: The total cost for all the clicks on your ads.

Obviously, the more impressions and clicks your ads receive, the better. You also want a high CTR, which indicates that viewers find your ads relevant and worth checking out.

Analyzing Individual Video Performance

As noted, the Dashboard by default displays aggregate data for all your Promoted Videos ads. You can, however, display this same data for each individual ad. All you have to do is click the ad's name in the My Promotions list; this displays the Promotion Detail page, shown in Figure 22.10.

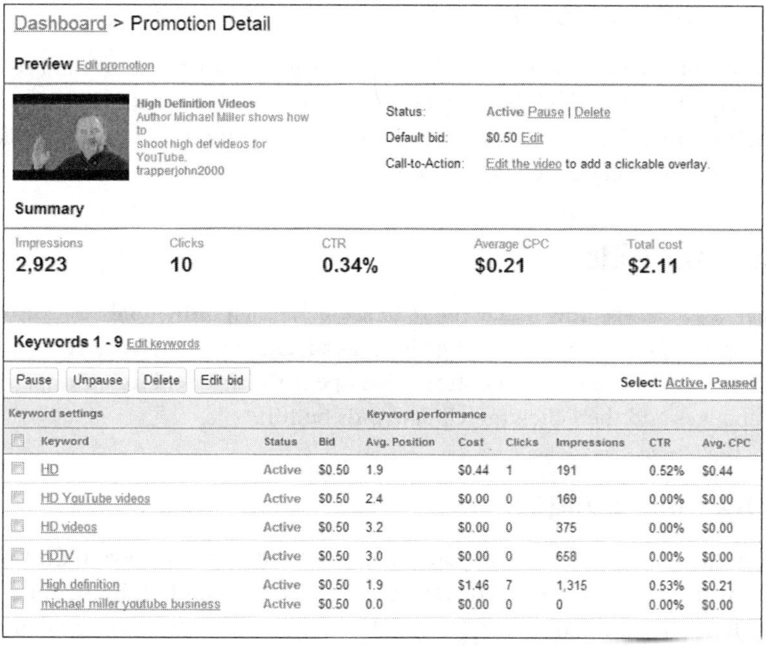

Figure 22.10   *The Promotion Detail page.*

At the top of the this page are the expected key metrics—impressions, clicks, CTR, average CPC, and total cost. Also of interest are the keywords listed on the bottom of the page; these are the keywords you choose to bid on for this ad. For each keyword you see the following data:

- **Status**: Either active or inactive

- **Bid**: The maximum amount you bid when you created the campaign

- **Average position**: The average position (from the top) that ads generated by this keyword achieved on YouTube search results pages

- **Cost**: The total amount you've been charged for clicks on ads generated by this keyword

- **Clicks**: The total number of clicks generated by this keyword

- **Impressions**: The total number of times ads generated by this keyword were displayed

- **CTR**: The click through rate for ads generated by this keyword

- **Average CPC**: The average cost per click paid for ads generated by this keyword

Editing Your Promotion

If you want to change the text or thumbnail image for any ad, go to the Promotion Detail page and click the Edit Promotion link near the top. This opens the title and text fields for editing, and displays all three available thumbnail images. Make your changes and then click the Save Promotion button.

Editing Your Bids

You can also change how much you're bidding for each individual keyword for an ad. Go to the Promotion Detail page for that ad, check the keyword you want to revisit, then click the Edit Bid button. This opens the Bid field for editing; make your changes and then click the Update Bids button.

Revising Your Budget

For that matter, you can change your daily budget at any time during the process. From the main Promoted Videos Dashboard, click the Edit link in the Budget box on the left. This opens the Max. Daily field for editing. Enter your new daily budget number and then click the Submit button.

Pausing, Resuming, and Deleting Ads

Finally, you can pause or delete an ad campaign at any point. From the Promoted Videos Dashboard, check the campaign you want to change and then click either the Pause button (to pause display of the ad), the Resume button (to resume display of a paused ad), or the Delete button (to totally delete a campaign).

The Bottom Line

When you want to get more notice for your YouTube videos, consider advertising them on the YouTube site, using YouTube's Promoted Videos feature. A Promoted Video appears on YouTube's search results pages when viewers search for keywords associated with that video. It's PPC advertising, so the advertiser pays only when a Promoted Videos ad is clicked—which then plays the associated video.

To create a Promoted Videos ad, you have to select a video to promote, write a title and short descriptive text, and select a thumbnail image for the ad. You also have to select which keywords to bid on, and how much you want to pay (on a CPC basis) for those keywords. You then set a daily budget and start the ad—the performance of which you monitor via the Promoted Videos Dashboard.

23

Using Call-to-Action Overlays on Your Videos

Throughout this book, I've stressed that there's no way to directly link from a video to your own website. That's true—with one very important exception.

That exception is something called a Call-to-Action Overlay, which you can add only to a Promoted Video. That's right, advertising a video has the added benefit of being able to link that video to your own website, outside of the YouTube universe.

Read on to learn more.

Understanding Call-to-Action Overlays

What exactly is a Call-to-Action Overlay? Put simply, it's a small band that is super-imposed across the bottom of a video, like the one shown in Figure 23.1 from charity:water (www.youtube.com/user/charitywater/). It's relatively small, relatively unobtrusive, but still noticeable—and it's clickable. That's right, viewers can click a Call-to-Action Overlay to be taken to the video producer's own website. It's the only way to link from a YouTube video to an outside website.

Figure 23.1   *A Call-to-Action Overly on a YouTube video.*

 Note

A Call-to-Action Overlay can also be turned off with a click. When viewer clicks the "X" at the top right of the overlay, the overlay disappears.

Each Call-to-Action Overlay includes a headline, two lines of descriptive text, and a destination URL—typically the home page on the host's website. An overlay can also include a small image, if the host desires. The overlay itself is clickable; clicking the overlay sends the viewer to a URL of the host's choice. (The click-to URL doesn't have to be the same destination URL displayed in the overlay.)

Know, however, that not just anyone can add a Call-to-Action Overlay to their YouTube videos. YouTube only enables these overlays when you advertise a video as part of its Promoted Videos program. That's right, you have to pay (via advertising) to gain the capability of linking from your video directly to your own website. If a video is *not* promoted, you can't add a Call-to-Action Overlay.

Note

Learn more about YouTube's Promoted Videos in Chapter 22, "Advertising Your YouTube Videos."

But here's the deal. It doesn't matter how big a budget you have, you still get to include a Call-to-Action Overlay. You can budget as little as $1.00 a day—and perhaps spend less, if no one clicks your ad—and gain the Call-to-Action Overlay feature.

For some businesses, then, this argues for a strategy that incorporates multiple low-cost Promoted Video ads. That is, you create a Promoted Video ad for each video you want to link back to your site, setting as low a budget as possible; the size of the budget doesn't matter, all YouTube cares about is that you're promoting the video. This lets you add Call-to-Action overlays at a very low cost.

With this strategy, you set a minimal promotional budget, get a little exposure for your videos on YouTube's search results pages, but then reap the rewards of viewers linking directly from those videos back to your website. It's not a bad deal.

Creating a Call-to-Action Overlay

You add a Call-to-Action Overly from the editing page for the promoted video. You only have this option, remember, if you go to a video that you're currently promoting. If you're not advertising a video, you don't have the Call-to-Action Overlay option.

To create a Call-to-Action Overlay, go to your My Videos page and click the Edit button for the selected video. When the video editing page appears, scroll to the Call-to-Action Overlay section, just below the video player, as shown in Figure 23.2.

Start by entering the overlay's title, no more than 25 characters. Then enter two lines of descriptive text, 35 characters maximum apiece.

If you want to include an image, typically your company logo, that image has to be sized at 56 × 56 pixels and hosted elsewhere on the Web. Enter the URL for this optional image into the Image URL box.

Next, enter the URL you want displayed on the overlay into the Display URL box. This does not have to be the same URL you link to. Instead, this should be a short and simple URL, typically the URL for your site's home page.

Finally, enter the URL for the page you want to link to into the Destination URL box. This can be a longer URL, to an individual page on your website. I recommend pointing to a special landing page on your site, so that viewers can click the link to get more information or purchase what you're selling.

Call-to-Action Overlay ▼

Headline:

| YouTube for Business Book | (25/25) |

Description line 1:

| Learn more about YouTube marketing | (34/35) |

Description line 2:

| From author Michael Miller | (26/35) |

Image URL (optional, 56 x 56 pixels):

http:// [   ]

Display URL:

http:// [www.molehillgroup.com]

Destination URL:

http:// [▼] [www.molehillgroup.com/youtube_for_bus]

The content of the Call-to-Action must abide by our Editorial Guidelines

Figure 23.2   *Creating a Call-to-Action Overlay.*

When you're done entering this information, click the Save Changes button. The overlay will now be displayed when people view your video.

 Tip

If you plan on adding a Call-to-Action Overlay to a video, you might need to rethink any onscreen graphics in that video. Because the overlay appears on the bottom quarter of the screen, avoid placing any graphics or other information in the bottom quarter of your video. This might mean repositioning other graphic overlays, such as your website URL, higher in the frame.

Tracking the Performance of Your Call-to-Action Overlays

How do you know if your Call-to-Action Overlay is working? There are several ways to track performance.

First, use your normal website analytics to track traffic from the overlay to the linked-to page on your website. This is easier if you designate a specific landing page for the overlay; all traffic coming to the landing page will be traffic from the overlay. Obviously, the more traffic you generate, the better.

You also want to track other website metrics leading from the overlay, including unique visitors, time on site, and conversions. This last one is particularly important if you're hoping to drive sales from viewers of your video.

Finally, YouTube generates key metrics for its overlays as part of the Insight analytics service. Go to the Insights page for the selected video and display the Call-to-Action tab, shown in Figure 23.3. This page displays the number of clicks the overlay received, as well as the most clicked URLs for the overlay. You can also view impressions and click-through-rate for the overlay.

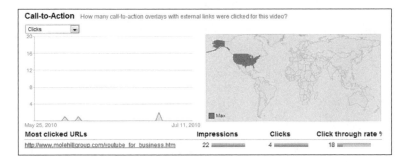

Figure 23.3   *Viewing Insight statistics for a Call-to-Action Overlay.*

The Big Picture

When you want to link directly from a YouTube video to your own website, your only course of action is to first advertise the video, using YouTube's Promoted Videos program, and then add a Call-to-Action Overlay. These overlays can only be displayed on promoted videos, and let you create clickable links to off-YouTube websites.

For this reason, many businesses are creating minimal advertising programs for their videos, for the sole purpose of then being able to add clickable overlays to those videos. It's a great way to drive traffic directly from a video to your website.

24

Generating Revenues from Your YouTube Videos

By this point in reading this book, you're no doubt convinced of the value of adding YouTube videos to your online marketing mix. But how, exactly, can you turn those videos into cash? How can you monetize the YouTube channel?

Probably the most common way to realize the revenue-generating potential of a YouTube video is to use it to drive direct sales of your company's products or services. The goal is to convert viewers into paying customers as quickly and as directly as possible.

Doing so requires a three-step process. First, you have to create a video with unique value, something that attracts viewers. Second, that video has to effectively (if subtly) promote your product and direct potential customers to your regular website. Last, your website has to offer your product or service for sale, enabling interested customers to finalize the purchase.

Let's look at all three steps.

Create a Video with Value

Not to flog a deceased *Equus caballus*, but the first step in any marketing-related activity on YouTube is to create a video that viewers actually want to watch. As I hope you've already learned, there are three ways to do this:

- **Create an *entertaining* video**: People love to laugh.

- **Create an *informative* video**: People like to get the latest news.

- **Create an *educational* video**: People need to learn how to do certain things.

If your video neither entertains, informs, nor educates, people won't watch it. That's the bottom line.

In all three instances, note that your video is *not* an overt advertisement for what you're selling. That's something else YouTubers won't watch: blatant commercials. They get enough commercials on regular television; they don't want to waste their Internet bandwidth watching more of the same. This is why your video has to attract attention through its subject matter; a commercial message doesn't have that type of valuable content.

So, work hard to produce a video that interests potential buyers of your product or service. Get inside your customers' heads and find out what they want to see. It might be something entertaining, it might be a bit of valuable information, or it might be a useful step-by-step how-to. In any case, you have to start with compelling content; anything less and your entire marketing plan falls apart.

Direct Viewers to Your Website

When you produce a video designed to directly sell a product, you need to incorporate selling pointers throughout the video. Think of your video as one of those late-night infomercials; yes, they're (sporadically) entertaining, but they also make it very easy for you to place an order.

How do you including selling pointers in your video? Here are some of the most common approaches:

- Include the URL of your website (or toll-free telephone number) upfront, in the title card for the video. The title card could also include the price of the product, any special offers, and other ordering instructions.

- Add a credits card at the end of the video, also with complete ordering instructions.

- Superimpose your website URL or phone number onscreen over the course of the video, such as the one shown in Figure 24.1 by Century 21 Redwood Realty (www.youtube.com/user/metroarlingtontv/).

Figure 24.1   *A video with website URL and phone number superimposed onscreen.*

- For longer videos, consider inserting a break somewhere in the middle that features a direct call to action by some onscreen personality—kind of like a PBS pledge break.

- Incorporate a subtle selling pitch in the script of the video, much the same way infomercial "hosts" plug their products as part of the onscreen presentation.

In other words, don't be afraid to talk about purchasing your product, but don't let the sales pitch get in the way of the content presentation. Suggest the sale, but subtly.

In addition, consider advertising your video, via YouTube's Promoted Video plan, and then adding a Call-to-Action Overlay to the video. (Remember, only promoted videos can include the overlay.) Use the overlay to link directly to a landing page on your website, where you can conclude the deal.

Finally, don't forget to include a sales pitch and ordering information in the video's text description. Don't make the viewer rewatch the entire video when he wants to place an order!

 Tip

Make sure you include ordering information on your main channel page, as well.

Close the Sale on Your Website

Now it's time to close the sale, which, because you can't sell directly from your YouTube page, you do on your own website. The URL you point to from your YouTube video should be a relatively hard-sell landing page. This means that you don't point to a generic page on your site or even to your site's home page; both approaches require unnecessary work on the part of the customer to place an order. Instead, link to a specific product page on your site, one that includes information about only the product shown in the video.

 Note

The *landing page* is the page that appears when a potential customer clicks an advertisement or search engine results link. This page should display content that is a logical extension of the advertisement or link. Depending on the nature and intent of the page, it should provide additional information, ask for information from the customer, or ask for the sale.

Why design a special landing page for viewers of your YouTube video? It's simple: You want to make it as easy as possible for them to give you their money. If you just dump potential customers on your site's home page, they could get lost. Or they might have trouble finding the product they want and give up. In any instance, you don't want them randomly browsing your site; you want them immediately responding to your specific offer.

Landing pages are all about presenting a consistent image to potential customers. You wouldn't get a lot of sales if someone clicked on an ad for blenders and landed on a page talking about your company's vast international manufacturing capability. That sort of inconsistent message is a surefire way to get people to click back to someone else's site.

For this reason, your product landing page should have the same look and feel of the video so that viewers sense the underlying connection. It doesn't hurt to include a screenshot or two from the video, or even an embedded version of the video in the case the customer wants to rewatch it. The page should also include more detailed information about the product than was possible in the video, as well as more detailed product photos.

Some experts recommend a more stripped-down landing page, with links to additional information if the customer needs it. The thinking is that anyone clicking to this page has already been convinced to buy; you don't want to introduce any element that might make her rethink her decision.

In any case, the most important element on the product landing page is the click-to-order button. Don't make the customer do a lot of work; make it easy to click one button to initiate the order process.

When the customer clicks the order button, she can move to your site's normal shopping cart or checkout section. For tracking purposes, make sure that you credit to your YouTube video any orders flowing from the specific product landing page.

 Tip

> Don't forget to suggest add-on or accessory sales to your new customer—ideally on the page immediately following the initial product landing page.

The Big Picture

Given that you can't sell products directly from your YouTube videos, there are ways to use those videos to generate revenues. For many sellers, the right approach is to direct customers from your video to a product landing page on your own website. This lets you convert viewers to purchasers—and you get to keep all the revenue! The key is to create a video that combines valuable content with a subtle selling message, much the way a good infomercial does; just make sure you include lots of pointers from your video (and its text description) to your website's URL.

Of course, not all companies want or need their YouTube videos to generate direct revenue. The best company videos work to build the company's brand and provide added promotion for the products and services the company sells. That's the magic of YouTube; with every viewer, you broaden your customer base. And it all happens at a relatively low cost.

That combination of efficiency and effectiveness makes YouTube an ideal marketing channel for even the smallest companies. In fact, YouTube is a great equalizer; a little guy can easily compete with the big guys without going broke.

Just remember to *think like the customer*. Create videos that offer unique value—that entertain, inform, or educate. Viewers will flock to useful and entertaining videos, as long as there's no hard sell involved. Offer value and sell subtly; that's the key to YouTube business success!

25

Using YouTube for B2B Marketing

Throughout most of this book, we've focused on using YouTube for traditional consumer marketing— business-to-consumer (B2C) marketing, in the lingo. But whenever I do a seminar about using YouTube for business, I inevitably get asked about whether YouTube can be used for business-to-business (B2B) marketing. It's obviously something that businesses are interested in.

To be honest, I didn't initially have a good answer for this question. It's easy to see how YouTube can be used to attract new customers from among the millions of consumers using the site each day. But are businesses also trolling YouTube in search of more information about suppliers they could be using? I wasn't sure.

Over time, however, I've developed an appreciation of how YouTube can be used as a B2B marketing tool. It's not quite the same as using YouTube to market directly to consumers, but it's worth considering, nonetheless.

Why Use YouTube for B2B Marketing

B2C marketing involves pitching a marketing message directly at the end con-sumer—the average folks who purchase products and services at the retail level. B2B marketing, on the other hand, pitches a marketing message not at consumers, but at other businesses. And marketing to businesses is a much different business than marketing to consumers.

First off, businesses are less influenced by promotional messages than are con-sumers; there's less impulse buying in the B2B market. Businesses tend to be more measured in their purchasing habits, and they certainly don't roam the retail aisles alongside individual consumers. Businesses are more likely to order direct from suppliers, from catalogs and websites and salespeople. They're also more likely to stay with a supplier once the purchasing process has been set up; routine is impor-tant.

As such, you're unlikely to attract new business customers via YouTube. Not only are businesses less apt to be looking for information about new suppliers on YouTube, they're also less apt to be viewing YouTube, period. In fact, many compa-nies prohibit employees from accessing the YouTube site on company time—and that includes employees in the purchasing department.

That said, many businesses *do* access YouTube, and for business purposes. Globally, YouTube reports that there are 1.5 million business searches of its site every day, which makes it the second-most visited destination for business-related searches. (Google is number-one, of course.) YouTube says it reaches half of all online small business owners; if that's who you're trying to reach, YouTube might be the way to do it.

Different Ways B2B Companies Can Use YouTube

Now that we know that more businesses than you might think are accessing YouTube, there's the issue of how exactly you can serve these potential customers via the YouTube platform. YouTube is primarily a consumer site, after all, and the types of videos that consumers flock to probably won't do much for the typical business customer.

First things first. What do you expect to achieve with your B2B YouTube videos?

Where most B2C marketers use YouTube to attract new customers, I think that's probably an unrealistic goal for B2B marketers. Few businesses will be looking at YouTube as a place to find new suppliers. Oh, a few might, but most B2B marketers trolling YouTube for new contacts are likely to be disappointed.

Instead, YouTube is best used to provide more information for potential customers, reinforce existing B2B relationships, and provide after-the-sale support. I'll elaborate on each of these points.

Using YouTube for Additional Information

You probably won't pick up a lot of new contacts from YouTube. However, you can direct contacts you acquire elsewhere to YouTube to provide additional information about your company, products, and services.

In this regard, think of YouTube as a giant brochure or presentation. In fact, you can create video brochures and video versions of your presentations for distribution on YouTube. Many purchasers prefer to watch rather than read, which makes YouTube ideal for putting more information in their hands.

Consider creating at least one video that introduces potential customers to your company, that creates the authority you need to present. Use other videos to provide more details about the various products and services you offer, including hands-on demonstrations, case studies, and the like. Use YouTube videos to help sell your company to prospective clients, and then let your salespeople follow through for the order.

Using YouTube to Reinforce Existing Relationships

B2B marketing is all about establishing and maintaining relationships. After you have a solid relationship with a client, future orders are likely to continue on a regular basis.

On this note, you can use YouTube to help make an otherwise impersonal relationship more personal. A video is great for putting a human face on your company. Let your company management speak directly to customers in videos, show products in use in the field, provide customer testimonials… you get the idea. Use YouTube to provide an ongoing conversation with your customer base.

Using YouTube for After-the-Sale Support

Many B2B products and services require a high level of after-the-sale support. You can minimize your support burden by providing a series of how-to videos that address the most common problems or issues.

For example, if you sell equipment that needs to be installed, you can produce a series of videos that walk customers through the installation process. If you sell a service that some find difficult to understand, you can produce videos that proactively address the most frequent questions. Talk to your technical or customer support people and find out what issues result in the most customer calls, and then deal with those issues upfront via your YouTube videos. Done right, you'll end up with happier customers and lower support costs.

Different Types of B2B Videos

In support of these various goals, there are a number of different B2B videos that you can produce and distribute via YouTube. Let's look at the most popular.

Product Demonstrations and Walk-Throughs

A good product demo or walk-through serves several purposes. First, it lets potential customers learn more about your offerings during the crucial decision-making process. In addition, it introduces existing customers to new products and services. In either case, a product demo provides much-needed information in a useful video format, and should be used to supplement the efforts of your salespeople.

How-To Videos

There are many uses for step-by-step videos in the B2B market. A good how-to video can aid in the decision-making process for potential customers. It can help new customers install and configure your products. It can even show existing customers how to get better use of the products and services they're already using. Be creative here; you can provide a lot of good ideas to help your customer base become more productive with what you offer.

Case Studies and Testimonials

It's always good promotion to showcase your success stories. Customers like to see how other customers are doing things; a video is a great forum for this information. Show your products and services at work in the real world, and let your customers tell each other how much they love what you're doing.

Conferences and Events

If your company sponsors or produces any conferences, seminars, or similar special events, you can use YouTube to both promote and distribute information about these events. Put together a teaser trailer to attract attendees for a future event, or record the event itself and put it (or selected highlights) online. You'd be surprised how many viewers you might attract—potential new customers among them—especially if you have well-known or interesting presenters.

Similarly, you can use YouTube to distribute videos of your internal sales conferences. Some customers might find these interesting in and of themselves, or perhaps you might want to limit access to your internal staff only. In either case, you can get more mileage out of these events by keeping them online for future viewing.

Management Messages and Video Blogs

Finally, don't forget the good old management message video—a talking head video of your company's president or CEO talking directly to the customer base. These are never my favorite videos, but if your CEO has a good presence, authority in the industry, or simply an established relationship with your customer base, this approach can work to reinforce existing connections—or make new ones.

This type of talking head video doesn't have to be limited to upper management. People at any level of your organization can help create an interesting video blog (vlog), talking about your company's latest product developments, industry trends, and the like. When marketing to other businesses, it's good to assume that you're dealing with people who are innately interested in their industry and other business-related topics. Feed that hunger with a vlog filled with information, advice, and even opinion. You might be surprised how many potential customers will take two to three minutes out of their week to hear what you're talking about.

Best Practices for B2B Marketing on YouTube

When utilizing YouTube for B2B marketing, there are some best practices to consider. Many of these practices are the same as for B2C marketers, but they bear repeating here.

Upload All Existing Video Assets

When it comes to B2B marketing, it's all useful. Take any existing videos you have— sales videos, how-to videos, you name it—and adapt them for viewing on YouTube. That might mean chopping up a single long video into a series of shorter ones, or pasting together several short related videos into a more cohesive longer one. If you think existing or potential customers might be interested in or find value from a video, make sure it's uploaded and available for viewing.

Publicize Your Videos

How will your existing customers find out about your videos? You have to tell them! Instruct your sales force to take advantage of this new resource and pass the

URLs for appropriate videos to their customers. Include your YouTube channel URL in all promotional materials, catalogs, and the like. Link to your YouTube channel and videos from your company website. You have to make sure that your customers know what's available, and how to get there.

Optimize Your Videos for Search

YouTube can also be useful in informing potential customers about your offerings. As such, you need to optimize your videos for search. That includes using appropriate keywords in your videos' titles, descriptions, and tags. It also means crediting notable speakers, partners, and customers in those descriptions and tags; someone well-known in a video can attract lots of new viewers.

 Note

> Learn more about video optimization in Chapter 21, "Optimizing Your Videos for Search."

Embed Your YouTube Videos on Your Own Website

Your video presence shouldn't be limited to the YouTube site. If your videos are truly useful to your customer base, you should also dedicate a portion of your company website for their viewing. Create a videos page and embed your YouTube videos there.

 Note

> Learn more about embedding videos in Chapter 18, "Incorporating YouTube Videos on Your Own Website."

Optimize Your Channel Page

For B2B businesses, just like B2C businesses, your home base on YouTube is your channel page. Customize this page to best reflect your company's visual image, and use the page as a gateway to all your videos on the site.

 Note

> Learn more about channel pages in Chapter 16, "Establishing Your YouTube Channel."

Keep Your Content Fresh

With a B2B business, you probably don't need to upload quite as many videos quite as often as with a B2C business, but you still need to keep your content fresh. Even business viewers expect fresh and timely content, so make sure you upload new videos on a regular schedule—and delete old ones that become outdated. If you're going to do the YouTube thing, you need to do it right.

Include a Call to Action

Finally, make sure you're getting the best use out of YouTube by including a call to action in all the videos you upload. This is probably a different call to action than in a B2C video (which is typically "Buy! Buy! Buy!"), but a call to action nonetheless. If what you want is the contact information for potential clients, then ask for that information—and then make sure you follow up with a call from a salesperson shortly after.

The Bottom Line

B2B companies can use YouTube just as B2C companies can—it's just a slightly different type of use. Instead of trying to create new customers from within the massive YouTube community, you use YouTube to reinforce the relationship with your existing customers—or provide reinforcing information to potential customers. There are a lot of different ways to do this, but the end goal is the same—to keep and grow your customer base. YouTube can be a great tool for achieving this goal.

Index

Numbers

3GP file format, 74

.3gpp extension, 74

.3gpp2 extension, 74

4K video, 71

720p resolution, 70

1080i resolution, 70

1080p resolution, 70

A

accentuating contrast, 143

Add as Friend link, 195

Adobe Flash Player Settings dialog box, 86

Adobe Premiere Elements, 126-127

Adobe Premiere Pro CS, 131

advanced metrics
call-to-action, 217
community, 216
demographics, 215
discovery, 214-215
hot spots, 216-217
views, 212-213

advertising videos, 235
CPM (cost-per-thousand) advertising, 244
PPC (pay-per-click) advertising, 244-245
YouTube Promoted Videos
budgets, 247, 254
CPC (cost per click), 250-251
creating, 246-251
defined, 244
explained, 245-246
keywords, 249-250
Promoted Videos Dashboard, 251-254

after-sale support, 269-270

All Contacts page, 195

analyzing individual video performance, 252-253

annotations, 162-164
annotating videos, 164-166
watching annotated videos, 166

Apple
Final Cut Express, 127-128
Final Cut Studio, 132

iMovie, 125-126

applying for brand channels, 189-190

approving comments and video responses, 173-174

ArcSoft ShowBiz DVD2, 128

attaching videos as video comments, 228-229

Audi, 31

Audio Video Interleave file format, 74

AutoDesk Inventor, 15

.avi extension, 74

AVS Video Tools, 77

B

B2B (business-to-business) marketing
advantages of, 268
best practices, 271-273

call to action, 273
case studies and testimonials, 270
conferences and events, 270-271
content, 273
embedding YouTube videos on company website, 272
explained, 267-268
goals, 268-269
  providing additional information, 269
  providing after-sale support, 269-270
  reinforcing existing relationships, 269
how-to videos, 270
management messages and video blogs, 271
optimizing channel page, 272
optimizing videos for search, 272
product demonstrations and walk-throughs, 270
publicizing videos, 271

background music, 137-138

background noise in webcam videos, 84

backgrounds, 97-98, 108

basic metrics, 210-212

benefits of online video advertising, 10

best practices, B2B (business-to-business) marketing, 271-273

bids, editing, 254

Blendtec, 58

blip.tv, 234

blocking viewers from leaving comments, 175

blogs
  blog marketing, 229-230
  vlogs (video blogs), 82, 101, 271

BMW informative videos, 41

brand awareness, 11-12

brand channels
  applying for, 189-190
  benefits of, 188-189
  explained, 186-188

Bruner, Rick, 10

budgets for YouTube Promoted Videos, 247, 254

bulletins, posting to subscribers, 193

Burns, Ken, 130

business video blogs, 33

business-to-business marketing. See B2B marketing

buttons. See specific buttons

C

Call-to-Action Overlays
  creating, 257-258
  explained, 255-257, 273
  metrics, 217
  tracking performance of, 258-259
  turning off, 256

Call-to-Action tab (Insight page), 217

camcorders
  camcorder storage, 91-92
  choosing, 92-93
  explained, 90-91
  lighting, 98
  mid-level camcorders, 94-95
  pocket camcorders, 93
  semi-pro camcorders, 95-96
  standard versus high definition, 92
  tripods, 96

cameras, 144

Camtasia, 34

case studies, documenting on video, 270

cassette tape, 91

categories, 157

Catspit Productions, 163

CCD (charge-coupled device), 90

Century 21 Redwood Realty, 263

channel pages
  linking from, 151
  optimizing, 272

channels
  brand channels
    applying for, 189-190
    benefits of, 188-189
    explained, 186-188
  channel pages
    linking from, 151
    optimizing, 272
  explained, 179-180
  linking to, 202
  personalizing, 181
    channel settings, 182
    colors, 182-183
    modules, 184-185
    themes, 182-183
    videos and playlists, 185-186
  subscribing to, 180-181
  viewing, 180

charge-coupled device (CCD), 90

Chen, Steven, 6

Choose Video page, 246

choosing
    camcorders, 92-93
    file formats, 75-77
    keywords, 238-239
    resolution, 72
    thumbnail images, 225-227
    video-editing programs
        ArcSoftShowBiz DVD2, 128
        free programs, 124-126
        high-end programs, 130-133
        mid-level programs, 126-130

close-ups, 109

closing sales on company website, 264-265

clothing and dress in videos, 112-113

Coca Cola, 188

codecs, 73

Coldwell Banker, 32

colors for channels, 182-183

comments, 171
    approving, 173-174
    attaching videos as video comments,
      228-229
    blocking viewers from leaving, 175
    comment voting, 172
    embedding, 172
    enabling, 170
    negative comments, 174-176
    optimizing for search, 242
    ratings, 172
    removing, 175
    reviewing, 210
    syndication, 173
    video responses, 172

commercials
    infomercials, 29-30
    repurposed commercials, 27-28

communications, employee communications,
  16

community (YouTube)
    bulletins, posting to subscribers, 193
    connecting with, 192-193
    friends
        adding, 195
        reading messages from, 196
        sending messages to, 195
    metrics, 216

Community tab (Insight page), 216

company introductions, 33

company seminars, 34

company websites
    closing sales on, 264-265
    directing viewers to, 262-263
    embedding YouTube videos on, 202-203
    landing pages, 264-265
    linking to YouTube
        linking to individual videos, 201
        linking to YouTube channel, 202

composing shots, 109-110

compression (video), 73

conference videos, 270-271

Confirm Promotion page, 251

confirming YouTube Promoted Videos, 251

connecting with YouTube community, 192-193
    adding friends, 195
    bulletins, posting to subscribers, 193
    reading messages from friends, 196
    sending messages to friends, 195

consumer video equipment
    digital camcorders
        camcorder storage, 91-92
        choosing, 92-93
        explained, 90-91
        mid-level camcorders, 94-95
        pocket camcorders, 93
        semi-pro camcorders, 95-96
        standard versus high definition, 92
    lighting, 97-98
    microphones, 99
    seamless backgrounds, 97-98
    tripods, 96
    video-editing equipment, 100-101

container format, 75

content
    in B2B (business-to-business) marketing,
      273
    targeted content, 225
    videos that entertain, inform, or educate,
      224

contests, 233

contrast, accentuating, 143

conversions, tracking, 219-220

converting
    file formats to YouTube format, 77
    video files, 138

coordinating online marketing activities, 65-66

CPC (cost-per-click), 244, 250-251

CPM (cost-per-thousand), 244

credits, inserting, 136

Cree LED Lighting, 16

customers
identifying, 22-24
wants and needs, 24
testimonials, 33, 83, 270

customizing channels, 181
channel settings, 182
colors, 182-183
modules, 184-185
themes, 182-183
videos and playlists, 185-186

CyberLink PowerDirector, 129

D

Dailymotion, 234

dashboards, Promoted Videos Dashboard, 251
analyzing individual video performance,
252-253
editing bids, 254
editing promotion, 254
examining key metrics, 252
pausing, resuming, and deleting ads, 254
revising budget, 254

deciding if video is right for your business
attracting eyeballs, 10
everybody's doing it, 11
low-cost online marketing, 9

deleting ads, 254

Delicious, 232

demographic groups, 8

demographics metrics, 215

Demographics tab (Insight page), 215

demonstrations, 31

descriptions, 156, 241

design for remixing, 149

Dickson, Tom, 58

Digg, 232

digital camcorders
camcorder storage, 91-92
choosing, 92-93
explained, 90-91

lighting, 98
mid-level camcorders, 94-95
pocket camcorders, 93
semi-pro camcorders, 95-96
standard versus high definition, 92
tripods, 96

Digital Video (DV) file format, 74

direct sales
marketing with YouTube, 14
tracking, 220

discovery metrics, 214-215

Discovery tab (Insight page), 214-215

dislikes, viewing, 210

.divx extension, 74

DivX file format, 74

Dixon, Dr. Patrick, 30

dress/attire in videos, 112-113

Drs. Foster & Smith Pet Supplies, 31

Drum Workshop, 45, 183

.dv extension, 74

DV (Digital Video) file format, 74

DVD-based camcorders, 91

E

Edit Bid button, 254

Edit Promotion link, 254

editing
bids, 254
promotions, 254
videos
combining shots, 134
old videos, 145
transferring to PC for editing, 105
video-editing equipment, 100-101
video information, 158-159

educational videos, 18
how-to videos, 50
producing, 53-55
product instruction videos, 50-51
project videos, 51-53
why they work, 50

effectiveness, measuring, 208
conversions, 219-220
direct sales, 220
interactivity, 218
traffic, 218-219

email marketing, 229

Embed button, 202

embedding
  comments, 172
  YouTube videos on company website, 272
  YouTube videos on company websites, 202-203

embeds, optimizing for search, 241

employee communications, 16

employee submissions, 34

entertaining videos, 19, 58-61

event videos, 270-271

Evian, Roller Babies ads, 59

executive speeches, 33

expert presentations, 33

extensions
  .3gpp, 74
  .3gpp2, 74
  .avi, 74
  .divx, 74
  .dv, 74
  .flv, 74
  .mov, 75
  .mp4, 74-75
  .mpeg, 74
  .mpg, 74
  .qt, 75
  .rm, 75
  .rv, 75
  .webm, 75
  .wmv, 75
  .xvid, 75

external microphones, 99, 107

F

Facebook, 230

files
  file formats
    3GP, 74
    Audio Video Interleave, 74
    choosing, 75-77
    comparison of, 73-75
    container format, 75
    converting to YouTube format, 77
    Digital Video (DV), 74
    DivX, 74
    Flash Video, 74

    H.264, 74
    MPEG-1, 74
    MPEG-2, 74
    MPEG-4, 75
    MPEG-PS, 75
    QuickTime, 75
    RealVideo, 75
    Windows Media Video (WMV), 75
    Xvid, 75
  uploading from your computer
    entering information about your video,
      155-158
    selecting files to upload, 154-155
    sharing options, 158

Final Cut Express, 127-128

Final Cut Studio (Apple), 132

fine-tuning efforts, 208

flash memory storage, 92

Flash Video, 74

Flip Video, 93

Flixya, 234

Fluval, 51

.flv extension, 74

Food for Life TV, 43

Ford, 186

free video-editing programs
  Apple iMovie, 125-126
  Windows Live Movie Maker, 124-125

friends
  adding, 195
  reading messages from, 196
  sending messages to, 195
  sharing videos with, 227-228

future activities, planning, 208

G

Gallagher, Mitch, 44

GData API (GoogleData Application
  Programming Interface), 204

goals of video content, 27
  business video blogs, 33
  company introductions, 33
  company seminars and presentations, 34
  customer testimonials, 33
  executive speeches, 33
  expert presentations, 33

humorous spots, 34
infomercials, 29-30
instructional videos, 31
product presentations and demonstrations, 31
real estate walk-throughs, 32-33
repurposed commercials, 27-28
user or employee submissions, 34
Google's acquisition of YouTube, 7
GoogleData Application Programming Interface (GData API), 204
graphics
    onscreen graphics, 137
    thumbnail images, 225-227
GUBA, 234

H

H.264 file format, 74
Harris Dental, 42
Harris, Dr. Joseph, 42
HD (high definition), 70
HDV format, 91
High Quality (HQ) videos, 71
high-end video-editing programs, 130
    Adobe Premiere Pro CS, 131
    Apple Final Cut Studio, 132
    Sony Vegas Pro, 132-133
hiring professionals, 145
history of YouTube
    early days, 6
    launch and acquisition of, 7
    today, 7-8
Home Depot, 13
hosting videos on YouTube, 200
hot spots, 216-217
Hot Spots tab (Insight page), 216-217
how-to videos, 50, 270
    producing, 53-55
    product instruction videos, 50-51
    project videos, 51-53
HP, 45
HQ (High Quality) videos, 71
humor, 34, 60, 147
Hurley, Chad, 6

I

identifying customers, 22-24
iframe embed code, 203
images
    onscreen graphics, 137
    thumbnail images, 225-227
immediacy in webcam videos, 83
infomercials, 29-30
informative videos, 17-18, 39, 102
    facts, 40-41
    news, 39-40
    producing, 41
        video newscasts, 42-44
        video product tours, 44-48
    why they work, 38-39
inserting
    titles and credits, 136
    transitions between scenes, 135-136
Insight panel
    advanced metrics
        call-to-action, 217
        community, 216
        demographics, 215
        discovery, 214-215
        hot spots, 216-217
        views, 212-213
    basic metrics, 210-212
instructional videos, 31
interactivity, 218
internal training, 15-16

J-K

judging likes and dislikes, 210
jump cuts, 135

Karim, Jawed, 6
kbps (kilobytes per second), 73
keywords
    choosing, 238-239
    defined, 238
    keyword research, 238
    for YouTube Promoted Videos, 249-250
kilobytes per second (kbps), 73
Kmart, 186

L

L cuts, 128
landing pages, 264-265
letterboxing, 70
lighting
    for semi-pro videos, 107
    in professional video shoots, 121-122
    in webcam videos, 84
    lighting equipment, 97-98
likes, viewing, 210
linking
    from channel pages, 151
    to individual videos, 201
    to YouTube channel, 202
links, optimizing for search, 241
live webcam video, uploading, 85-87
location shoots, 103-105, 119-120
lossless codecs, 73
lossy codecs, 73
Lowe's project videos, 52

M

M2Convert Professional, 77
makeup, 120-121
management message videos, 271
Mantia, Bryan, 45
marketing, 11
    B2B (business-to-business) marketing
        advantages of, 268
        best practices, 271-273
        call to action, 273
        case studies and testimonials, 270
        conferences and events, 270-271
        content, 273
        embedding YouTube videos on company website, 272
        explained, 267-268
        goals, 268-269
        providing after-sale support, 269-270
        how-to videos, 270
        management messages and video blogs, 271
        optimizing channel page, 272
        optimizing videos for search, 272
        product demonstrations and walk-throughs, 270
        publicizing videos, 271
    brand awareness, 11-12
    deciding if video is right for your business
        attracting eyeballs, 10
        everybody's doing it, 11
        low-cost online marketing, 9
    direct sales, 14
    employee communications, 16
    internal training, 15-16
    marketing mix, formulating, 65
    product advertising, 12
    product support, 14-15
    recruiting, 17
    retail promotion, 13
    strategies, 21
        defining YouTube's role, 64
        messages, 25
        online marketing activities, coordinating, 65-66
        purpose of your video, 22
        television marketing and YouTube, 66-68
        what are you promoting, 24-25
    marketing videos
        advertising, 235
        attaching videos as video comments, 228-229
        blog marketing, 229-230
        email marketing, 229
        posting to other web forums, 230
        running contests, 233
        sharing videos with subscribers and friends, 227-228
        targeted content, 225
        thumbnail images, 225-227
        traditional promotion, 233-234
        uploading videos to other video-sharing sites, 234
        video titles, 225
        videos that entertain, inform, or educate, 224
        with social media, 230-232
measuring
    effectiveness, 208
        conversions, 219-220
        direct sales, 220
        interactivity, 218
        traffic, 218-219
    results of videos, 26
    views, 209-210

messages
  marketing strategies, 25
  reading, 196
  sending to friends, 195
Metacafe, 234
metrics
  advanced Insight panel metrics
    call-to-action, 217
    community, 216
    demographics, 215
    discovery, 214-215
    hot spots, 216-217
    views, 212-213
  basic Insight panel metrics, 210-212
  for YouTube Promoted Videos, 252
microphones, 99, 107
mid-level camcorders, 94-95
mid-level video-editing programs
  Adobe Premiere Elements, 126-127
  Apple Final Cut Express, 127-128
  ArcSoft ShowBiz DVD2, 128
  CyberLink PowerDirector, 129
  MoviePlus, 129
  Nero Vision Xtra, 129
  Pinnacle Studio, 129
  Roxio Creator, 130
  Sony Vegas Movie Studio HD, 130
  Ulead VideoStudio, 130
MiniDV format, 91
modules (channel), 184-185
.mov extension, 75
Movavi VideoSuite, 77
movement in semi-pro videos, 108-109
MoviePlus, 129
.mp4 extension, 74-75
.mpeg extension, 74
MPEG-1 file format, 74
MPEG-2 file format, 74
MPEG-4 file format, 75
MPEG-PS file format, 75
.mpg extension, 74
multiple camera trick, 43
multiple takes in professional video shoots, 122
music, background music, 137-138

N

needs of customers, 24
negative comments, 174-176
Nero Vision Xtra, 129
news, informative videos, 39-40
Nike, Bootcamp Drill videos, 12
Norton Internet Security, 58
notes, 162

O

offices, shooting videos in, 103-104
Old Spice, 12
on-the-scene reports, 103
online marketing activities, coordinating, 65-66
online video advertising, benefits of, 10
onscreen graphics, creating, 137
optimizing
  channel page, 272
  videos for search, 272
    comments, 242
    descriptions, 241
    embeds and links, 241
    explained, 237-238
    keywords, 238-239
    ratings, 242
    tags, 239-240
    titles, 240
    views, 241

P

pauses
  annotations, 162
  pausing ads, 254
pay-per-post (PPP), 230
pay-per-click (PPC), 244-246
Pepsi, 183
performance
  of Call-to-Action Overlays, tracking, 258-259
  tracking
    call-to-action, 217
    community, 216
    conversions, 219-220

demographics, 215

direct sales, 220

hot spots, 216-217

importance of, 208

interactivity, 218

judging likes and dislikes, 210

measuring views, 209-210

metrics, 210-215

reviewing comments, 210

traffic, 218-219

of YouTube Promoted Videos, 252-253

personalizing channels, 181

channel settings, 182

colors, 182-183

modules, 184-185

themes, 182-183

videos and playlists, 185-186

Pinnacle Studio, 129

pixels, 70

planning future activities, 208

playlists, choosing for channels, 185-186

pocket camcorders, 93

Post Bulletin pane, 193-194

posting to other web forums, 230

Power Video Converter, 77

PowerPoint presentations, converting to video, 34

PPC (pay-per-click), 244-245

PPP (pay-per-post), 230

preparing for professional video shoots

lighting, 121-122

makeup, 120-121

multiple takes, 122

shooting angles, 121

presentations

company seminars, 34

experts, 33

privacy, 158

privacy-enhanced mode, 203

producing

entertaining videos, 61

how-to videos, 53-55

informative videos, 41

video newscasts, 42-44

video product tours, 44-48

product demonstrations, 12-15, 31, 50-51, 102-103, 270

product tours, 44-48

professional videos

advantages of, 116

disadvantages of, 117

preparing for professional video shoots

lighting, 121-122

makeup, 120-121

multiple takes, 122

shooting angles, 121

shooting in studio, 118-119

shooting on location, 119-120

professionals, hiring, 145

project videos, 51-53

Promoted Videos Dashboard, 251

analyzing individual video performance, 252-253

editing bids, 254

editing promotion, 254

examining key metrics, 252

pausing, resuming, and deleting ads, 254

revising budget, 254

promoting products, 12

promotional videos

educational videos, 18

entertaining videos, 19

informative videos, 17-18

Prompt!, 112

publicizing B2B (business-to-business) marketing videos, 271

Publish button, 87

publishing webcam videos

live webcam video, 85-87

video files, 85

purpose of videos, 22

Q-R

.qt extension, 75

QuickTime file format, 75

ratings

comments, 172

optimizing for search, 242

reading messages, 196

real estate walk-throughs, 32-33

RealVideo file format, 75

Record button, 86

Record from Webcam link, 85

Record Video from Webcam page, 85-86

recording videos. *See* shooting videos

recruiting, 17

recycling old videos, 145

reinforcing existing relationships with B2B marketing videos, 269

relationships, reinforcing with B2B marketing videos, 269

removing
  videos from YouTube, 160
  viewer comments and responses, 175

repurposed commercials, 27-28, 67

RER Video Converter, 77

resolution, 106
  4K video, 71
  choosing, 72
  comparison of, 71-72
  high definition, 70
  standard definition, 70
  supported resolutions, 70-71

responding
  to immediate issues, 82
  to negative comments, 175-176

responses, removing, 175

resuming ads, 254

retail promotion, 13

revenues, generating from YouTube videos, 261
  closing sale on company website, 264-265
  creating videos with value, 262
  directing viewers to company website, 262-263

reviewing comments, 210

revising YouTube Promoted Videos budget, 254

Revver, 234

.rm extension, 75

Roller Babies ads, 59

Roxio Creator, 130

rule of thirds, 109-110

running contests, 233

.rv extension, 75

S

sales
  closing on company website, 264-265
  direct sales, tracking, 220

Save Changes button, 87

saving video files, 138

scenes, inserting transitions between, 135-136

screens, shooting for smaller screens, 142

scripts, 42

SDTV (standard definition television), 70

seamless backgrounds, 97-98

search engine optimization (SEO), 237

search, optimizing videos for
  comments, 242
  descriptions, 241
  embeds and links, 241
  explained, 237-238
  keywords, 238-239
  ratings, 242
  tags, 239-240
  titles, 240
  views, 241

Seattle Coffee Gear, 45

selecting files to upload, 154-155

semi-pro camcorders, 95-96

semi-pro videos
  informational videos, 102
  on-the-scene reports, 103
  product demonstrations, 102-103
  shooting
    backgrounds, 108
    close-ups, 109
    composition, 109-110
    digital video, 106
    in office, 103-104
    lighting, 107
    on location, 104-105
    microphones, 107
    movement, 108-109
    resolution, 106
    rule of thirds, 109-110
    shooting angles, 109
    shooting to edit, 111
    subjects' clothing and dress, 112-113
    teleprompters, 111-112
    tripods, 106

transferring to PC for editing, 105
video blogs, 101
when to use, 101
Send Message button, 195
sending
bulletins to subscribers, 193
messages to friends, 195
SEO (search engine optimization), 237
Set CPC page, 250
sharing videos with subscribers and friends, 158, 227-228
shooting videos
like a pro, 144
professional videos
advantages of, 116
disadvantages of, 117
in studio, 118-119
on location, 119-120
preparing for professional video shoots, 120-122
semi-pro videos
backgrounds, 108
close-ups, 109
composition, 109-110
digital video, 106
in office, 103-104
lighting, 107
on location, 104-105
microphones, 107
movement, 108-109
resolution, 106
rule of thirds, 109-110
shooting angles, 109
shooting to edit, 111
subjects' clothing and dress, 112-113
teleprompters, 111-112
tripods, 106
for smaller screens, 142
webcam videos, 83
background noise, 84
immediacy, 83
lighting, 84
simplicity, 83-84
shooting angles, 109, 121
shot lists, 111
Sign Warehouse, 14
simplicity in webcam videos, 83-84
slideshows, 145
Snickers Super Bowl ad, 28

social media, marketing YouTube videos with, 230-232
Sony Vegas Movie Studio HD, 130
Sony Vegas Pro, 132-133
special effects, 138
speech bubbles, 162
speeches, 33
spotlights, 162
standard definition, 70
Stop button, 86
storyboards, 46-48
studios, shooting professional videos in, 118-119
subscribers
posting bulletins to, 193
sharing videos with, 227-228
subscribing to channels, 180-181
success, measuring, 26
Sweetwater Sound, 44
syndication, 173

T

tags, 6, 157, 239-240
targeted content, 225
TelePrompTer, 111
teleprompters, 111-112
television marketing, co-existing with YouTube, 66
extending and expanding, 67
repurposing, 67
starting fresh, 68
testimonials, 33, 83, 270
themes for channels, 182-183
thirds, rule of, 109-110
thumbnails, 156, 225-227
tips
for better-looking videos, 142
accentuate contrast, 143
breaking rules, 146
hiring professionals, 145
investing in quality equipment, 143
look professional, 145
recycling and editing old videos, 145
shoot for smaller screens, 142

shoot like a pro, 144
slideshows, 145
slow and steady, 143
using multiple cameras, 144
for generating sales
   include URLs in accompanying text, 151
   include your website address, 149-150
   link from channel pages, 151
for improving video content
   avoid the hard sell, 148
   be entertaining, 146
   be informative, 146
   communicate a clear message, 148
   design for remixing, 149
   humor, 147
   keep it fresh, 149
   keep it short, 147
   keep it simple, 148
   stay focused, 148
titles, 156, 225
   inserting, 136
   optimizing for search, 240
TOMS Shoes, 186
tracking performance
   Call-to-Action Overlays, 258-259
   conversions, 219-220
   direct sales, 220
   importance of, 208
   interactivity, 218
   judging likes and dislikes, 210
   measuring views, 209-210
   metrics
      basic Insight panel metrics, 210-212
      call-to-action, 217
      community, 216
      demographics, 215
      discovery, 214-215
      hot spots, 216-217
      views, 212-213
   reviewing comments, 210
   traffic, 218-219
traditional promotion, 233-234
traffic, tracking, 218-219
training, internal training, 15-16
transferring videos to PC for editing, 105
transitions, inserting between scenes, 135-136
travel reporting with webcam videos, 82
tripods, 96, 106

turning off Call-to-Action Overlays, 256
Twitter, 230-232

U

Ulead VideoStudio, 130
uploading
   files from your computer
      entering information about your video,
         155-158
      selecting files for upload, 154-155
      sharing options, 158
   to other video-sharing sites, 234
   webcam videos
      live webcam video, 85-87
      video files, 85
URLs
   including in accompanying text, 151
   including in videos, 149
user submissions, 34

V

Vegas Movie Studio HD (Sony), 130
Vegas Pro (Sony), 132-133
Veoh, 234
Viator Travel, 29
video annotations, 163-164
video blogs (vlogs), 33, 82, 101, 271
video equipment
   digital camcorders
      camcorder storage, 91-92
      choosing, 92-93
      explained, 90-91
      mid-level camcorders, 94-95
      pocket camcorders, 93
      semi-pro camcorders, 95-96
      standard versus high definition, 92
   lighting, 97-98
   microphones, 99
   seamless backgrounds, 97-98
   tripods, 96
   video-editing equipment, 100-101
Video File Upload page, 85
video newscasts, 42-44
video product tours, 44-48

video responses
adding background music, 137-138
  approving, 173-174
  comments, 172

video-editing equipment, 100-101

video-editing programs, 124, 133
  adding background music, 137-138
  creating onscreen graphics, 137
  editing together different shots, 134
  free programs
    Apple iMovie, 125-126
    Windows Live Movie Maker, 124-125
  high-end programs, 130
    Adobe Premiere Pro CS, 131
    Apple Final Cut Studio, 132
    Sony Vegas Pro, 132-133
  inserting titles and credits, 136
  inserting transitions between scenes,
    135-136
  mid-level programs
    Adobe Premiere Elements, 126-127
    Apple Final Cut Express, 127-128
    ArcSoft ShowBiz DVD2, 128
    CyberLink PowerDirector, 129
    MoviePlus, 129
    Nero Vision Xtra, 129
    Pinnacle Studio, 129
    Roxio Creator, 130
    Sony Vegas Movie Studio HD, 130
    Ulead VideoStudio, 130
  special converting and saving video files,
    138
  special effects, 138

videos, 17
  advertising, 235
  annotated videos, 166
  annotating, 164-166
  B2B marketing videos. See B2B (business-
    to-business) marketing
  Call-to-Action Overlays
    creating, 257-258
    explained, 255-257
    tracking performance of, 258-259
    turning off, 256
  case studies and testimonials, 270
  choosing for display on channels, 185-186
  codecs, 73
  compression, 73
  conference and event videos, 270-271
  editing
    old videos, 145
    transferring to PC for editing, 105

video information, 158-159
  video-editing equipment, 100-101
  educational videos. See educational videos
  embedding on company websites, 202-203
  entering information about, 155-156
    categories, 157
    descriptions, 156
    privacy, 158
    tags, 157
    thumbnails, 156
    titles, 156
  entertaining videos, 19, 58-61
  file formats
    3GP, 74
    Audio Video Interleave, 74
    choosing, 75-77
    comparison of, 73-75
    container format, 75
    converting to YouTube format, 77
    Digital Video (DV), 74
    DivX, 74
    Flash Video, 74
    H.264, 74
    MPEG-1, 74
    MPEG-2, 74
    MPEG-4, 75
    MPEG-PS, 75
    QuickTime, 75
    RealVideo, 75
    Windows Media Video (WMV), 75
    Xvid, 75
  generating revenues from, 261
    closing sale on company website, 264-265
    creating videos with value, 262
    directing viewers to company website,
      262-263
  hosting, 200
  how-to videos. See how-to videos
  informative videos. See informative videos
  linking to, 201
  management messages and video blogs, 271
  marketing
    advertising, 235
    attaching videos as video comments,
      228-229
    blog marketing, 229-230
    email marketing, 229
    posting to other web forums, 230
    running contests, 233
    sharing videos with subscribers and
      friends, 227-228
    targeted content, 225

thumbnail images, 225-227
traditional promotion, 233-234
uploading videos to other video-sharing sites, 234
video titles, 225
videos that entertain, inform, or educate, 224
with social media, 230-232
measuring results of, 26
optimizing for search
    comments, 242
    descriptions, 241
    embeds and links, 241
    explained, 237-238
    keywords, 238-239
    ratings, 242
    tags, 239-240
    titles, 240
    views, 241
pixels, 70
product instruction videos, 50-51
professional videos
    advantages of, 116
    disadvantages of, 117
    preparing for professional video shoots, 120-122
    shooting in studio, 118-119
    shooting on location, 119-120
project videos, 51-53
purpose of, 22
recycling, 145
removing from YouTube, 160
resolution
    4K video, 71
    choosing, 72
    comparison of, 71-72
    high definition, 70
    standard definition, 70
    supported resolutions, 70-71
semi-pro videos
    informational videos, 102
    on-the-scene reports, 103
    product demonstrations, 102-103
    shooting, 103-113
    transferring to PC for editing, 105
    video blogs, 101
    when to use, 101
sharing with subscribers and friends, 227-228
thumbnail images, 225-227

tips for better-looking videos
    accentuate the contrast, 143
    breaking rules, 146
    hiring professionals, 145
    investing in quality equipment, 143
    look professional, 145
    recycling and editing old videos, 145
    shoot for smaller screens, 142
    shoot like a pro, 144
    slideshows, 145
    slow and steady, 143
    using multiple cameras, 144
tips for generating sales
    include URLs in accompanying text, 151
    include your website address, 149-150
    link from channel pages, 151
tips for improving content
    avoid the hard sell, 148
    be entertaining, 146
    be informative, 146
    communicate a clear message, 148
    design for remixing, 149
    humor, 147
    keep it fresh, 149
    keep it short, 147
    keep it simple, 148
    stay focused, 148
titles, 225
uploading, 85-87, 234
video content, goals of, 27
    business video blogs, 33
    company introductions, 33
    company seminars and presentations, 34
    customer testimonials, 33
    executive speeches, 33
    expert presentations, 33
    humorous spots, 34
    infomercials, 29-30
    instructional videos, 31
    product presentations and demonstrations, 31
    real estate walk-throughs, 32-33
    repurposed commercials, 27-28
    user or employee submissions, 34
video information, editing, 158-159
viral videos, 60-61
webcam videos
    explained, 79-81
    shooting tips, 83-84
    uploading to YouTube, 85-87
    when to use, 82-83

YouTube Promoted Videos
  budgets, 247, 254
  CPC (cost-per-click), 250-251
  CPM (cost-per-thousand), 244
  creating, 246-251
  defined, 244
  explained, 245-246
  keywords, 249-250
  PPC (pay-per-click), 244-245
  Promoted Videos Dashboard, 251-254
VideoStudio (Ulead), 130
VIDEOzilla, 77
viewers, 8-9
  blocking from leaving comments, 175
  directing to company websites, 262-263
viewing
  channels, 180
  likes/dislikes, 210
views
  measuring, 209-210
  metrics, 212-213
  optimizing for search, 241
Views tab (Insight page), 212-213
Vimeo, 234
viral videos, 19, 60-61
vlogs (video blogs), 33, 82, 101, 271

W

wants of customers, 24
watching annotated videos, 166
webcam videos
  explained, 79-81
  shooting tips
    background noise, 84
    immediacy, 83
    lighting, 84
    simplicity, 83-84
  uploading to YouTube
    live webcam video, 85-87
    video files, 85
  when to use
    customer testimonials, 83
    responses to immediate issues, 82
    travel, 82
    video blogs, 82
webcams, 142
.webm extension, 75

websites
  company sites. See company websites, 264
  including in videos, 149-150
"Will It Blend?," 58
Williams-Sonoma, 52
Windows Live Movie Maker, 124-125
Windows Media Video (WMV), 75
wireless mics, 100
WMV (Windows Media Video), 75
.wmv extension, 75
Write Your Promotion page, 248-249

X-Y-Z

Xilisoft Video Converter, 77
Xvid file format, 75

Yahoo! Video, 234
YouTube
  co-existing with television marketing, 66
    extending and expanding, 67
    repurposing, 67
    starting fresh, 68
  history of, 6
    early days, 6
    launch and acquisition of, 7
    today, 7-8
  size of, 1
  viewers, 8-9
YouTube Promoted Videos
  budgets, 247, 254
  CPC (cost-per-click), 250-251
  CPM (cost-per-thousand), 244
  creating, 246-251
  defined, 244
  explained, 245-246
  keywords, 249-250
  PPC (pay-per-click), 244-245
  Promoted Videos Dashboard, 251
    analyzing individual video performance, 252-253
    editing bids, 254
    editing promotion, 254
    examining key metrics, 252
    pausing, resuming, and deleting ads, 254
    revising budget, 254
    YouTube usage, 8

que®

Biz-Tech Series

Straightforward Strategies and Tactics for Business Today

The **Que Biz-Tech series** is designed for the legions of executives and marketers out there trying to come to grips with emerging technologies that can make or break their business. These books help the reader know what's important, what isn't, and provide deep inside know-how for entering the brave new world of business technology, covering topics such as mobile marketing, microblogging, and iPhone and iPad app marketing.

- Straightforward strategies and tactics for companies who are either using or will be using a new technology/product or way of thinking/ doing business

- Written by well-known industry experts in their respective fields— and designed to be an open platform for the author to teach a topic in the way he or she believes the audience will learn best

- Covers new technologies that companies must embrace to remain competitive in the marketplace and shows them how to maximize those technologies for profit

- Written with the marketing and business user in mind—these books meld solid technical know-how with corporate-savvy advice for improving the bottom line

Visit **quepublishing.com/biztech** to learn more about the **Que Biz-Tech series**

FREE Online Edition

Your purchase of **YouTube for Business: Online Video Marketing for Any Business** includes access to a free online edition for 45 days through the Safari Books Online subscription service. Nearly every Que book is available online through Safari Books Online, along with more than 5,000 other technical books and videos from publishers such as Addison-Wesley Professional, Cisco Press, Exam Cram, IBM Press, O'Reilly, Prentice Hall, and Sams.

SAFARI BOOKS ONLINE allows you to search for a specific answer, cut and paste code, download chapters, and stay current with emerging technologies.

Activate your FREE Online Edition at www.informit.com/safarifree

> **STEP 1:** Enter the coupon code: IZVUNCB.

> **STEP 2:** New Safari users, complete the brief registration form. Safari subscribers, just log in.

If you have difficulty registering on Safari or accessing the online edition, please e-mail customer-service@safaribooksonline.com